SAMANTHA   TRENOWETH

THE
FUTURE
OF GOD

Personal adventures

in spirituality with

thirteen of today's

eminent thinkers

MILLENNIUM   BOOKS

First Published in the U.S.A. & Canada in 1996 by
Millennium Books
an imprint of E. J. Dwyer (Australia) Pty Ltd

Distributed in the U.S.A. by
Morehouse Publishing
P. O. Box 1321
HARRISBURG, PA 17105
Ph: 1 800 877 0012
Fx: (717) 541 8128

Distributed in Canada by
Novalis
49 Front Street East
2nd Floor
Toronto, Ontario
CANADA M5E 1B3
Ph: 1 800 387 7164
Fx: (416) 363 9409

National Library of Australia
Cataloguing-in-Publication data

Trenoweth, Samantha, 1961-.
The future of God : personal adventures in spirituality
with thirteen of today's eminent thinkers.

ISBN 1 86429 023 4

1. God. 2. Spirituality. 3. Religions. I. Title.

291.4

Edited by Leonie Draper
Cover design by Rockin' Doodles Design
Typeset in Goudy 11.5pt
Printed in Australia by Gillingham Printers

10 9 8 7 6 5 4 3 2

00 99 98 97 96

CONTENTS

TO ANN AND PAUL TRENOWETH

ACKNOWLEDGEMENTS

*My gratitude to all those who shared their lives and hopes and beliefs with me
for this book, particularly to Elisabeth with whom I began this journey.
I also thank . . .
For patience, organisation and assistance: Ken Ross, Rita Ward,
Marie Devlin, John Allen, Jeffrey Kammins, Rosie Westerman,
Lezlee Christianson, Mary Genovese, Heather Duff, Bernadette Khourie,
John Clearly, Tenzin Geyche Tethong, Tsering Tashi and Lhakdor.
For encouragement: Ann and Paul Trenoweth, Eva Melocco, Ivy Jenkinson,
Michele Williams, Michele Walker, Cicely Whiteman, John McRae, Rhyl Draper,
Sheila Griffiths, Pat Burgoyne, Japetus, Paul Dengate, Ari Powell, Tennyson Yiu,
Neville Drury, Robert Wood, Steve Broadbent, Richard Jones, Carlo Du Bois, David Mills,
Joan Miura, Alice Walker, Catherine Hammond, Carol Floyd and Anthony Dwyer.
For liberation: Giovanna Trenoweth, Mark Baxter.
For humor: Sean and James Trenoweth.
For insight: Rosie Heritage and Amber St Clare.
For impetus: Malcolm Harrisson.
For the title: John O'Donnell.
For research and transcription: Samantha Clode and Jillian Daniels.
For flight: STA Travel.
For support, pancakes and encouragement way beyond the call of duty:
Lesa-Belle Furhagen and Anthony Sive.
For flexibility: All at Terraplane Press.
For vodka, tarot and sympathy: Ruth Hessey, Helen Lutz, Heather Vaile,
Kirsten Smith, Margaret Merton, Susan Olle, Ann Gordon, Claudia Castle.
For all these things, as well as understanding, editorial advice, courage,
pasta, adventure and true love: Toby Creswell.*

*Thanks also to HarperCollinsPublishers Australia for permission to reprint the extract from
"The Beginning of Life" in* STRADBROKE DREAMTIME, *by Oodgeroo Nunukul.*

PREFACE

THIS BOOK HAS DRAWN ITSELF AROUND ME OVER MANY YEARS. IT IS THE RESULT of seventeen years' work as a journalist and a lifetime of captivation by the spiritual impulse. The first interview that would later grow to become a chapter was with Elisabeth Kübler-Ross, in 1985. Yet, I can trace the threads of this book further still — back to their source in the daydreams of my childhood.

In spite of a family who lived on the borderline between agnosticism and Protestantism, I was one of those romantic children who pore over the lives of saints. Not that saints were really the thing in our house. The only religious book we possessed was an enormous, illustrated Bible, which was maintained exclusively as a filing system for birth certificates and locks of hair. I do, however, remember seeing a film about St Francis of Assisi and lolling about enraptured for days and I remember, very clearly, coming upon my mother's cache of Tibetan books, which included the Dalai Lama's autobiography, Heinrich Harrer's *Seven Years in Tibet* and a dubious Lobsang Rampa paperback.

A little later, my parents took up Italian lessons with a Franciscan father, who visited on Mondays after dinner and sat in the kitchen, drinking Irish whisky, while my parents struggled with tense and gender. He drank, he laughed, he exuded warmth, he taught us St Francis' prayer for peace, he had his whole monastery pray for my brother when he was critically ill. He was everything our local minister (whom I'd met once or twice) was not and henceforth we referred to him as our family priest.

In essence, that was my childhood religious instruction. A haphazard combination of Hollywood movies, Tibetan adventure paperbacks and the chance acquaintance of an Irish-Australian Catholic priest.

Some time in my fifteenth year, I developed a social conscience. I announced to my parents that I was a socialist, read the Seventies feminists obsessively and dipped into works of Gandhi and Martin Luther King. There was also pop music: Bob Dylan, John Lennon, George Harrison, Melanie Safka, Patti Smith's poetry. That was the religious instruction of my teens.

After school, I took up a position on a rock magazine and two years later, decided to try freelancing, which left ample time for explorations in Buddhism, the New Physics, meditation, Kriya yoga, Hatha yoga, hallucinogenic drugs, the peace and environment movements, left-wing politics, Anthroposophy, the Goddess thing, the reading of tarot cards and auras. I came to write exclusively on spirituality, social justice and green politics and eventually to edit a green/New Age magazine.

Not surprisingly, there were passages of rough sailing. The New Age movement is uncommonly susceptible to purveyors of snake oil. There was a spiritual healer who could direct rays of energy through brick walls, over mountain ranges, across oceans — indeed halfway around the world — but not through a woman's blouse. There was the personal growth organisation with which a friend was involved until, pushed to her limits, she suffered a minor breakdown and not a soul from that place turned up to visit her in hospital.

There were also meetings with truly remarkable human beings and from these, this book has sprung.

I am not a theologian, I am not a philosopher, I am not a scientist. I am someone who has, from time to time in her life, sensed the presence of divinity and sought an explanation. Most often, that presence has crept up on me in moments alone with nature. Once or twice, as a teenager, I felt strongly the answers to prayers. Later, that presence washed over me in meditation. Occasionally, I have watched it light up the eyes of fellow human beings.

Some of those human beings have shared their lives and dreams and hopes with me in the making of this book and have enriched my life immeasurably through our meeting.

This book is a mirror to my spiritual wanderings, to my search for a spiritual home. Each person whom I have interviewed represents a stopover en route to my own Olympus. It is by no means an objective assessment of the state of theological discussion today. Rather, it is a very personal exploration of ideas which have shaped my faith and which I believe — in some cases, I hope — will influence mainstream religious thought in years to come.

The recovery by indigenous people of their own native spiritual traditions has been of inestimable significance, not only to the Native Americans, Aboriginal people and others immediately involved, but to all of us.

It was a privilege to spend time with the great Australian poet, Oodgeroo, before her death. Always a proponent of mutual education and understanding, she believed firmly that there were elements of indigenous spirituality — particularly as regards the relationship between humanity and the land — which white Australians would do well to observe. Like the Native American actor and songwriter, Floyd Westerman, she did not take kindly to Europeans appropriating indigenous beliefs, lock, stock and barrel. She did, however, believe that some of the values which lie at the heart of Aboriginal religion could enrich European culture and increase the harmony with which we all live together on this one small planet.

The environmental crisis of recent years has radically altered notions of our role in the natural world and needs to alter them still further if our future is to be secure. A tremendous shift in understanding is under way, pushed along by a few courageous souls at the far frontiers of the green movement. John Seed is one of them. Borrowing from indigenous traditions and from contemporary developments in science, he has done more than anyone to propagate the burgeoning eco-spiritual movement known as Deep Ecology.

Even within mainstream Christianity, biblical attitudes to the natural world are being reassessed. As the Uniting Church minister, Dorothy McRae-McMahon points out: "The Christian community has a responsibility to release Western society from a view which is related to the first chapter of Genesis, which talks about human beings having dominion over the earth. I think what's meant there is a sense of responsibility for the earth but I don't think that's the way we've seen it. I think we've seen it as ruling the earth and it's high time we gave a lead to the community in releasing that."

Dorothy, too, speaks of tapping into "the spirituality of Aboriginal people, who understand the God who goes down deeply into the earth and is their mother."

As one of the first women to be ordained in the Uniting Church in Australia, she is well aware of the changes being wrought by the growing involvement of women at every level of religious life. For the first time in many thousands of years, Western religion is coming to worship a God who is as female as male — if, indeed, gender description is any longer applicable.

Moreover, the expanding roles of women are altering the very way we worship. Rabbi Kushner once mentioned to me the revelation of observing a Shivah ceremony created by a female rabbi after the miscarriage of a congregant's child. No male cleric of any faith, he suspected, could have designed such a ritual because no male cleric could have understood so intimately that mother's loss.

Yet institutions move slowly and there are those who will not wait. The women's spirituality movement flourishes in a revival of the Wiccan faith and renewed interest in the pre-patriarchal religions of Europe and the Middle East. Bernadette Cozart's life changed forever when, one day, she looked in the mirror and saw reflected there the face of the "One Most High." Just as the recovery of indigenous beliefs has affirmed the purpose, dignity and strength of those communities, so there has been nothing so liberating, for women like Bernadette, as the acknowledgment of a female deity.

Liberation theology is another area through which religion has a very real impact on the secular world and my introduction to liberation theology came through a man who knows, better than anyone, its spiritual and political power. The Archbishop of Capetown, Desmond Tutu, is among its best known exponents. He has worked tirelessly for justice in South Africa because, he believes, his religion demands it of him. His God, he insists, is concerned with equality and righteousness and his Bible, he says, is a radical tool for change. Every political action the archbishop has taken has been steeped in theology and South Africa's bold struggle today is, in part, the fruit of his religious effort.

When first I began my spiritual wandering, however, I knew nothing of liberation or feminist theology. My very meagre understanding of the faith in which I'd been raised allowed me to appreciate few of its redeeming qualities. Besides, I, like so many others, was shopping for an experiential spiritual path and nothing in my religious education classes had led me to believe Christianity had that on offer.

Fortuitously, at just that time, Tibetan lamas, who had been exiled from their homeland, were making their way from Nepal and northern India to the West. They joined a lengthy parade of Indian gurus, Thai monks, Chinese Taoists and others, leaving an indelible imprint on the Western psyche. Not only have they multiplied the options for the Western seeker, they have also, I suspect, encouraged the Judeo-Christians to lift their game. It's a little like a free market economy. No longer does a congregation simply walk in from the streets every Saturday or Sunday morning. The maintenance of a healthy congregation requires remaining abreast of the competition and offering spiritual insight and a path to transpersonal experience which is comparable in quality, if not in substance, with the ashram or gumpa across town.

Increasingly, Westerners require more from religion than a moral code, and spiritual experience is only one element of that. Crucial also is a cosmology which is capable of igniting the soul without affronting the rational mind.

There has been a variety of approaches to this problem, particularly within Christianity. There are those, like Barbara Thiering, who choose to jettison myth, magic, mystery and even the divinity of Jesus as incompatible with their considerable intelligence. There are others, like Matthew Fox, who seek a holistic cosmology within the deep mystical tradition of their own Christian faith.

The search for a satisfying cosmology has resulted, in part, from the recent evolution of scientific thought, which has opened the doors to new definitions of divinity while leaving others utterly redundant.

The very best scientists and mathematicians are engaged in a spiritual discipline, the physicist and author, Paul Davies, asserts. In following the scientific method and seeking to understand the laws by which the universe works, he believes, we come to know a little of the mind of God. That there is what he calls a Designer behind this world, he has little doubt. The Designer's signature is written, in clear mathematical language, into the laws which govern the universe and even into the workings of our nimble and logical minds. Paul Davies' Designer is not the God of the fundamentalists but it bears more than a passing resemblance to notions of divinity described by the Dalai Lama, John Seed, Harold Kushner, Matthew Fox and others at the cutting edge of contemporary theology.

We do, indeed, live in interesting times. The God we worship today (if we elect to worship one at all) is markedly different from the God of our grandparents. As often as not, our God today is androgynous and increasingly our God sides more solidly with the oppressed than the oppressor. Our God is a shape-shifter. When we envisage God, she is as likely to be the colour of chocolate as the colour of snow and might sit high on a cloud or lie curled beneath the earth, birthing the forests, the animals, the mountains, the oceans and, over and again, the human generations. Or perhaps, as the Dalai Lama would have it, we envisage no God at all, for the one true reality lies in blissful emptiness, perfect peace.

We have options — more options than ever before — and we have a freedom, unthinkable in generations past, to create our own religious framework. If there is one common element to each of the interviews in this book, it is that all of these people have, at some time, approached a crisis of faith and been forced to redefine their beliefs, their notions of divinity, the manner in which they imprint meaning upon the world.

The invasion of his homeland by the Chinese military and his subsequent flight into exile has enabled His Holiness the Dalai Lama to reassess his understanding of Tibetan Buddhism as the one true faith. The discovery of the Dead Sea Scrolls and the hidden language they contain has forced Barbara Thiering to reconsider the divinity of Jesus and the Christianity of her youth. The suffering and death of Harold Kushner's son hurled him towards a theological abyss and made him question both the power and the righteousness of his deity.

Each chapter recounts the story of such a struggle and reflects, I think, the struggles of many. This is a time in which hierarchies are rocking, much that has been held sacred is crumbling and our beliefs are less often dictated from on high. The effort to define a belief system which is, at once, spiritually, intellectually and morally satisfying is now more an individual responsibility than an institutional one.

Those who have shared their personal battles in the following pages are, I believe, pacesetters, paradigm shifters, adventurers at the frontiers of new spiritualities. Barbara Thiering wonders whether anything that we can call religion will survive the present upheavals. I believe that it will, and that it will be defined by people like Paul Davies, Bernadette Cozart, Matthew Fox and Desmond Tutu.

Where does this leave my personal quest for a spiritual home? In much the same place, I suspect, as many of my generation.

I am tired of chanting in languages which are not my own, yet I can't make sense of the world, can't reconcile human suffering with a compassionate God, unless I incorporate a philosophy of reincarnation. I love the rich earthiness of the Goddess religions. I love the way they speak directly to my female experience of the world, the way they honour life and fertility, change and growth. Yet all logic in me riles at the notion of a deity of either gender. I am attracted to the figure the Jesus — to his compassion, his courage, his fear, his humanity, the way he is born and dies, journeys through the underworld and lives again, like Osiris in Egypt, like the great heroes of mythology. Yet Christianity requires a leap of faith of such magnitude that I feel I must parcel up all reason and leave it on the far side of some rocky gorge.

So I choose not to throw in my lot with any single theology. I practise yoga, read Christian and Buddhist texts with equal interest and pray to a God who is no less real for its diverse husbandry. If, however, I was forced to take a stand, it would be with Matthew Fox's heroic effort to fan the spark of a Western mystical tradition. We in the West need, as much as anyone, to reclaim our spiritual roots and to uncover, beneath the thousand-year weight of dogma and institutional oppression, a religious framework that will encourage us to feel at home on this earth and to acknowledge as relatives all its people of different cultures and appearances and colours. Indeed it was for revolutionaries like Matthew Fox, who are battling, at great personal cost, to enrich Western spiritual life, that this book was written.

Archbishop Desmond Tutu

RATTLING HEAVEN'S GATE

I have seen the affliction of my people who are in Egypt and have heard their cry
because of their taskmasters; I know their sufferings and I have come down to
deliver them out of the hand of the Egyptians, and to bring them up out of that land
to a good and broad land, a land flowing with milk and honey ... Now, behold,
the cry of the people of Israel has come to me and I have seen the oppression with
which the Egyptians oppress them. Come, I will send you to Pharaoh that
you may bring forth my people, the sons of Israel, out of Egypt.

EXODUS 3: 7–10

IT IS 5 PM ON A SUNDAY AFTERNOON IN AUGUST 1993. A SHINY BMW SPEEDS ALONG expressways over Cape Town. It passes a village of corrugated iron and cardboard. Machine-gun toting soldiers guard the road against residents who have recently taken to hurling rocks at cars. It passes a huge cement complex where Crowded House, a New Zealand rock band and one of the first international acts to tour with approval of the African National Congress (ANC), played last night to a packed arena of screaming, dancing, singing, sweating, fainting South African fans.

On past the bay and along the coast, the car heads south through eucalypts and along towering cliffs where great white mansions perch, looking out to sea. Down a winding road, flanked by stately homes, comes the BMW. It is driven by Erwin Law, an ex-army man (he worked in counter-insurgence) turned mercenary security guard, who carries a gun in his money pouch and sticks to the members of the band (on which I'm here to report), like glue.

The car swerves to avoid a gaggle of teenagers and screeches to a halt by a convenient but illegal stretch of curb. Erwin swaggers down a precarious incline and stands fully clothed in the sand, legs astride, arms folded, waiting for the troupe of New Zealanders to tire of the sea.

This is my first day in Cape Town. I have taken the assignment in the hope that I might combine this story with one on the Anglican archbishop Desmond Tutu. However, he is in Belgium. Desmond Tutu, it transpires, can most often be found almost anywhere in the world but Cape Town. Indeed, his schedule has been such in recent years, that he laughingly refers to himself, not as "the Archbishop of Cape Town" but as "the Archbishop from Cape Town".

Erwin shepherds us to an enormous hotel: mirrored ceilings in the lobby, suites three times the size of most township homes and great verandahs overlooking the sea. The band has been in the country a week and the search for "the real South Africa" has become a quest for them. Apartheid no longer exists in legislation but South Africans have yet to bridge the divide. Black and white cultures carry on in virtual isolation. The band has resorted to cornering hotel maids and room service staff to make some small connection with black South Africa. They want to visit a township. The tour promoters are terrified that something will go awry.

Just last month, a date was confirmed for this country's first democratic national election. Also last month, four armed men burst into a Sunday service at a church in the suburb of Kenilworth. They threw hand grenades into the body of the church and showered the congregation of one thousand with automatic rifle fire. Eleven people were killed and more than fifty were injured.

At an inter-faith rally four days later, the archbishop, along with other Christian, Jewish and Muslim leaders, led the people of Cape Town in a desperate call for peace.

"If these people, who did what they did on Sunday, think that they have succeeded in separating us," his deep voice rang out through city hall, "let us say to them: 'No! You have failed. You have succeeded in bringing us together.' We, as we have always said, are the rainbow people of God. We are beautiful because we are the rainbow people of God and we are unstoppable ... This South Africa belongs to all of us, black and white."

MONDAY, 3 PM: I WANDER INTO THE ARENA WHERE THE BAND IS TEST-DRIVING some new material before the show. The entrance is flanked by conspicuously armed guards. Erwin paces the auditorium. Soon a sniffer dog will arrive to check for explosives.

Across town, the lighting director has taken his quest for South Africa on a tour of city market stalls full of carved zebras, giraffes, elephants and strings of wooden beads. He stops at an outdoor cafe. Biscuits and hot chocolate arrive with an over-abundance of cream. The cream is scooped onto a saucer and put to one side, where it is spied by an Indian boy. The lighting director hands over biscuits and cream and the boy runs, laughing, back to his mother's knee.

This is the parish of Archbishop Desmond Tutu. It is a parish bubbling variously with elation, horror, hope, desperation, fear and grief.

The archbishop might not be in town at present but his influence is felt everywhere. He is adored, he is reviled, he is never ignored.

"Oh," I am told by a white cab driver, "he is so ambitious — far more concerned with advancing his career than advancing the cause." Quite the opposite picture is painted by a Franciscan missionary nun, who came here from Hong Kong, at his behest, to help build bridges in institutes of higher learning.

Whether they are for him or against him, Capetonians embrace this outspoken, articulate, headstrong Nobel Laureate as their own. Everyone has an opinion and a story. The Tutu joke is a thriving cultural phenomenon and one from which the archbishop, himself, derives much delight. He has memorized a whole string of them. One of his favorites runs something like this ...

"The archbishop died and made his way straight to heaven because, naturally, that was where he thought he ought to be. When he got there, however, he was greeted and told that, no, he was in the wrong place. He had to go to the other place, the warmer place. So, off he went. Then, a fortnight later, there was a frantic knocking on the gates of heaven and, when St Peter opened those pearly gates, there was Satan, standing on the threshold. 'What are you doing here?' asked St Peter. 'Well, since you sent Tutu down to me,' Satan replied, 'he's been causing so much trouble that I have come to ask for political asylum'."

Desmond Tutu's sense of humor and unrelenting faith have seen him through the darkest days of apartheid.

"When Christian missionaries first came to Africa, we had the land and they had the Bible," he often recounts. "Then they said, 'Let us pray.' So we closed our eyes and when we opened them, they had the land and we had the Bible .... Perhaps we got the better end of the deal."

BORN IN 1931 IN KLERKSDORP, A GOLD-MINING TOWN IN THE TRANSVAAL, WEST of Johannesburg, he was baptised Desmond Mpilo Tutu at the Methodist missionary school where his father was teaching. His grandmother added the name Mpilo, which means health and life, because he was so ill as a child that his family was unsure whether he would survive.

"She was trying to counteract the forces of death and disease," he chuckles, "and she seems to have succeeded because here I am, sixty-three years later."

His father was a stern disciplinarian and a dedicated teacher. His mother, a domestic worker, he remembers as gentle and kind, with an unbending sense of justice. It was from her, he suspects, that he inherited his determination to fight for the underdog.

Young Desmond was bright and dreamed of studying medicine. Although his grades were high, his parents were unable to afford the tuition fees, so he completed his schooling in Johannesburg and graduated to become, like his father, a missionary teacher.

By all accounts he was a fine teacher but, between 1953 and 1957, the government phased in its Bantu (black) education system, under which church schools were closed or placed under tight controls and all African education was dictated by the state. The system was designed to ensure that black South Africans received an inferior education. The minister responsible admitted as much in the national parliament, accusing the previous church schools of misleading young Africans by introducing them to the "green pastures" of European society on which they would never be permitted to graze. The solution implemented by the government was that each black child's education was allocated around one-tenth of the funds provided for the education of each white child.

Tutu, in whose own life education had been a passion, resigned his position in protest and, as the state had become the only employer of teachers, was forced to contemplate a new career.

His choice of theology was influenced by two factors. On the one hand, he had a young family to support (he had married Nomalizo Leah Shenxane in 1955) and he could sidestep into a position in the ministry with relative ease. On the other, he had long held a deep respect for Christian ministers, inspired by a childhood encounter with the Anglican priest and civil rights advocate, Trevor Huddleston. He was a small boy, walking to work with his mother, when a white man, in the garb of a priest, approached. As the man passed by, he raised his hat to Desmond's mother — a sign of respect so rare that it etched itself indelibly into the young boy's mind.

"In life," he says now, "you depend on other people. They help you to grow, they present challenges and they show you possibilities. You may not always be aware when you are emulating somebody. Perhaps unconsciously you have someone as a role model, someone who impressed you. You didn't know, at the time, that they had impressed you, especially if it happened when you were young. It is only much later that you discover it."

So Desmond Tutu enrolled in theological college and was ordained a priest in 1961. He spent eight years studying in England (several of them at King's College) and later returned to London to work for the Theological Education Fund of the World Council of Churches.

Here, he and his family were overwhelmed by their acceptance into the white community. For the first time, the Tutus tasted freedom and understood, by comparison, the impact of apartheid on their compatriots at home. It was also during his tenure with the World Council of Churches that Tutu received his first "dose," as he calls it, of liberation theology and came to realize that "the Bible is actually the most radical political manifesto there is."

Back in South Africa, meanwhile, apartheid's grip was tightening. As the growing black consciousness movement spawned campaigns of defiance, the government resorted to bloody massacres at demonstrations and abandoned any pretense of a commitment to civil rights. Opposition parties (most notably the Pan Africanist Congress and the ANC) were outlawed and many key political figures (including Nelson Mandela) were imprisoned for indefinite terms.

On Tutu's return to South Africa, he rose quickly through the ranks of the Anglican church. In 1975, he was appointed Dean of St Mary's Cathedral in Johannesburg. His first political act in his new position was to choose to live with his family in Soweto, rather than in the more luxurious Anglican deanery.

In 1976, he was promoted to Bishop of Lesotho. In 1978, he was elected General Secretary of the South African Council of Churches and thus spokesperson for all South Africa's thirteen million Christians, bar those whose allegiance was with the white Dutch Reformed churches.

In 1984, he was awarded the Nobel Prize for Peace. In 1985, he became Bishop of Johannesburg and in 1986, he was enthroned as Archbishop of Cape Town, the highest Anglican church position in the land.

At a time when the majority of black leaders had been exiled, silenced or imprisoned, Desmond Tutu became the loudest, most insistent and most eloquent voice for justice in South Africa and took a prominent place on the international stage.

At the time of his election to archbishop, he threw his, by then considerable, political weight behind calls for economic sanctions against South Africa. He repeatedly called on government leaders to abolish the pass laws, which restricted movement of black and white citizens between their designated zones; to end the policy of the forced removal of black South Africans to impoverished townships or ghettos; to establish a uniform education policy; to lift all bans on political organisations; to release political prisoners; to permit exiles to return and to begin a process of negotiation towards a representative, democratically elected government in South Africa.

The archbishop also took to the streets in protest, often placing himself in genuine danger as he stood between demonstrators and platoons of heavily armed South African police.

Broadcaster, John Cleary, tells the story of one such occasion in 1990. He was in Modderpoort, South Africa, to cover a meeting of Anglican bishops for ABC Radio in Australia.

"I was with the archbishop and the bishops when they received word that twenty-one people had been killed in Sebokeng, about three hundred miles away," he recalls. "Immediately, the archbishop said, 'We will go to Sebokeng.' So the Anglican bishops of South Africa drove to Sebokeng and I jumped in a car and followed.

"Driving through the outskirts of the town, we saw burnt-out cars, rocks across the road. The archbishop visited the burnt-out hostels, he visited the hospitals full of people who had been maimed the night before. Then, he said to the bishops, 'We will go to be with these people.'

"As the convoy of cars moved off, my driver and I managed to grab a whole lot of young, black boys and girls in choir robes and stuff them into the back of our car. We figured we'd be safe with a bunch of seven-, eight- and nine-year-olds leaning out of the car and shouting, so we went off in convoy towards the main township.

"There was a major crossroad in the center of the township and as we reached it, the crowd converged from every side, blocking the convoy of cars. The crowd was angry and chanting — some of them chanting pretty ugly things — so the archbishop got out of his car and stood on the running board. Then he said, 'What do we want?' and the crowd said, 'We want victory.' He said, 'We want peace.' and the crowd said, 'We want peace.' Gradually, there were other slogans: 'We want education,' and so on.

"I heard a noise and looked around and coming down the road was the one thing that you dread when you're in that situation, a convoy of casspirs, the big armored vehicles, with machine guns on top. You know they're loaded with police and tear gas, and you think, 'What is going to happen now?'

"By this time the other bishops had moved out of their cars and were pressing through this crowd of two or three thousand people. I could no longer see them but I heard the archbishop say, 'Let us pray.' Then the noise of the vehicles stopped. The crowd went quiet. There was no sound from the casspirs, no sound of tear gas canisters. So I looked around and there, behind me, were the Anglican bishops of South Africa — black, white, colored, old, young — standing between the crowd and the casspirs, with their arms outstretched. In that moment, I understood a little about what the Christian vision for a new South Africa cost people. I'd never witnessed that sort of courage before."

For the remainder of my time in South Africa, I join the band on its increasingly frustrating quest. The promoters steer us, for a night on the town, to a very young, very white, very affluent beer barn called Bertie's Landing, where we watch a passing parade of South African teens drink, listen to rock music, eat fish and chips and take one another home or to the beach or the back seats of their cars.

In a flagrant breach of security procedure, the intrepid lighting director and I board a "black bus" and career through language and accent barriers with a noisy mob of passengers making their way from jobs in beachside homes back into the city and then to townships on the outskirts of Cape Town.

We fly to Durban. The band plays on to packed houses which are almost exclusively and disappointingly white. The drummer suggests setting free tickets aside and providing buses, at the band's expense, for school children from outlying townships. The promoters are politely bemused. Negotiations begin for an impromptu free show in Soweto. They come to nothing, as does my personal quest. Desmond Tutu has still not returned to South Africa.

Back in Sydney, I begin a long, determined correspondence with the archbishop's media secretary, John Allen. The archbishop, I learn, will be in Australia in October.

STANDING ON THE STEPS OF ST JAMES' CHURCH IN SYDNEY, I WATCH DESMOND Tutu make his way through the forecourt, in a vast ecumenical procession. The great church is packed to standing room capacity.

"We pray for the people of South Africa," a single voice calls quietly. "Hold them in your loving hands as they await the dawn of justice, peace and freedom. Help us to commit ourselves to stand with the South African people in their struggle."

"In the power of the spirit, we commit ourselves," the congregation responds.

"To be a voice for the silenced," adds the worship leader, "to share the burden of the need for resources, to pray for gifts of courage, wisdom, energy and healing, to announce with them God's commitment to an end to the evil of racism, to surround them with our love as they sing their songs of determination and hope."

"Change is coming to South Africa," the archbishop announces and his words roll over the crowd, squeezing shoulder to shoulder and overflowing into forecourt and street. "We will be free and yes, it is of God's doing, but without you — without all of you who prayed for us, who protested on our behalf, campaigning for sanctions, for boycotts — without you, we would not be where we are today. I used to go around the world, asking for help in our struggle. It is an incredible privilege to be able to return and say, 'You know, we came asking for help, you gave that help and hey, we are succeeding.' Thank you for all you have done. Thank you.'

As the congregation parts and the procession files sedately to the door, a local African choir strikes up. Two songs into their repertoire, a handful of stragglers and African music enthusiasts has gathered around them. Moments later, all eyes turn to the left. The archbishop has slipped away from the procession, and is sneaking back in through a side door. In an instant, the half-filled church is singing and dancing, swaying and clapping with him. This evening was, after all, billed as a "celebration."

I meet the archbishop several days later. At five foot five, he is smaller in reality than I'd imagined. His head is covered in tight, salt-and-pepper curls. His handshake is firm and energetic, his smile wide and his dark eyes lively and welcoming. He is extraordinarily approachable.

Yes, he would like to read a little of my manuscript. Yes, the idea of an interview interests him. His schedule is, of course, full to the gills but his media secretary will be in touch.

So my correspondence with the long-suffering John Allen continues through the rest of 1993 and into 1994.

In November 1993, inter-party talks finally agree on an interim constitution for South Africa. In December, the establishment of a Transitional Executive Council, designed to monitor government up until the election, puts an end to exclusive white minority rule. In April 1994, South Africa holds its first truly democratic national election and Nelson Mandela is elected president.

The archbishop, along with millions in South Africa and around the world, is elated. He feels, he says, as if he has fallen in love. The sun shines more brightly, the birds sing more sweetly and the people he sees in the street appear more beautiful. Moreover, in this vindication of his struggle, he sees the working of the hand of God.

"Yes," he announces, "we have a new South Africa. Just before our election, we were gritting our teeth in fearful apprehension of what was likely to happen. Most of us were scared that we were going to be overwhelmed by a bloodbath. Most of us believed that we were on the brink of an awful civil war. As you know, right up to the last week before the election, a major role player in the whole process, the Inkatha Freedom Party, led by Chief Buthelezi, was boycotting the election. All of us were scared that we were in real trouble, that we were, as the Americans say, up a creek."

As always, he has a story to illustrate:

"Have you heard," he chortles, "about the guy who was going to make his first parachute jump? They told him, 'Don't worry, you just jump out of the aircraft and there are two cords. Pull on the first cord and the parachute will open. In the unlikely event that it doesn't open, you have a second cord. It is really foolproof. You will almost certainly not need to use the second cord.' Well, he made his jump. He pulled on the first cord. Nothing happened and he was hurtling down towards the ground. So he tried the second cord. Nothing happened again. The air was coming past him at breakneck speed, when someone shot past him, heading in the opposite direction. So this guy yelled out, 'Help, do you know anything about parachutes?' The other guy called back, 'No, do you know anything about pressure cookers?' "

This parachutist's predicament, the archbishop explains, is analogous to a nation about to embark on a new course of democracy.

"Then, the election happened," he smiles. "You saw endless lines of people waiting to enter the polling booths. All sorts of things were going wrong. There were not enough ballot papers. You couldn't have had a worse scenario. After I had voted for the first time in sixty-two years, I went around to survey what was happening and I saw those long lines. It would have taken just two people with AK47s to have created the most awful mayhem. It didn't happen. These long, long lines did not turn to chaos, disgruntlement, anger, as one might have expected. An incredible kind of alchemy was at work.

"As people stood in these long, long lines — sometimes in baking heat, sometimes in the rain — South Africans of all races began sharing picnic lunches, sharing newspapers, sharing stories. Suddenly, they discovered one another. The scales fell off their eyes and they made what, to you, would appear so obvious but, for them, was a very profound discovery: 'Hey, we are fellow South Africans. Skin color is indeed a total irrelevance.'

"They found that they wanted the same sorts of things. They wanted a safe environment for their children, they wanted a nice home, they wanted a good job, they wanted good schools. Ethnicity and skin color didn't even enter the equation.

"Elections in almost every other part of the world are political, secular events. Our election turned out to be a deeply spiritual and a deeply religious experience. Indeed, it was a mountain-top experience, a transforming experience.

"Each of us went into the polling booth as one type of person and came out the other side a totally transfigured, transformed person. The white person went in carrying a heavy burden of the guilt that comes from enjoying, so unjustly, the many privileges afforded by apartheid. They came out on the other side, a different person: 'Hey, I'm free. The burden of guilt has been lifted.' The black person went in weighed down by the anguish and the pain of having had their dignity trampled under foot, their humanity rubbed in the dust. They came out changed, transfigured, transformed: 'Hey, I am free. The burden has been removed. My dignity, my personhood have been acknowledged.'

"An incredible miracle has taken place. Even the most secular of us have to admit that only religious language can truly describe what has happened. It is a miracle. We scored a spectacular victory over an awful system and one of the wonderful things was that nobody, after the election victory, gloated. Nobody said, 'We blacks have beaten you whites.' People were saying, 'It is a victory for justice, it is a victory for South Africa.'

"South Africans have, ever since, walked tall, with a new pride. No more skulking in foreign lands, seeking to hide the fact that they come from what has, for so long, been the pariah of the world. I have seen so many people wanting to deny the fact that they were South African. Many of us now have lapel badges of our new flag. You wouldn't have seen me dead with the old flag. I have this new flag on my desk. It's incredible how patriotic we've all suddenly become."

MY PUBLISHER'S DEADLINE COMES AND GOES AND STILL JOHN ALLEN AND I exchange fortnightly faxes. Mine grow increasingly demanding, his increasingly conciliatory until one morning in December when the message reads: "The archbishop will be in Sydney on Saturday. Will you be free at 10 am?"

"You've been very persistent," Desmond Tutu grins by way of greeting.

So has he. Waiting sixteen months for an interview diminishes in significance when set against a wait of sixty-two years to cast a ballot in a national election.

He rises from the desk at which he has been working on a speech and makes his way to an over-stuffed hotel couch which threatens to consume him. His bright African shirt indicates this might have been intended as the archbishop's morning off. The constant ringing of the phone hints otherwise. The supremely dedicated Mr Allen bounds from phone to desk to doorway. Desmond Tutu bows his head and whispers a quiet prayer.

Those of us who live in Australia or Europe or America have come to know, almost exclusively, the political face of the archbishop. Largely, I think, that is because of the types of questions we have asked. For so long, he was the lone free voice heard internationally for black South Africa. We could not trust the voice of his oppressors. We wanted him to tell us about the reality of life for his people at home.

However, every political act Desmond Tutu has taken has been steeped in theology. He thinks deeply, every day, about the implications of his religion. He has been involved in the struggle for justice in South Africa, quite simply, because he believes his God demands it of him. His argument against apartheid was, in his own words, that it was "unbiblical, unchristian, immoral and evil." It was an argument that he was happy to support, once quoting vast tracts of the Bible to the ostensibly Christian then president, P.W. Botha.

"It's mind blowing, really," he says of the notion that all humanity is created in God's image. "I think some of these truths reveal their profundity especially to those in situations that are not comfortable. I think many religious truths have a particular significance for times when life is rough. Most of the Bible is written either out of or into situations of suffering.

"Look at Exodus and Genesis. The first account of creation is written to Jews in exile who were feeling really rotten and badly let down by God. They were in a land where it seemed so clear that the gods of the Babylonians had succeeded and they were surrounded by huge monuments to these Babylonian deities. This account of creation is actually a propaganda piece. It is incredible theology, yes, but it was written, very largely, to lift the morale. It says, 'You are sitting amongst people who have won, who have a pantheon of gods. You have one God. They need several gods to carry out all the divine functions. Your God embraces all.

"There was a story in Babylon about how creation happened. It happened when the god, Marduk, overcame the goddess, Tiamat. He killed her and, from the pieces of her carcass, sprung all creation. The incredible story in Genesis adopts some of those mythical elements but it uses them to convey a different set of truths.

"On one side are many gods. On the other is one God. On this side, creation happens as a result of a bloody struggle between two gods. On that side, God just has to speak and things happen. God just says, 'Let there be,' and there is. It's a wonderful account. In Babylon, the moon and the stars are thought to be deities who have an horrendous influence on human beings. The Jewish God says, 'I have created them for you, to provide light for you.'

"Then, at the end, comes this extraordinary event: God creates human beings in God's own image and likeness. In the Babylonian account, human beings are created to be the scavengers of the gods. You are not important and the gods are capricious. The first human being is created from the clots of Tiamat's blood. Now, Tiamat is a goddess of evil, so, according to the Babylonian account, you already have an evil element within you. In the biblical account, you are created good. It does not just say that what God saw is good. It says very good. Everything that God created is very good and human beings are God's stand-ins, God's viceroys, God's representatives to hold sway over all of creation on behalf of God."

This is the cornerstone of Desmond Tutu's faith. It is the passage which sent him to the barricades and around the world time and again. It led him to kneel in the dirt and gaze down the barrels of automatic weapons. It led him to comfort the wailing, fifteen thousand strong crowd at Stephen Biko's funeral with the words, "If God is on our side, who can be against us?"

"I said this account was propaganda," he continues, "and to a great extent, it is. It's saying, 'Your God, you Jews, is the real McCoy God.' It's saying that this God is Jewish because God rests on the seventh day. God is a good Jew. God keeps the Sabbath. However, if that account was pure propaganda, you'd expect the author — who was a Jew writing for Jews — to have said, 'only Jews, and maybe only Jewish men, were created in the image of God.' Perhaps a sign that this account is actually inspired by God is the fact that it says that every human being is created in the image of God. It is an incredible assertion that you and I, however we may be — it has nothing to do with status, it has nothing to do with race — were made in God's image. It is of universal application to every human being.

"So, this saying is dynamite in any situation of injustice and oppression. We are treated like dirt, for whatever reason, or we are told we are not important. The Bible says, 'Nuh-uh. Any attribute that is isolated and can belong only to one set of people is a horrible irrelevance and you count with a worth that is infinite just because you are a human person created in the image of God.' Its political significance is mind boggling. It is one of the most radical things that you could ever find. No political manifesto can match the Bible for radicalness."

The political nature of his ministry has been the focus for a continuous stream of right-wing criticism but this has not for a moment diverted the archbishop from his course. At its very core, he asserts, the Judeo-Christian tradition is political.

"When we read it," Desmond Tutu explains, "the Bible starts with creation but that is not where it actually began. That is not how the Israelites came to experience God. They experienced God, first of all, in an act that was not religious in a narrow sense. They didn't meet God in church. Their first experience of God was when God helped them to escape from bondage. It was the exodus.

"Then, it was when they were reflecting on this experience, this political encounter with God, that they extrapolated backwards. They decided that a God who could do the things that this God did in the exodus must be a God who is in charge of creation. Therefore, if this God is in charge of creation, this God must also have started it all. They worked backwards and also forwards. They said, 'This is our primordial, our founding, paradigmatic experience of God. God is a liberator God. God is a God who is on the side of the weakest.'"

When surrounded by oppression, Desmond Tutu insists, careful reading of the Bible demands activity for justice. In the history of Israel, he says, we see the workings of a God who has no qualms about uprooting the powerful and unjust.

Moreover, Jesus did not spend his life praying on a mountain top. Far from it. He sided with the weak, the downtrodden, the oppressed and poor. Jesus went about the work of restoring unity between one human being and another and between humanity and God.

Even more extraordinary, the archbishop believes, is that this God of justice is also a God of unparalleled compassion. Desmond Tutu's God cares when people die in custody, when children starve in a land of plenty or are gunned down on their way to school. Indeed, this God of his is so compassionate as to intercede for us, whether we have earned it or not. This God did not liberate the Jews because they were particularly virtuous. This God acts on our behalf and ahead of our deserving.

"It was not because this bunch of slaves deserved to be saved," he insists. "They didn't deserve it. It was a gratuitous act on the part of God. That is why Paul says, 'Whilst we were yet sinners, Christ died for us.' That's incredible. God — who upholds all morality and goodness and value, who ought to be the paradigm of virtue — does not choose the good, does not side with the good. Grace is at the heart of it all. When you read Deuteronomy, constantly God is reminding the Jews that it was not because they were good, it was not because they were important, it was because I am God and I did what I did because 'I am the kind of God that I am.'

"Jesus was constantly trying to tell this story. Do you remember the parable that he tells of the laborers in the vineyard?"

I admit that I don't.

"It's an incredible story," he says and, thirty-three years after graduating to the ministry, his eyes still light up as he recounts it.

"A man goes out one morning, looking for laborers to work in his fields for the day. He meets up with some people who are looking for work and bargains with them and says, 'I will give you the normal wage for the day.' So they go off and they work. Then he goes out again, maybe three hours later, at midday, and finds more people to work for him. He goes out again at three o'clock. Then, finally, when only one hour is left of the normal working day, he goes out and he finds another bunch of people and says, 'Come.' They don't bargain with him. They just come and they don't know what to expect.

"When the day is over, he says to the person in charge, 'Now, pay everyone, starting from the last bunch,' and to the last bunch of people he gives a full day's wage. So, these guys, who came in right at the beginning and bore the burden of the day, expect to be paid more but they're paid exactly the same amount as the lot who worked just for a few moments. They grumble. They say, 'We did most of the work and we were here under the burning sun and you are paying us the same amount that you pay to these people who have done nothing.' The man says, 'Yes, but we agreed on this wage.' Then he says, 'Don't I have a right to do with what is my own as I wish?'"

The Bible, says the archbishop, is teeming with instances in which God's love has no strings attached. He thinks immediately of those who were closest to Jesus.

"'Look at this guy,' said his critics. 'He is supposed to be a prophet but who does he consort with? Prostitutes, sinners. I mean, those are the people who sit at his table. What kind of a person is he? Did you see how he behaved with that woman who came in? She's a woman of the streets and she made an embarrassing scene. There she was, the whole time through that meal, sitting at his feet, crying and wiping his feet with her hair. If he had been a prophet, he would have known what an awful character she was.'"

"Christianity is actually an incredible thing," Desmond Tutu adds softly. "We've turned it around. We've made Christianity a religion of virtue, whereas Christianity is, in fact, a religion of grace. God says, 'I don't love you because you are lovable. You are lovable because I love you and nothing — but nothing — is going to change that love that I have.'"

His faith in that love accounts, perhaps, for his irrepressible optimism. Throughout his long and public battle with apartheid, he was sustained by a conviction that justice would come to South Africa, whether South Africans deserved it or not.

"God's purposes are certain," he would often say. "God's intention to establish his kingdom of justice, of love, of compassion, will not be thwarted."

He was fond of quoting, to government ministers, Psalm 72, in which God outlines the basic requirements expected of rulers: "To judge thy people with righteousness and thy poor with justice" and "from oppression and violence redeem their life."

He truly believed that divine justice would have its way in South Africa, just as today he is convinced that South Africa will emerge from the turmoil of transition to become, not only an exemplary democracy, but a virtual paradise on earth.

"My hope," he confesses, "is that South Africa will become one of the most wonderful countries in the world, with everyone having a place in the sun. I hope that it will be a gentle country, with people who do not think that the most important thing is to succeed, but that the most important thing is to be caring and loving and compassionate. I hope that we will show our greatness by how we deal with the weakest and the most marginalized and how we use our economic and military powers, which are fairly substantial, not to threaten others but to give them space.

"We now have a democratic government and we have the best president in the world but that is just one stage in the process. Now, that goal has to be turned into tangible energy. It has to be turned into homes for the homeless; it has to be turned into clean, running water for people who, for so long, have not had running water at all; it has to be turned into electricity; it has to be turned into good schools, good jobs; it has to be turned into a safe environment and into a society that will embrace all.

"Apartheid was a society that sought to alienate, to separate, to set apart. Now, we must attempt to embrace everyone, so that no one feels marginalised or pushed to the edges of society. That is why we have eleven official languages. What other country that you know has three national anthems? We want a society which will celebrate diversity, so there will be no discrimination on any grounds — not on the basis of race, of culture, of gender, of sexual orientation, of faith, of anything. We want a society that is compassionate and gentle and caring, a society that says people matter more than things, people matter more than profits."

Once again, the archbishop does not entertain a moment's doubt that this will come about.

"We have some very serious problems," he acknowledges, "but we are going to succeed. Not so much because we are smart or conspicuously good — obviously, having produced a system like apartheid, we have not been — but we will succeed largely because God wants us to succeed for the sake of the rest of the world.

"God wants us to succeed because we are such an unlikely bunch. Who would ever have thought that South Africa could be used as a symbol of unity, of reconciliation? God wants to be able to hold up this new South Africa as a beacon of hope to Liberia, to Bosnia, to Rwanda, to Somalia, to the Sudan and say, 'Hey, you know, over there, they too had a nightmare. It was called apartheid. It was a mess but it has ended. Your nightmare will end. They had a problem which was thought to be intractable. It had been on the agenda of the world since 1948.

It is being solved. No problem can ever again be described as intractable.'

"So, we will succeed because God is going to set us up as a paradigm, saying, 'If it could happen in South Africa, then it can happen everywhere else in the world.' We used to say, 'We are going to be free, all of us, black and white together, the rainbow people of God.' Now what we say is, 'We are free, all of us, black and white together, the rainbow people of God.'"

The price of that freedom was unspeakable. In just twenty months, between August 1984 and April 1986, twelve hundred black South Africans were killed, primarily at the hands of official security forces. A further thirteen hundred people died in political unrest during 1986 alone. In the last six months of that same year, twenty-five thousand people were detained under emergency regulations.

In the weeks leading up to the 1994 election, a car bomb near ANC headquarters in Johannesburg killed nine people and injured ninety-two. In Germiston, a bomb at a taxi rank killed ten people. Two people were killed when a bomb exploded in Pretoria and sixteen died in an explosion at Johannesburg airport.

This is merely a random selection of events. Much of the archbishop's life has been lived under a weighty cloud of violence and fear. While Desmond Tutu was actually imprisoned only briefly, it was a threat which hung perpetually over his head. His son, Trevor, was sentenced to jail under anti-hijacking legislation following a publicity stunt at an airport. The Tutus were forced to send all four of their children abroad for an education which was denied them under the South African system. Moreover, the archbishop's life was under constant threat, as was highlighted when a car he was to travel in was tampered with, following his return from Mozambique in 1987.

Yet, he forgives. Indeed, he is bemused by the difficulty I have comprehending this forgiveness.

"How do you forgive? You forgive by forgiving," he mutters, with furrowed brow. "You simply forgive.

"I was actually thinking this morning that life without forgiveness is virtually impossible — on a personal or societal or national or international level. I mean, if blacks had found it difficult to forgive whites for slavery, how would they ever have been able to live together? You have to. Forgiveness is saying, 'I am opening a door for you to walk out and start again.' How can life, for a married couple, continue if there is no forgiveness? How are they going to survive in Rwanda if, ultimately, they do not forgive? How would we ever have a new South Africa? How could we ever have a future, if there was no forgiveness?

"I was reading, in your interview with Oodgeroo [Chapter Four, "Say It Loud"], that an elder once told her how the Earth Mother does not permit Aboriginal people to hate. That reminded me of a concept in our African world view, called *ubuntu*, which is the essence of being human. Our understanding of being human is that it is corporate. I can't be human in isolation. I need other people. We say that a person is a person through other persons. I am because I belong, and one of the highest values is harmony in the community. Anything that undermines that harmony is bad. It's bad for the community and it's bad for the individuals who make up the community. Resentment, anger, revenge are self-destructive because, when you undermine that harmony, when you undermine another person, you inexorably undermine yourself. Hatred and anger are corrosive.

"So, after Mau Mau in Kenya, people expected that the Kenyans would go on an orgy of revenge against whites. It never happened. They expected it to happen in Zimbabwe after Mugabe's victory. It didn't happen. They expected it to happen in Namibia. It didn't happen. In South Africa, they are surprised at the capacity to forgive, highlighted particularly by Nelson Mandela but he's not the only one. It's a gift. It's not something that we can boast about. It's not our achievement. It is something that God has given us which maybe we can share with the world. It is the capacity to be magnanimous.

"In fact, you see, it is ultimately the best form of self-interest because, if I destroy the society in which I live, how am I going to survive? Since the being who I am is caught up in the being who you are, when you are diminished, whether I like it or not, I am diminished. So I have to forgive. If I am going to have a future, it is because you also have a future."

It is interesting to speculate what might have become of the archbishop had he remained a teacher, and what might have become of South Africa. Would democracy have come later, with more bloodshed? Would Desmond Tutu have found his way into politics? Would he, in fact, have evolved such an astute political consciousness without the overwhelming influence of his Christian faith?

"I am," he has said, over and over, "a pastor, not a politician. I am a church person who believes that religion does not deal just with one compartment of life."

There are many who believe that, if the church has a future, it is in just this brand of liberation theology. There are others who feel that, as the religion of the oppressors, Christianity has no place in Africa nor in other indigenous cultures around the globe. This is one issue on which, the archbishop is happy to admit, his approach is not so radical.

"I have learned one or two little things about religion over the years," he smiles conspiratorially. "Human beings are incredible creatures, with remarkable capacities for nobility. We can achieve truly sublime things. Just think of some of the ways people have given of themselves on behalf of others, the compassion and the love, the great achievements in science and the creations of artists and composers. When you see or experience them, you think God must rub God's hands in an incredible self-satisfaction and say, 'That really justifies the risk I took creating these creatures.'

"Then, there is the other side — our capacity to be evil, our capacity to turn goodness into something horrendous. On the one hand, science has achieved remarkable breakthroughs in medicine but scientists also produced the atom bomb.

"We humans have an ability to choose. When I give you a knife and you use it for cutting up bread to make sandwiches which you then give to a hungry person, a knife is a good thing. When I give you that knife and you stick it in somebody's guts and you kill them, then the knife is a bad thing. On its own, it is actually morally neutral. It is what you do with it.

"Religion is the same. Religion is not, in and of itself, a good thing. What you do with religion determines its worth. So, yes, religion has been a remarkably glorious liberator but it has also been horrible when, in the hands of some, it has been used for malevolent, evil purposes. It is not the religion that is good or bad. It is we.

"Whenever we Christians have risen to the best that is possible in us through the inspiration of our faith, we have been able to do incredible things. However, equally, invoking the same religion, we've done horrendous things. Remember what GK Chesterton once said. He said, 'The trouble is not that Christianity has failed. The trouble is that Christianity has never been tried.' He is exaggerating but you can understand what he means."

I stand to leave and the archbishop, lurching for the phone, calls out, "God bless you."

John Seed

2

A VOICE FROM THE WILDERNESS

YOU ARE WALKING THROUGH THE FOREST A MOMENT BEFORE SUNRISE ONE MORNING in summer. To the west, the sky is still indigo. A handful of dim stars dip towards the horizon. To the east, mountains and sky glow pink. Twigs crack underfoot. The earth feels cool. The first birds call across the great gash of a valley into which the path you're traveling winds. Otherwise, there is only silence. You reach the valley floor and, looking around, notice a rustling form emerge from a mound of leaves, just the way street people do from newspapers about this time every morning. It stands for a moment, facing west, losing itself in the infinity of blue. As it turns to the east, the sun crests the valley wall, flooding everything in watercolor light. The form begins its climb out of the valley, towards the sun.

    This is your first encounter with John Seed. Mine, however is less picturesque. It's about five on a fiercely hot afternoon. A man in the carport points his spanner up the stairs to a darkened room in which bodies are strewn on couches, on cushions, on the floor. One of these belongs to John. The others belong to his son, his son's friends, his friend's sons. They all went surfing at dawn. They collapsed about twelve. They stumble blearily to their feet before piling back out the door beachwards. Only John remains. Slowly, he rises to his feet, smooths the creases from a magenta sarong, ruffles his short cropped grey hair and offers tea. This is the first time he has spoken. His voice is soft, barely more audible than a whisper. He boils water and, while he's there, begins to make dinner for the boys.

Flitting from stove to fridge to chopping board, he chats animatedly about Ecuador, where the Rainforest Information Center funds a project which has saved more than half a million acres of rainforest. John founded the center in 1979, shortly after his first involvement in direct action. It was a demonstration to save a small patch of Australian coastal forest at Terrania Creek. The protests went on for months, stirring the environmental conscience of a nation and changing the lives of those involved — none more than John's.

"I went in there thinking that I was going to save the forest," he's often said, "and walked out knowing that the forest had saved me."

John Seed has been described by his peers as "one of the genuine heroes of the international environment movement" and "someone who has been personally responsible for saving more rainforest than anyone else we know." His Rainforest Roadshows (in which he traveled the globe, singing, speaking, showing slides and videos about the state of the environment) inspired the formation of the Rainforest Action Network, which organized the groundbreaking Burger King boycotts in America.

Today, he lobbies governments and corporations around the world, implements sustainable forestry practices in Pacific island nations, raises funds to support campaigns from Siberia to Ecuador and is among the most influential and creative thinkers in the new environmental religious philosophy called Deep Ecology.

The term Deep Ecology was first used by Arnae Naess, Emeritus Professor of Philosophy at Oslo University, to describe a cosmology which draws on influences as diverse as Eastern and indigenous religions, Spinoza, Thoreau, the Neo-Platonic mystics and recent developments in physics and the biological sciences. Deep Ecology sees the root of the current environmental crisis in the anthropocentricism of much Western philosophical and spiritual thought and sees the world, not as a pyramid with humans teetering on top, but as a web of which *homo sapiens* is a single strand.

"It went IBM, LSD, meditation and community," John smiles, explaining the evolution of his own thought towards Deep Ecology. In the 1960s, he "turned on, tuned in, dropped out," leaving a lucrative position as a systems engineer with the international computing giant to take drugs, explore Eastern mysticism and get back to nature on the Australian east coast.

"I grew vegetables for a few seasons — the experience of placing a seed in the ground and growing a tomato and taking a seed from the tomato and putting it in the ground and growing another tomato," he recalls. "Then, I helped to conceive a child and birthed that child with my partner. Finally, ecology swept me away. I had a very powerful spiritual experience of the environment through Terrania Creek, Franklin River, the Daintree rainforest and all those direct actions.

"Each of those things gradually transformed my life, until I finally surrendered to the earth. Now, I find myself asking for guidance and direction and energy and wisdom from the earth, knowing that I am part of the earth, knowing that I'm a cell in the body of the earth. I just go back to the forest, lie down on the forest floor, cover myself in leaves, imagine an umbilical chord going from my belly deep down into the earth and pray for nourishment, wisdom and guidance. There I find energy and an ability to act, to inspire other people, to think, write, dream, make films and do all of these things."

John compares the notion of "a god with a human image" to the once-firm conviction that the earth was the center of the universe and all else revolved around it. It comes, he says, from the same mindset, but neither belief is logical nor particularly productive in the world in which we live today. We let go of the idea that we were the center of the solar system and discovered a vastly more complex and interesting universe to explore. In much the same way, John postulates, we can discard this notion that we are the crown of creation (evidenced by a god who is much like us) and find ourselves part of an intricate web sustained by a force whose wealth, diversity and generosity are unlike anything we have imagined.

"When I think of divinity, I think of four thousand million years of evolution," he says. "I think of the Milky Way. Virtually all the stars we see are the Milky Way. We can barely see anything else with the naked eye. What we call the Milky Way is just the center of the Milky Way. It's all Milky Way. We are Milky Way and that's one of hundreds of billions of galaxies.

"So, when I think of sacredness, I think of the expanding universe and the propensity — you might even say desire — of that universe to articulate itself, to become more conscious, to become more complex."

He speaks of this vast web as though it were alive and intelligent. Each of its threads is unique but none is indispensable. Humanity is magnificent but no more or less important than anything else.

"It's so huge," he insists, "and the human circuitry is such a tiny fragment of it. It's like a hologram. One human being, in a sense, contains it all, though with less clarity. One human being is an attempt to articulate and to give expression to that force which you might call the universe or god or nature."

He can see no end to the web of creation but individual strands must come and go. He perceives no menace in the violence of nature and is comfortable with the notion that he, and all humanity, will one day return to the earth, leaving no trace but fertile soil. He claims he's not afraid of death.

"I don't see what difference it makes," he grins impishly, "whether all my constituent molecules go back into the great cycle, out of which they emerged, with or without some trace of my soul. I understand reincarnation, genetics, near death experiences. I know that people come back from them and people remember past lives in rebirthing or under drugs. I've had intimations of this, that and the other myself but I don't understand what the fuss is about. It's all miraculous and 'I' am miraculous but 'not-I' is just as miraculous as 'I', so who cares?"

All this, John relates matter of factly, as he busies himself about the kitchen. By far the most important thing on his mind at the moment is that the vegetables begin steaming. Musing about cosmology is a pleasant distraction but a distraction nonetheless. It is only when he begins to speak about a particular campaign that passion informs his every word.

In the Solomon Islands and Papua Niugini, he has been instrumental in the introduction of a whole new approach to forestry. As multinational lumber companies swept in, striking deals with indigenous people to deforest their neighborhoods, John Seed heard of a product called the Walkabout Sawmill. These tiny mills are just the right size for island villagers to operate their own sustainable forestry industries. In conjunction with ecological forest management, they can bring economic development to villages without destroying the integrity of the forest. Teaming up with a local non-government organisation, the Rainforest Information Center convinced the Australian government to fund the introduction of well-managed Walkabout Sawmills, protecting hundreds of thousands of acres of rainforest which had been slated for industrial logging.

Even other activists are in awe of his boundless energy. He is, they say, possessed. The burnout rate amongst those who try to keep pace with him is enormous. Over twenty years, his passion for the environment has not abated. The reason, he says, is that he has never been fighting for anything but himself. As an activist, he says, he represents the earth.

"This is difficult to discuss," he admits, "because, 'I represent the earth,' can sound terribly arrogant. When I tell you I represent the earth, I mean that, when you don't represent your ego and when you don't represent Australia and when you don't represent Christianity and when you don't represent humanism and when you don't represent anything else, then that's automatically what you represent. I don't think of it as something I've constructed so much as, when you pull all the other things away, that's what's left because that's what's always been underneath it all. The sense of separation from nature, which everybody in this society suffers, is an illusion.

"I'm not talking, here, about anything more mysterious than trying to hold your breath for three minutes. The fact that we can't hold our breath for three minutes totally demonstrates our interdependence. That's our relationship with the air. Then there's the water and the soil and all the other earth cycles which move through us and which define us. The psyche grows out of this soil and out of this water and out of this air.

"It's no big deal to represent those things because that's who we are. As soon as you know that, what else can you do? What else can you represent? It's not like, 'I'm a very noble person because I represent the earth.' No, I'm totally self-centered and self-absorbed like everybody else. It's just that most people don't know what their selves actually consist of. Recent cultural influences have led us to see ourselves as separate from and superior to the rest of nature. Common sense and even elementary high-school science, however, tell a different story. We all started out as stardust. Every single thing around us is a relative."

"We've been evolving here on earth for thousands of millions of years," John explains. "I've been evolving here for thousands of millions of years. Every cell in my body has been evolving here for thousands of millions of years. To represent the thrust of that today is my task. In order to do that, I need to recognize the conditioning that makes me identify with something smaller than that, whether it's a country or a religion or an ideology or my ego. Rather than representing those tiny things, I aim to represent the big picture, in the same way that every ant and every mosquito and every little microbe does. There's nothing grandiose about it. It's just that humans, it seems to me, are the only ones who have some choice in the matter. We can choose not to represent that life force.

"Ever since we grew this big bulge above our nose and developed self-reflective thought, it's been possible for us to see ourselves as separate from the rest of it. Along with that possibility, comes the freedom to represent anything we can imagine. So people imagine that they are fundamentalist Christians or Fascists or Socialists or Buddhists and they live certain kinds of lives. Humans are very fragmented. Millions of different human cultures have developed.

"Indigenous cultures, through regular rituals which lie at the very root of their social organisation, are able to maintain a spiritual connection with the matrix out of which humanity and everything else has evolved. However, modern human beings, having dispensed with all that in their arrogance, no longer have any way in which to articulate and experience the connections between themselves and the rest of the earth or between themselves and their evolutionary journey. Our evolutionary journey becomes like a story in a book or one branch of science rather than being the root of our existence.

"I remember, there was this thing when I was at university. It was a black box with a switch on it. You turned the switch and there was a creaking of gears, a door opened, a hand came out and it switched itself off. Today, we're in a position to represent that. We can switch ourselves off if we want to."

BY NOW, STEAM IS RISING FROM A BEVY OF POTS IN THE KITCHEN AND JOHN IS SITTING on the couch, cradling his tea. He seems envious of ants and microbes, envious of the ease with which they play their integral roles in the scheme of things. Surely, I suggest, there must be some reason for the evolutionary path we've trodden. There must be some advantage to this perilous facility for choice.

"The place we've come to has certain characteristics," he says, then pauses. "Which of those are advantageous, I guess, depends on your point of view. I see some advantage to the experience of love, to the experience of spiritual upliftment and consciousness. Our human circuitry is capable of experiencing and expressing certain states which, as far as I can tell, are unique. To me, they have value but so do the characteristics of decomposing bacteria.

"A species is defined by the fact that it has certain characteristics which other species don't. I expect that every species, if it could reflect on such things, would find its own characteristics particularly delightful. So, as a human being, I feel that the highest qualities of my species are particularly marvellous but, objectively, the qualities of decomposing bacteria must be more marvellous because, without them, organic life would cease. It's easy to see the beauty of the earth going on without any mind capable of reflecting on it. Without the decomposing bacteria, however, you can forget it, it's just a lump of rock."

The disadvantages of this condition we've evolved to are, for John, far simpler to identify.

"The disadvantages are our anthropocentricism and our arrogance in thinking that we are the measure of all being and that we alone were created in the image of God. I like James Lovelock's way of putting it. He says it's as if the brain thought it was the most important organ in the body and started mining the liver. It's not to say that the brain isn't as miraculous as the liver or anything else. It's just that it's part of a body and it has no existence outside that body. To start mining the liver doesn't show what a powerful brain it is, it shows what a stupid brain it is. It's like a tree with a billion leaves and one leaf thinks that the sole purpose of the tree is to be a place for that one leaf to grow. It's ugly and embarrassing and the consequence, if this attitude is lived out with our current technology, is that we start to destroy the tree on which we're growing. We believe in our own independence, even when ecology clearly shows us our extraordinary interdependence. We behave as though we could profit by chopping down this tree, even though we're actually a leaf on one of its branches."

"Is it stretching it too far," I ask, "to say that, for you, the whole tree is made in the image of God?"

"The whole tree is God," he insists. "I have no experience or evidence or reason to postulate God is outside it. That's just unnecessarily cumbersome. The tree is God-like, in the sense that it's mysterious and powerful and creative and fertile. I'm in awe of the numinous possibilities of the universe. It stretches out to infinity in all directions. I can't sense any limit to it. That's the web."

I NEVER CEASE TO BE STRUCK BY THE POWER NATURE HOLDS OVER THE PSYCHE. A very urban, very cerebral child, it was not until my early twenties that I first stepped into a forest and felt it was alive.

It was not until I met John Seed that I realized most of my epiphanies have hit while I've walked along beaches. John has spent more time than most of us in nature. His office, his church, his family is the forest. Yet it still fills him with wonder. Have people always been awe-struck by nature or is it because we've distanced ourselves from it that we're so often overwhelmed in its presence?

"I think," John suggests, "that our ability to experience may have evolved. I'm not sure how much other life forms can experience. It seems to me that it might be a human phenomenon which has developed as our leisure and our time to philosophize and think and experience things has increased.

"Then again, perhaps trees are in a constant state of awe. How would one know? That sense that everything is singing God's praises all the time and that we've just forgotten, grown too busy to remember. Modern humans have an incredible distrust of feeling. There's this idea that all our intelligence is in our thinking and that this is betrayed by feelings, that we need to be objective about things and not get emotional. We're unconscious of the fact that we survived for thousands of millions of years before thinking came along, which must have taken extraordinary intelligence. I came from my mother's womb and she came from her mother's womb and it goes back through womb after womb until wombs were invented. Before that, reptilian eggs and before that, spores.

"At every step of the way, each ancestor of mine and yours had to somehow survive long enough to reproduce before being consumed. At every step along the way, millions died without being able to do that. How many eggs does a fish have? Well, we had a zillion fish ancestors, one after the other, and every one of those had millions of eggs, of which two or three survived. At each generation, our ancestor was one of those. There's incredible intelligence in that, yet it had no thinking associated with it at all. It was feeling, intuition, instinct."

John has co-authored a book on Deep Ecology called *Thinking Like a Mountain* and that is, to some degree, his aim.

"Has intuition been totally replaced by our linear thinking," he asks, "or is it possible for us to surrender to it once again? I believe we can. In order to do that, we have to see through humanism and the idea that human beings are more special than anything else. We must drop that and recognize the tiny part we play and deliberately surrender the idea that we're so smart and we know what's going on. Then we can start to hear the music that everything else is dancing to and that offers the possibility of living harmoniously with it all.

"At the moment, we can't smell anything except our own stench. We can't hear anything except our own thoughts and voices. We've forgotten that anything else speaks. The world is reduced to human beings and resources. It's a horrible idea but, when we let go of that, we can once again harmonize with the incredible choir of nature and that is what has the longevity, that potentially lives forever. By cleaving to that, we've thrown heads every single toss of the coin, every generation, for four thousand million years. We haven't thrown tails once. We think we can replicate that exquisite intelligence with our thinking but there's no evidence of it. Can we create a system where the very thing that the leaves exhale is what we inhale? Can we create the tide?

"We've evolved in the middle of this exquisitely complex, beautiful thing and, if we destroy it, I have no confidence whatsoever that we can replace it with machines. So, I think, the first step is to experience the awe and also to experience the embarrassment at having been so childishly arrogant."

This is not to say we should throw the baby out with the bath water. Interestingly, for someone who communes with his God by burying himself in leaves, John is not an extremist. Asked once by the American psychologist and mystic, Ram Das, to justify his travel by jet, John told this story:

"The only thing that helps me in this," he began, "is a metaphor from a cowboy movie that I saw in my childhood. All the cowboys are asleep, and the fire's gone out and the clouds come over. Then there's a bolt of lightning and all the cattle stampede towards the cliff. The cowboys jump on their horses and they don't ride in the opposite direction, they ride straight towards the cliff, even faster than the cattle. Now, their aim is not to go over the cliff but they realize that only by keeping pace with the whole thing can they turn the herd around. So I use a computer and I know the chips were cleaned using CFCs. I'm prepared to get my hands dirty with sawmills and aeroplanes and anything at all but I'm also prepared to let go of them."

Likewise, John will cheerfully use linear thinking to serve his ends. Indeed, he believes it has a role to play in serving all our ends.

"The role of our intelligence," he says, "is that — at incredible cost to the species we've killed and things we've dismembered and destroyed and the landscape that's been trashed — we've built up a certain set of skills and attributes and knowledge about ourselves. With that, I hope, we can now construct a place for ourselves on the earth that will allow the earth to continue.

"I think rational, linear thought is a good servant. If it's accompanied by good will, if it's accompanied by love and a concern for the big picture, then it's incredibly clever. I'm full of admiration for it and I believe it's even clever enough to dig us out of this hole into which we've dug ourselves.

"I believe that we either already have the technology or have proved our ability to create the technology to enable us to live extraordinarily well within the limits of the biological systems in which we find ourselves.

"The trouble is that, by seeing only our own cleverness, we've tricked ourselves. We can't succeed while we refuse to see the intelligence and generosity of nature. I used to break my teeth on those hard roots and then I delved into the nature of things and found a way to turn them into the fat, soft orange carrots that I now eat. I can either see that as a sign of how clever I am or I can see how incredibly generous nature is. Whatever question we put to her, this mother, this thing that nourished us through all the ages, she'll say yes to it. We want to dig up a bit of dirt and turn it into a wire to carry our messages all the way around the world. She says yes. There's this incredible generosity, this incredible intelligence. Our intelligence is the tiniest fragment of all of that. All we need is the humility and the willingness to cooperate with it.

"I believe that our arrogance is actually a reaction. Deep down, we feel miserable and useless and we have no self-esteem whatsoever. So we react to that by crowing, 'I'm so fantastic, I'm so great,' without really believing it. We need to let go of that, to experience the pain of being very little and ignorant.

"Really, we don't know anything. If I cut my skin, it heals by itself. It has nothing to do with me. We're helpless. It supports us, it keeps us alive and has always done so. When we see how miraculous that is, then we know that there's no way out of it, we're part of that. We evolved here. The composition of our blood is akin to the composition of sea water four hundred million years ago, when our ancestors crawled from the ocean. All the evidence suggests that we evolved here. Therefore, if that is miraculous and awe inspiring and beautiful and intelligent, then so are we. Once that's understood, there emerges the possibility of conscious cooperation between the tiny fragment and the whole. Then we can hear the music of the earth and can find a way to bring our own human sound into harmony with it again."

WHEN NEXT I SEE JOHN SEED IT IS ON THE EIGHTH STOREY OF AN APARTMENT block in central Sydney. Outside the window, the harbor is a highway for ferries, submarines, pleasure craft, containers of goods from around the world.

The foreshores are packed, shoulder to shoulder, with highrise structures like this one. Asphalt butts up against the water. Witnessing John Seed in my apartment makes me suddenly aware that I am one hundred feet above the ground. If I'm ever likely to be susceptible to vertigo, it will be today. His precious earth is barely visible. John looks like an elf who's been plucked from the forest and abandoned in the central business district.

He arrives mid-morning, leaving me ample time to scan the headlines, read of tragedy in Bosnia and Rwanda and a bomb in an Israeli embassy. So we begin by discussing humanity.

"When you see a school of fish or a flock of birds moving as one," he explains, "they're not all thinking about what they're going to do. They just do what they feel like and, in doing that, they're harmonious with their fellows. There's a feeling I've had from the environment movement — and I think it's true for almost everything — that, when numbers of human beings align themselves with one spiritual direction or one philosophy, a certain harmony is possible between them.

"However, that harmonious group then becomes disharmonious with another group that has aligned itself with something different. Then you get the Christians fighting the Muslims and you get the Christian Catholics fighting the Christian Protestants and you find one kind of Catholic fighting another kind of Catholic and the whole world is in flames.

"There's only one thing that human beings could identify with that would really unite everybody and that is that we are earthlings. All of us are standing with our feet on the earth. We all have a navel and two nipples in common, not just with other humans, but with all other placental mammals as well. We have our toenails. If they became the badges of what we believed in, we wouldn't have to work so hard to build community. Then, if we had community and love, we wouldn't need all these objects, these displacement phenomena.

"We feel there's something missing and we feel this horrible, anxious hole inside ourselves and society teaches us that you deal with that by filling it full of stuff. We dig up the earth to make microwave ovens and electric toothbrushes that we sacrifice to this bottomless pit inside us but, no matter how much we throw in there, we are still empty and incomplete. If we could be natural — in the sense of natural relationships, natural food, natural sex, natural everything — that would be totally satisfying and enduring. That would have a future.

"The craving only disappears," he continues, "when we find that place of humility, that place of love for the earth, that place where I am the earth. Then we know that whatever beauty we can see out there has to be in us because, if it wasn't, we couldn't see it. I can't get out of the fact that I'm part of all this and, if it's magnificent, so am I. The earth is alive and generous and wants to nourish us and that's why we're alive, because she's nourished us all the way along, without a moment's pause. We only have to stop breathing for three minutes and we're dead. I don't even have to remember to breathe. I can breathe when I'm asleep. So she's pushing that air in, she's breathing me all the time and I'm too arrogant to notice it. All I can think of is, 'Aren't I fantastic.'"

This morning, as I look out the window and realize that the earth is still alive under the weight of this city, John strikes me, not as a prophet of doom, but as an emissary from some Tolkien tree creature with a message of hope. The fact that we come from generations and generations of successful adaptors speaks to me of a resilience in our species and a resilience in the planet.

"Exactly," John concurs cheerfully. "I've steeped myself in the prophecies of doom from the scientists — the number of species becoming extinct every day, what's happening to the atmosphere, the intractability of nuclear waste. On the one hand, I realize, there is no way that the environment movement can get us out of that. It's so huge and the momentum is so fast. On the other hand, my ancestors survived ice ages, my ancestors learned how to walk the land after being fish, my ancestors went from being inorganic to being organic.

"When you identify with all that, there's this fantastic pedigree, this unbroken record of survival and success and it becomes difficult to completely lose hope, even in the face of what seems like a hopeless situation. We've demonstrated our ability to face the odd crisis in the last four hundred million years and the fact that we're here talking about it is, to me, irrefutable proof of that. So, I think there must be a resilience there — in humanity and certainly in the biosphere."

The difference, however, between myself and this elf in my living room is that, while I'm cheering for humanity, he's cheering for the biosphere and if that must survive at the expense of his species, so be it.

"When the early plants in the water began producing oxygen and gradually pushed methane out of the atmosphere, ninety percent of all species died," he relates dispassionately. "Our ancestors didn't die. It's another example of how incredibly clever we've been. At the same time, ninety percent of everything died and that was fine. It might have seemed a tragedy if you'd been up close to it but, looking back now, everything went on fine.

"So, I could let go of humanity and even complex life on earth without feeling it was an utter tragedy. I could let go of organic life too because all those molecules and atoms existed before there was any life on earth. It was just hot gas once but it had the propensity — and we must say the desire — to evolve. There's nothing we can do that's going to touch that. That's who we are.

"We're the whole thing. We're the clouds of hydrogen gas, we're the big bang, we're all of that. It has recently articulated itself into this form and I like this soft stuff. I like flesh, I like organic life, I like humans, I like consciousness, I like love. I like all those things so, if I get to vote on it, I will vote for it to keep evolving on from here but I don't know whether I get to vote on it or not. If I do, I'll vote for this because I like it but not because of some terrible abyss that will be left if it all disappears. Nothing goes on forever, except possibly the matrix out of which things are born and die. So, I don't feel particularly hopeful but I certainly don't feel desperate. I just feel that, any time someone gives me a chance to choose between vibrant life and microwave ovens, I'll vote for life."

IT IS THE NIGHT BEFORE DEMONSTRATORS WILL CONFRONT LOGGERS IN A PRISTINE patch of forest in south-eastern Australia. Just outside the township of Eden, they have pitched tents and gathered in a field under a starry sky. They have come together, in preparation for the morning's demonstration, to honor the earth and reaffirm their connection to nature in a ritual known as the Council of All Beings.

John developed the Council of All Beings, with anti-nuclear campaigner Joanna Macey, as an experiential extension of Deep Ecology which, up until then, had been an exciting but nonetheless mostly cerebral affair. Through guided visualisation, movement, drama and dance, they aimed to create a very personal sense of connection with all of nature.

"I had been steeped in the philosophy of Deep Ecology," John recalls, "but I felt that it wasn't enough just to think these things. I felt that, unless we could move from having ecological ideas to having an ecological identity, it wouldn't change our behavior. So, through meeting Joanna Macey, doing one of her Despair and Empowerment workshops, combining some of those philosophies and techniques with Deep Ecology, came the Council of All Beings. It's a series of processes that dispel the illusion of separation between human beings and nature. It's ritual and ritual touches us at a deeper place than our intellect. We resonate with it.

"The Council of All Beings is a spontaneous expression of something that is very deeply human," John explains. "I haven't been able to find any indigenous culture that doesn't, at its very core, have a Council of All Beings or some such ritual. These have been practiced since time immemorial and are held to be what defines and creates the society. That suggests that the propensity to lose the connection must go very deep, that it's not a modern phenomenon. Otherwise, why would people whose lives are embedded in nature need to remind themselves, through these rituals, that human beings aren't fundamentally different from anything else? Why would we need to put on the mask of bear and wolf and speak for bear and wolf if there wasn't some doubt, some danger there?

"For a long while, I thought of the Council of All Beings as a therapy. Arnae Naess spoke about the need to move from ecological ideas to ecological self to ecological identity. To accomplish this, he suggested the creation of community therapies. To begin with, I thought, 'Hey, that's the Council Of All Beings.' It's performed in community. It's a therapy that moves us from this skin encapsulated ego to an expansive, ecological self.

"Then, I visited a Hopi village, which was the longest continuously inhabited village in the western hemisphere. They had their masks and drumming. It was much more splendid but they'd been doing the Council of All Beings for thousands of years, and still their 'therapy' wasn't complete. That's when I decided that the Council of All Beings isn't a therapy. A therapy is like, 'I'm sick now but I'm going to be well and the therapy's just a temporary thing.' Ritual, on the other hand, is something that we need to keep reaffirming and renurturing every season, every moon, every generation, all the time. It's like eating food. You don't say, 'Well, now I've eaten, I never need to eat again.'

"The Council of All Beings is a modern interpretation of this ancient phenomenon. It comes very naturally to people because it's archetypal, it's universal and it's only quite recently that we've forgotten it."

Scores of facilitators on three continents now offer these workshops and many more take place spontaneously, like the one at Eden, in times of celebration or confrontation. Like everything John's involved with, Councils of All Beings are fundamentally democratic. He refuses all credit for their inception and is happy to take a back seat if he happens to be around as one unfolds.

"Anyone can perform Councils of All Beings," he says. "No qualifications are required. It's a useful adjunct to direct action. It grounds direct action. If I know for sure, because I've just had that experience, that I'm speaking for the trees and the animals, then there's a different quality to my voice. I can stand up to the police. I can stand up to the Prime Minister. My constituency is vaster and more powerful than anything they can throw at me. It changes the confidence with which I present myself. If I just think, 'I've got my opinion — I'm an environmentalist, and you've got your opinion — you're a developer,' then it's my opinion against yours and there's no real power there. If, however, I know I'm speaking for the earth, that's a very strong place to be coming from."

Deep Ecology is a philosophy, an ideology, a gateway to the transpersonal and an impetus to action. There is, however, some dispute amongst its adherents about whether Deep Ecology is a religion.

"It depends who you ask," John laughs mischievously, "but you're asking me, so, sure. I would say that those people who don't experience Deep Ecology as a religion haven't experienced the best of it."

For John, Deep Ecology is not so much a way of thinking about the world as a way of being in the world. He might be sitting in my living room, sorting through my discs to find his favorite one by Leonard Cohen, or chained to a bulldozer on a muddy logging track a day's drive from anywhere. He might be walking defiantly into a boardroom at Mitsubishi or catching a wave off the point at Byron Bay. In every instance, he is a Deep Ecologist. Every cell of his being grew up from stardust. Every moment of the day, he aims to act and think and feel from a core that's conscious of that.

"I'm talking about living it," he smiles, "and I'm also talking about being awe-struck. You don't have to do a hell of a lot of reading or take too many drugs to know that there are heights of ecstasy, of which human beings are capable, that hardly anyone these days can experience through their political life or their work or their sexuality or anything. Some people think this is the experience of Jesus and other people think that the Buddha showed us the way to enlightenment but I think that these things come from the earth, just the same way that Jesus and the Buddha did. If Jesus and his followers and the Buddha and the Sufis have been capable of this extraordinary, elevated, high, high experience, that's because one of the qualities of the earth is the ability to create that.

"If there's any reason whatsoever why I'd be sorry to see human beings go, it's because I think that experience has more value than anything else I know. That's the religion of Deep Ecology. Deep Ecology says that experience comes from the earth. The earth offers many gifts, like food and water and air. One of the ones I like the best is enlightenment."

Dr. Elisabeth Kübler-Ross

3

CHOOSE LOVE

IT'S THE SUMMER OF 1985 AND I AM STANDING IN A HOTEL CORRIDOR UTTERLY immobile. Feet riveted to carpet, eyes fixed to the number on the door, heart racing, palms sweating. Samantha, why are you trembling at the door of a fifty-nine year old woman from Switzerland via the Virginia hills?

Frankly, I have no idea. She arrived in the country last week and I decided I had to interview her. My passion to meet her became all-consuming. I tried the regular channels. I made a lifelong friend of the secretary of her association. I sent flowers. Then finally more flowers and a note that said I was willing to sit in the hotel foyer day and night until she found time. Would she please call? She called before it came to that.

So here I stand, with ten foolscap pages of questions and a tape deck. When finally I knock, the door is opened by a tiny, grey-haired woman with the firmest handshake on earth. The smoke in the room is thick. She smokes Marlboros. I gave up last week. My resolve crumbles instantly. Then we talk. We talk for hours. We drink strong coffee, we smoke a pack of cigarettes, we eat Swiss chocolates that her son has sent in the mail. We stroll around shops buying gifts for her friends. We run through all ten pages of questions and then some and still I'm in awe.

"One thing I would like to share with people," she says, "is that they really don't need to be afraid that the planet is going to be destroyed because the tide has already changed and they can help to keep it changing. People need to know that they have an incredible effect on what happens to the planet and though it may seem very ridiculous that, if you are full of love and peace, you're going to change the planet earth, it is really true.

"You can almost verify that in your own daily life. Like, if you get up and you're a sour-puss and you scream at your husband, he steams out, furious, without a cup of coffee. Then you bash the kids and they leave without breakfast. By the time they're outside the door, they've already kicked the dog. Then they kick their friends, irritate the teacher, the teacher sends them to the principal and the principal sends them home with a letter. It's a chain reaction of horrible things.

"All you need to do is, at the end of each day, take an inventory of how many lives everybody has touched. It's an incredible effect. That's what you do at the end of your life when you're in the presence of that light. You look, literally, at the inventory of every deed, word and thought and you'll be totally overwhelmed by how many lives you've affected. With a change of one degree in you, you change one hundred and eighty degrees in so many people. If you imagine that a million people would become aware of that, this place would be gorgeous.

"I feel very enthusiastic," she adds later in the afternoon. "This is probably the most important decade in the history of humanity. Things have changed so fast and if you begin to understand that all the changes are happening, not in a linear but in an exponential way, then you can imagine what the world will look like at the end of the century. It's very exciting.

"Now we need to heal people so we can heal the planet, and that is my big dream before I make my transition. If we become less destructive in ourselves, then we are also less destructive with the earth. There is an old saying: 'as above, so below'. People must learn to treat the earth as a living organism, like another human being, and to treat their fellow human beings with more respect and love.

"We will do it," she says. "I'm very optimistic. It will be paradise on this planet very soon."

By the time I leave, I am convinced that I have met a truly extraordinary human, the sort who surfaces maybe once in a generation and who cannot leave the world unchanged. Which is striking because, in so many ways, Elisabeth Kübler-Ross and her special brand of down-home wisdom seem thoroughly ordinary. I also leave with a conviction (which hasn't left me yet) that, in some ill-defined but very permanent way, this woman has touched my life.

ON THE EIGHTH OF JULY 1926, ELISABETH BURST INTO THE WORLD (THE FIRST-BORN of triplets) and has barely stopped for breath since. She coped with the restrictions of childhood tolerably well but, as soon as she was able, took off to work as a volunteer in war-torn Europe. Returning to Switzerland, she put herself through medical school, emerged a physician and emigrated to the United States with her American husband in 1958. It was then that her life's work really began as she found herself moving into the much neglected area of the care of terminally ill patients, their relatives and friends.

Since then, she has been called a vulture and a saint. Medical students have lined up to kiss her hand and she has been spat at in hospital corridors. She has received countless honors and awards for her service to humanity, while being ridiculed for her research into life after death and almost hounded from her home county for her work with children who have AIDS. That a small, gently spoken Swiss doctor has incited reactions like these is testimony to the revolutionary nature of her work.

The experiences of so many patients she has sat with at the moment of death and her own "mystical encounters" have convinced her not only of life after death — which she describes as the spirit butterfly emerging from the physical cocoon — but also of the existence of spirit guides or guardian angels and the fact that, to heal the planet, what we all must do is increase our own individual capacity for love.

To this end, she has spent much of her life traveling the globe — up to fifty weeks of every year — lecturing to overflowing halls, visiting patients and holding workshops to aid in the release of people's pent-up "negativities," banishing fear of death with a contagious love of life. In between, she's found time to write more than fifteen books, countless papers, chapters and reviews, and to set up a farm in the woods of Virginia which, until recently, functioned as a center for her workshops and massive international organisation, as well as her sanctuary and home.

Yet this woman who, in the course of her much heralded career, has almost single-handedly changed the medical profession's view of death and vast numbers of individual lives, still describes herself as a "Swiss hillbilly".

I SEE ELISABETH AGAIN IN 1986 AND THEN IN 1987. SHE TELLS ME HER TRAVELING days are numbered, that she's settling into her farm in the woods, that she wants to write her memoirs. I laugh and say I'll believe it when I see it. Elisabeth is hardly the settling kind. She has more nervous energy per inch than anyone I've met, and she uses it. She brings out snapshots of rolling hills and sheep and tells me of her dream to open the farm up as a center for children with AIDS.

"You see, these babies are mostly the offspring of heavy drug-using mothers who are not bad people but they are only just surviving. They manage okay while the child is well but the child gets sick and they take it to a city hospital and they're told their baby has AIDS. They can't survive financially themselves if they can't work. So, in order to have the child get medical attention, they leave their baby in the hospital and disappear without a forwarding address.

"These babies are the poorest of the poor. They are handled by nurses who are very ambivalent about taking care of them. So they're maybe six months old and they'll die when they're two and they're doomed to stay in city hospitals. There isn't one single facility in the United States that takes care of these children and we must get ready because we're going to have more and more of them until, one day, the hospitals won't be able to cope."

To you and me, this is a tragedy. To Elisabeth, it's a personal responsibility.

"So I want to open up a hospice for rejected AIDS babies but, when I conceived of this, I had no idea how much hostility and anguish it would cause in a community that truly feels it is immune to AIDS. They see AIDS as an illness only of gay men in San Francisco and New York. They're petrified that, if we start this center and it becomes known, the real estate prices will go down, tourism will go down and the whole county will be viewed like a lepers' colony.

"We needed local government approval for re-zoning if we were to start this hospice, so we brought in a local physician and a navy physician — you know, associated with the military, very much in the spirit of this whole community — and we brought someone from the Health Department of the State of Virginia and we held a public meeting. Nobody could hear any of the speakers. The people screamed and yelled and hollered and they were ready to lynch us, physically. We had to be escorted home by the sheriff. They threatened to burn down the farm.

They treated us worse than anything you can imagine.

"I thought it was interesting how my life had prepared me for all this. Years ago, people would spit in my face when I started working with dying patients. Twenty years later, I got honorary degrees from those same institutions. Then I started to talk about life after death and fundamentalist Christians said that I was of Satan and I should be eliminated — in the name of Christ, mind you. Now, this is my third big project and reactions are a hundred times worse than they were twenty years ago."

That's not the half of it. I've met born-again Christians whose eyes have lit up with an unholy passion while recounting imaginary tales of black magic rituals in Elisabeth's lucerne fields and rumors of this really quite conservative Swiss grandmother cavorting naked in the moonlight with new age channelers from the west coast. She's had to retain her sense of humor, obviously, but how, I ask, in the face of such constant hostility, does she hold onto her commitment to this or any project?

"From a practical point of view, this hospice has no chance," she says, with her cryptic, crinkly smile, "but from my point of view, naturally, there is a chance. I have never given up. I know the universal laws and if you know the universal laws, then you go with the flow and you know that you're going to win because love is always stronger than fear."

I hang onto these words every moment for the next five days.

IT'S BEEN TWO YEARS SINCE ELISABETH AND I MET. I'VE WRITTEN A NUMBER OF articles about her life and work. We get on like we've known each other forever. Yet I've never attended one of her workshops. Now she invites me to come along as her guest on what I swiftly discover is the retreat from hell on the outskirts of Sydney. That my car breaks down on the way is probably an omen.

Elisabeth developed these workshops (originally called "Life, Death and Transition", now known as "Working It Through") in the 1960s, to help the terminally ill and their caregivers deal with unresolved emotions and move on to live each day more energetically, joyfully, peacefully, whether those days stretch out indefinitely or might cease tomorrow. Increasingly, participants are also drawn from the wider community. Physically, as often as not, they're fighting fit. Emotionally, they carry burdens of trauma, abuse and loss. In an understanding environment, guided by Elisabeth's experienced, supportive team, participants come along to do battle with the past, clear out cobwebs, throw open doors and windows and watch freedom rush in.

You cannot imagine the courage this takes. I look around our group each morning and am in awe of these people's resilience and trust. Seventy people have gathered here to exorcize their demons. The days merge into one great mass of pain. There is no relief from the sound of wailing, crying, sobbing and screaming. Someone has brought a guitar and we break from time to time to sing something desperately uplifting. This (along with tea and biscuits and late night raids on the kitchen) gives us the strength to face another session.

There are people here who have terminal illnesses, there are doctors and nurses, nuns and priests and many carrying long concealed scars from unforgivable childhood abuse. The fear is tangible and thick and engulfing. I spend a long time in front of a mirror one night, trying to remember who I was before I walked into this well of fierce emotion, touching my arms and legs, relieved that they still feel the same and that some things are secure. I travel with these people through an underworld of agony that I had not imagined possible. I wonder whether any of us will emerge unchanged.

Immediately following Elisabeth's workshop, I suffer ten months of panic attacks, leave my boyfriend of nine years and enter into thirteen months of therapy. This might not sound like a fabulous advertisement for her work but Elisabeth speaks often of the pebbles thrown into the tumbler which emerge polished rather than crushed. I like to think of it as a polishing experience.

"Until some years ago," she explains mid-way through the longest week of my life, "there were many times when I was ready to quit but always, when you're at the end of the rope, something, it can be something very small but always something very significant, happens. Then you make it through another day. At the beginning of my work with dying patients, I existed that way every single day.

"Maybe the biggest help I got was from a black cleaning woman. That woman must have saved my whole life's work. Every time I walked into a room where this cleaning woman had been, something happened that I couldn't pinpoint — I just knew that my work was very easy in those rooms.

"One day I saw her in the hallway and I was just dying to ask her so I walked over and I said, 'What in the world are you doing to those patients?' You understand, I meant it in a very curious, almost envious way, but she became almost paranoid. She looked at me and she said, 'I'm not doing anything. I only clean the floors.' She didn't trust any white person. So I stepped back but, from that day on, we kind of snooped around each other.

"Then, one day, after weeks of snooping around, this woman — and it took a lot of courage for a black cleaning woman and I was the white assistant of psychiatry — she grabbed me and took me into a back room which was like a walk-in linen closet and she shared the story of her life.

"She grew up without enough food, no medication. She had several children. One after the other died literally of poverty and neglect. One day, she took her three year old to the emergency room and they refused to see him because she hadn't paid the bill from the visit before, and then she described how she walked all the way to the county hospital in the middle of the city, carrying this very sick child, and how she sat for three hours in the waiting room and watched her little boy die of pneumonia, waiting in a hospital.

"Finally I said, 'Why are you telling me all this? What has this to do with my dying patients?' And she said, 'You see, Dr Ross, death is not an enemy to me any more. He is like an old, familiar friend and sometimes I walk up to the rooms of those dying patients and they look so scared, I can't help but walk over to them and touch them and try to convey to them that it's not so terrible.'

"You understand that I promoted this woman to my first assistant, much to the dismay of my academic colleagues, because this was the first time it dawned on me that you can tell people anything from your head, if it's not true for you inside it will go in one ear and out the other and if I could find people who were really not afraid to die, who have gone through the tumbler of life a thousand times and come out, not crushed but polished, then they don't need words because my patients will know.

"She was a gift from heaven and I always thought of this woman when things got really bad and then I made it through another day. It's people like this who are your teachers. It's not the ones you think are your teachers."

Elisabeth has retained the rich Swiss-German accent of her childhood, deepened an octave by countless packs of cigarettes and warmed by years in America. She speaks softly and slowly and patiently. I've never heard her raise her voice, though I've heard it's possible. With this voice and a grab-bag of adopted Americanisms, she dips into an archive of stories she's been collecting all her life.

"I want to tell you about an AIDS patient we had in one of our workshops," she says later in the week. "I want to tell you some of the things he shared with us about his life. He came from North Carolina, from a very fundamentalist Christian family. Many fundamentalist Christians believe AIDS is a punishment sent from God and this guy grew up in such a family — very strict, very puritanical, very judgmental.

"He told us how, when he was a young man, he knew he was homosexual. He tried not to be, he tried to be with girls but he just knew he was not a heterosexual guy. So his family called the religious community to pray over him — a public experience to humiliate him — and everyone in the village knew about him and pointed the finger and said they wanted to pray for him. He knew he couldn't survive that, so he left home and swore he would never set foot in this community again.

"Then he told us how he lived in San Francisco and how, after a time, he was diagnosed as having AIDS. So he was in the San Francisco General Hospital, which has an AIDS ward where three hundred of his buddies spent their last days. Now he was there and he knew he was going to be next.

"He was very close to death and when you're close to death, there are two things that will go through your mind. He thought about all the windstorms of life, and he'd had lots of those. The windstorms are the experiences that help to strengthen you to grow, to make it through the next windstorm. It's like the Swiss fir tree that's been shaken by the avalanches and storms. It may not look very pretty on the outside but, boy, it has roots and they're solid. He decided he felt very much like a fir tree on the mountain.

"The other things you will review when you come close to death are the special moments, the memories of the times when you've experienced unconditional love. Do you understand what those moments are? When a busy, busy father one day plays hooky and takes you fishing. You may be on your deathbed and you may remember one afternoon when your father put all his business away and took an hour out to go fishing with you.

"So he went through those moments and he couldn't believe it because every moment had something to do with his Mom and Dad, and he just knew that he couldn't die without telling his parents that, despite all the judgmental, horrible, ugly stuff, those were the moments that he was remembering. So, after years of not speaking to them, he phoned home. He just told one white lie — he told his mother that he was in hospital in San Francisco dying of cancer — that's the only lie he told — and he explained that he needed to come home once more to say goodbye.

"Then he described North Carolina and going home and by this time, everybody at the workshop was sobbing — that whole room was totally in tears. He told us how he walked across the meadow towards his old log home. Nothing had changed. It was like time had stood still. His Mom saw him coming and she dropped everything and started walking towards him, and he was stumbling towards her. Then his Dad caught up — dads are always about three feet behind — and they were both walking to meet him. He'd forgotten all the nightmares — all he felt was this incredible love.

"Then, just as they were getting really close, his fear came up and he thought, 'Oh my God, when she sees my face, she's going to stop and drop her arms,' but he knew he had to take that as a challenge. So he stumbled on until he and his mother were in each other's arms — she never stopped — and there they were, cheek to cheek, and his mother whispered in his ear, 'Son, we know you have AIDS and it's okay with us.'

"Do you know what that meant for fundamentalist people in North Carolina? Much more than if somebody had grown up in San Francisco. It was an enormous step those people had to make. What did that story do for my other AIDS patients in the room? What gift did that mom and dad give to all the other AIDS patients? It gave them hope. If that family was able, at the end, to love their son without strings or hooks attached, if that family could do it, then the hope was, for my patients, that maybe they would find one human being who would be big enough to love and accept them at the end. You can be that person for any AIDS patient.

"I'm sure that, twenty-five years from now, we'll see AIDS as an incredible blessing," she adds, "because it forces you — it literally forces you — to take a stand and make a choice based either on love or fear."

There are some things in life about which Elisabeth is uncompromising and this is one of them. Love and fear are polarized, she says. With every decision that faces us, we can ask ourselves if we're making a choice from a basis of love or from the clutches of fear. Always choose love, she insists, and you can't go wrong.

"There are a lot of different ways you can react to AIDS. You can get paranoid. You can walk around with goggles and boots and overalls and masks and gloves and not touch anybody — and if you do that, you'll probably get sick anyway. Maybe you won't get AIDS but all that fear is bound to make you ill. Or you can say, this is an opportunity to practise unconditional love, and then you go out and stick your neck out and you help those people. You don't judge where they come from or how they got it because that's not your business. What is your business is that this is a suffering fellow human being whom you can help. If you stick your neck out, you'll move forward. If, like an ostrich, you put your head in the sand, you're bound to get stuck. It's your choice. Choose love and you'll be blessed beyond anything you can imagine. Choose fear and it could quite literally kill you."

IT'S JULY 1990. THE SUN IS SETTING THROUGH THUNDERHEADS ON A HOT SUMMER night in Virginia. Elisabeth has just come in from an afternoon harvesting beans. She looks out over fields to a cluster of buildings which, in just three days, on her sixty-fourth birthday, will open as a center for her work. Already she, her staff and volunteers have begun baking to feed the multitudes who are expected to come and help celebrate these two auspicious events. The Swiss hillbilly in her is insisting on providing a home-cooked dinner for her guests, even though they're likely to number more than two hundred.

Elisabeth's hospice for children with AIDS never became a reality — community opposition held sway — but over the years she has organized for many of her friends and supporters to foster these children. The center that does exist will offer workshops and a retreat environment for members of the medical profession, those under their care, relatives, friends and the growing numbers of people who are simply interested in Elisabeth's work.

"We hope hospitals will send thirty or forty people at a time to come here and have conferences and workshops and relax. It's a gorgeous environment. It reminds me of the Swiss Alps. We grow our own food and I hope to do the cooking for some of the workshops. I have vegetables here for about one hundred people, and I have my Noah's Ark, with two animals of each kind. There are llamas and sheep and cattle and peacocks. At the moment, the mother llama is pregnant. In a few weeks our calves will begin to be born. It's a healing environment. You know, my sister has been in a wheelchair and then was walking with a cane all the time. She was here for two weeks and left her cane on the farm when she went. She says she doesn't need it any more."

The opening of this center feels somehow like a culmination, a celebration of years of struggle and a truly remarkable life. Elisabeth's birthday seems an appropriate time to look back over those years and try to identify the spiritual impulse that has propelled her through them.

Elisabeth's work with dying patients led her gradually and seamlessly into what was then considered a thoroughly eccentric field — research into life after death. What began as an innocent partnership with a Protestant minister at the University of Chicago grew to become an area of study which has spawned pop religion books, investigative theses and motion pictures around the world. It was during the early years of these investigations that Elisabeth first began to feel what she believes was the guiding hand of God, nudging her subtly along a path, leaving clues strewn at her feet and directions when she came to crossroads.

"I was working with dying patients," she recalls, "and I needed to find some-body who could talk to them about God because many of my dying patients wanted to know what would happen when they died and I always passed the buck and said, 'You have to ask the minister.' When the hospital ministers were called, they never helped my patients. They opened a little black booklet, read some psalms and took off fast, before the patient was able to ask any questions.

"So I decided to find someone who could help. I did my research, eventually met a wonderful minister and asked him if he would join forces with me so, if my patients asked medical and earthly questions, I could answer but if they asked religious stuff, then he could answer. We became a superb team. He was a man, I was a woman. He was black, I was white. He was very religious and I was very scientific.

"He and I would philosophize late into the night and, one night, we sat for hours talking about how important it would be for our patients if we could understand more about death and what occurs after death. I was still very grumbly about ministers because I'd had bad experiences with Protestant minis-ters in my childhood. So I said to him, 'You stand on the pulpit every Sunday and say, "Ask and you will be given," but you don't believe a word of it. That is the big farce about religion. I am going to ask God now, in front of you, to please help me to do research into death so that I can help our patients.' I pointed to the ceiling and asked God, as if he was sitting up there, and the minister smiled, knowing damn well that he preached that all the time.

"Then, five days after I made this request, my very first patient had a near death experience. That was many decades ago, in the 1960s. There was no book on life after life and we didn't even have a word for near death experiences or out of body experiences. Nobody knew anything about it. So this restored my faith that there is a God who can hear you, who you can talk to and that, if you make a request with the right motivation and if you really need this thing, you will get it."

From that day on, Elisabeth and her minister friend began investigating cases of near death experiences with a passion. By the time they were through, she says, they had collected thousands.

"Our fantasy in those naive days was to get twenty cases," Elisabeth smiles, "so we could publish them in a very prestigious medical journal and change medicine overnight. We never published them because our first patients all said that they would share with us only if we promised never to use their names, never to tell anybody. They were afraid they would be sent to a psychiatric hospital. There was such a paranoia in those days that it was impossible to publish. Then we collected so many cases that we didn't need any more. They all repeated the same thing. There are some cultural and religious differences but they are very small. The basic issues are all the same. That was the beginning of my research into life after death."

Shortly after Elisabeth's research was complete, she was approached by a doctor called Raymond Moodie who had heard of her work and begun research in the same area. His bestseller, *Life After Life*, for which Elisabeth wrote the foreword, was published in 1975.

Yet the publication of Moodie's data posed as many questions as it answered and Elisabeth determined to take her own work one step further. Again, she recalls gleefully, the hand of fate was on her side.

"I asked God for some help to go beyond Moodie's near death experiences. I simply asked the question in my mind and, a few days later, I came upon the case that would lead me along my next path.

"She was a Native American girl who had been hit by a car. Hundreds of people drove by. This girl was lying on the curb. She did not look externally injured but she had a lot of internal injuries. One man, who I call the Good Samaritan, stopped and asked if there was anything he could do and she said, with great serenity, that there was nothing anyone could do. He didn't get it but he stayed with her. He did not desert her. Then, after about fifteen or twenty minutes, she looked at him again and said, 'Maybe there is something, one day, that you can do for me. If you ever get to the Indian reservation, visit my mother.' She gave him her name and the name of the reservation and said the message was that she was okay, that she was, in fact, very happy because she was already with her dad.

"Then she died in the arms of this total stranger and he was so moved that he was at the right place at the right time that he drove seven hundred miles to visit the woman at the reservation, who was not totally devastated to hear about the death of her daughter but was very happy and explained that the reason why she was happy was that her husband, the girl's father, died on the reservation, one hour before the car accident, of a totally unexpected coronary.

"That was the answer I received when I asked, how can I go beyond Moodie's book? I got the message that I had to find people who are near death and who see somebody who preceded them in death but they could not have possibly known it."

For years, Elisabeth had sat with terminally ill patients at the moment of death, offering comfort or courage or merely a familiar presence. Now she began to visit children who were brought into the hospital following fatal and near-fatal road accidents.

"There are so many family accidents where one, two or three people are killed but the injured children are never told who died at the scene of the accident. I visited many of them and I sat with them for a while and I asked them if they were willing to share with me what they experienced. One little boy I remember, whose story was much like so many others, told me with great serenity and calm, 'Everything is okay now. My mommy and Peter are already waiting for me.' Mommy, I knew, was killed at the scene of the accident but Peter had been sent to another hospital that specialized in burns. Then, as I left the intensive care unit, the nurse waved to me and said, 'We have a message for you from the burns unit. Peter died ten minutes ago from his burns.' The only mistake I made was I said, 'Yes, I know.'

"In fifteen years of research, I have never heard a child mention somebody who did not precede them in death by ten minutes or more. So my research just went on and on. Every time I finished one project, I asked for help. I never got a voice or an answer that I could hear but I was connected with a case that gave me the answer."

Elisabeth looks into the gathering darkness, listens to the stillness and the distant rumblings of the storm. In the autumn of her life and following a stroke in recent years, she now finds her own death creeping near enough to contemplate. Smiling, she says she hopes it will be "terrific ... my life has been so full, so packed that, looking back, at least I can say I've done my best. I want to live to the end of 2003. I have another ten years. Then, I'm determined not to come back. This time I picked a lulu."

Despite her well-publicised research into near death and out-of-body experiences, it has only been quite recently that Elisabeth's personal spiritual beliefs have taken a prominent role in the public side of her work. I ask when she first became conscious of a spiritual dimension in her life, which naturally inspires another story.

"It sneaks in on you," she begins. "Like, fifteen years ago, I had what I would call my first mystical or spiritual experience and I had no idea what it was. I just knew it was indescribable, it was bliss.

"Then I had to go to California to a transpersonal psychology meeting. I hadn't really shared my experiences with anyone but I looked at all these strange people and suddenly I knew that they would understand what I was talking about. So I went on the stage and I shared some of my mystical experiences and I said, 'You know, all I want to tell the world is that, if this can happen to me, it's going to happen to all of you because I'm square, I'm straight, a scientist and a very rational research person. I've never taken drugs. I can't even meditate — I have ants in my pants, I can't even sit the right way. I've never been to India. I've never done the right things. If somebody had said I was trying to reach higher consciousness, I would have said, 'Oh, these Californians!'"

"Then, one of these orange-clad people — I guess he was a Buddhist monk or something — said to me, 'No, that is not correct. You are a great meditator.' I said, 'Me, a meditator? I can't even sit on a plane without knitting.' He said, 'When you're with dying children and you're totally tuned in to them, that's a form of meditation.' Well, people don't know that. At least, I didn't know that. I thought you had to sit, with your legs folded up, trying not to think. Yet, it's true, I've spent thousands of hours with dying children and they could have an alarm going or a page system and I wouldn't hear it. So people have their own ways. I think, if you do what feels right to you — you don't do it to please somebody else — then you are in the right spot at the right time and things begin to happen."

A few years later, Elisabeth decided to put these experiences through some tests. It began when a woman showed her a photograph which she insisted was of a fairy.

"The woman brought out the photograph and she asked, 'What do you think of it?' I said, 'It's very interesting but, you understand, I don't believe in any of this.' She insisted that it was absolutely mandatory that we knew of the existence of things that our eyes couldn't see. So, with her Polaroid camera, I took a picture of a bush in her garden and, by golly, there was such a thing on it. Naturally, I still didn't quite believe it.

"Anyway, that night my husband came in with a very fancy hospital camera — like, thousand dollar equipment — and asked me to carry it on the plane with me back to Chicago because he was driving back with the children and didn't want to take it with him. The last thing he said to me — very typical — was, 'Be careful, it's very expensive and you know you're not very careful with material things.' I said, 'Don't worry, I'm not going to even touch it.'

"Then, the moment they left in the car, I thought of that woman's photograph. I grow the biggest cabbages and the biggest sunflowers and I think my cabbages are bigger than Findhorn's. So fairies are just not my cup of tea, but I'd always heard about guides or guardian angels — my children talked to their invisible playmates and, to me, that's all the same — and I would've given anything in the world to know if I really had a guide. So I checked this fancy camera and it had three pictures left and I took a picture of a meadow with a forest behind it. Then, with the second last picture, I said, 'To whoever hears me, if it is really true that I have such guidance, would you please, please make yourself visible? I am now taking the exact same picture of the meadow and the forest.' So I knew I had taken two — one without request and one with request.

"About a month later, I was coming home from somewhere and I got on an earlier plane. So I dashed home and made a really good dinner to surprise my family, and my husband called up and he was really grouchy. Instead of saying, 'That's great, you're home early,' he said, 'You did it again.' I said, 'Did what again?' He said, 'You know very well.' I said, 'I don't know what you're talking about.' Then, finally, he said, 'This is a most expensive camera and you cannot superimpose pictures with it.' The moment he said superimpose, I knew what he was talking about and I said, 'Honey, come home.' I couldn't wait for him to come home. So he comes home with these pictures. One is of a meadow with trees behind it and the other one is the absolutely identical picture but superimposed on the pine tree is an enormous figure standing with his arms folded across his chest, looking straight in my eyes. I was so excited.

"Then, for a while, I was able to take these photographs. Like, if I would photograph you and in my thoughts ask to see your guidance, I would be able to take your picture with your guides around you. I was able to do that for about six months and then it disappeared. When you lose something, however, something better always comes along. You should not cling to it. You also can't misuse it because, if you misuse it, you lose it. That's how things happen in life. If you lose something, you always get something else and it's always better than what you lose."

Elisabeth was and, unlikely as it may sound, still is, a highly rational, down-to-earth individual. At the time, she was also just developing a very successful career in thanatology. Not surprisingly, she was hesitant to go public with her spiritual convictions.

"I didn't share it for years," she admits, "and then it happened without my doing anything about it. I was on a stage in North Carolina. My old stuff, the conservative stuff, I shared and at the end of the lecture, a woman came up, totally distraught, and said, 'Dr Ross, I only came for one question. Do you know what happens at the moment of death?' I heard myself say, 'Oh, that's very easy.' It was not under my control and you could've heard a pin drop. Then I explained how you just step out of your body and go through the different phases, and this woman dashed up on stage, took the second microphone and shared with me her experience with the death of her three-year-old child who then made a come-back and told his story to her.

"The next day, naturally, there were headlines: 'Psychiatrist Discovers Life After Death.' My husband didn't talk to me for three days and I didn't know why because I'm always out of town when the newspaper articles appear. So, you see, it wasn't me deciding in my head when it was time to talk about life after death. The right woman was at the right place at the right time to give me a kick in the pants and that's how my whole life is. I think that's the most important thing, that you trust that this will happen, that you're not deciding everything on your own. You need to listen to your intuition or to whatever guidance you get."

IN A CUPBOARD IN HER TWO-STORY WEATHERBOARD COTTAGE (HALF VIRGINIA hillbilly, half Swiss chalet), Elisabeth keeps a great stack of diaries under lock and key. At present she's wading her way through them with the aim of putting together an autobiography.

"I have about twenty-five diaries," she says. "Each time I have an experience of an extraordinary nature, when it happens, I write down exactly what I remember from every point of view and then, weeks later, as I get more insight into what it was all about, I write that down. The diaries are more a reference in terms of chronology because, when you live this way, you have absolutely no time concept and I couldn't tell you what year I had my first out-of-body experience or first saw my own guide or guardian angel or when I had my first materialisation, spontaneously, at a time when I didn't believe in any of this. I did absolutely everything to verify that it was not true, only to come to the conclusion that this really happened.

"I'd known this woman very well. She was my first patient who shared with us a near death experience, long before any of this was published. Then, eleven months after her death, I saw her standing in the hallway and she asked to walk me to my office. I was so blocked. I absolutely blocked out that this was Mrs Schwarz. I mean, that just didn't exist in my life experience. That didn't exist in my scientific comprehension of the world. I remember walking down the hallway of the hospital next to her and she had this all-knowing smile on her face which drove me up the wall. I remember touching her hand to see if it was warm but the other part of me didn't even have the courage to say why I touched her hand. I was functioning like on three or four different levels at the same time. I was an observer of what was going on here but my head could not yet accept that reality.

"I always tell my psychiatric patients, if they have a visual hallucination, 'I know you see that Madonna on the wall but I don't,' and I try to help them with their reality testing. Well, I did that to me. I said, 'I know you see this woman next to you but ...' but, by golly, she was there. Then I thought, by the time I get to my office, I open the door and it's my familiar paper stuff on the desk, then this whole vision will disappear. However instead of me opening the door, this woman opened the door and said, 'I had to come back and thank you and Reverend so-and-so for what you have done for me.' By then we'd moved inside the office and she closed the door and she stood next to my desk and said, 'Can you hear me?' I said, 'Yes.' Then she said, 'You cannot give up your work now.' This was the day I wanted to give notice at the University of Chicago. 'Your work has just begun. You will know when it is completed.'

"Then I did something very shrewd. I gave her a piece of paper and a pen and I said, 'Reverend so-and-so is no longer here. Would you mind terribly sending him a little message?' What I needed was something in black and white, so I would have proof that this woman was actually in my office. I didn't have the nerve to read what she wrote. The minute she wrote it, I turned it over. She said, 'Promise that you won't give up your work,' and the last thing I said to her was, 'I promise.' Then she left and, the moment that she walked out of my office, I became a psychiatrist. I dashed after her. I wanted to see how she walked. What kind of shoes did she wear? All the more distant kinds of observations. I opened the door and she was gone. It was a long hallway. There was no way she could have disappeared without … just disappearing.

"I went back into my office and I made an incredibly long list of what I needed to do, as a scientist, to prove that the woman who was buried eleven months earlier can stand in my office and talk to me. I had to exhume her body to be sure it was her they buried. I had to do fingerprints. I had to do graphological analysis. Oh, I was terrific in forensic psychiatry. Yet, the longer the list became, the more I realized that I was only doing this to prove it to other people because I knew that she was in my office and stopped me from making the most horrible mistake I would have made in my life. Then I turned over the sheet of paper and she said she was 'at home, at peace.' I sent that note to the minister. He still has it and he keeps it on his desk under glass and he doesn't quite know what to do with it.

"That was my first horrendous kind of experience and, within weeks, I was asked to write the book, *On Death and Dying*. Within weeks everything happened and I wrote that book in the mornings between one and three am, two or three nights a week and it typed itself. I just sat there and typed with two fingers and never read it. I gave the book to my minister friend to read and see if it felt right and he said it felt right and they published it just as it was typed. That's how my first book was born and, if I had not listened to that woman, to that materialized Mrs Schwarz, I would've given notice and I would never have written the book. I would've gone into some other kind of work."

A FEW DAYS BEFORE CHRISTMAS OF 1993, IT'S ONE AM IN SYDNEY AND SIRENS ARE wailing in the dark and stifling heat. I am thinking about Mrs Schwarz. I am thinking about Elisabeth. I am thinking that this tale encapsulates the quality which continues to draw me to her. I am intrigued by Elisabeth's faith.

In Virginia, the sun is battling through winter skies, newborn llamas shiver as they climb onto unsteady hoofs and Elisabeth sits by the phone waiting for her son, Kenneth, to call. I call instead. She disguises disappointment fabulously.

I ask, is she happy?

"Ja," she replies.

Are you sure?

"I have too much work. If I didn't have the mail, I would be happy. I am drowning in mail, which is an eternal problem for me. I dictate letters until three in the morning. Every room is stacked full of mail and the fax machine drives me crazy. We have a big workshop here every month and I cook for fifty people. On Thursdays, I do the teaching and somebody else keeps an eye on the oven."

Twelve months ago, her ex-husband, Manny, died. It was a test of faith but one which has served to strengthen her.

"I wanted to be there so badly," she admits, "but I was told, a long time before he died, that would not be possible. I said, 'Make sure he's in good hands, that he's not alone, that he does not suffer.'

"I spent three weeks in Arizona. Kenneth moved down there to be near him and Barbara [Elisabeth's daughter] was there and we had three wonderful weeks. Then all his organs began to deteriorate and he was really in bad shape. He started to hallucinate and I listened to every word so I would not miss anything. He laughed and apologised and said, 'I'm hallucinating. I'm not making any sense. Don't pay so much attention.' Then the doctors came and said they had to put him on kidney dialysis.

"After the dialysis, he was totally normal again and I said, 'Do you want to live this way? You know, one system falls apart, then they fix that one up, then the liver falls apart, then the heart.' He said, no, he did not want his life prolonged with all these machines. I said, 'Okay, I will talk to the doctor and we will see if we can take you home.' Then he started hallucinating again, so we did a second dialysis and he stopped hallucinating but he would have required a kidney dialysis three times a week.

"So, after the second one, I talked to the doctor in Manny's presence and Kenneth's, and we said we'd take him home with a promise that I would give the dialysis. He granted us this wish and Manny prepared to go home.

"Kenneth was staying in Arizona. I had to go to California for a day. So, when Kenneth was able to take him home, they had an absolute ball because Manny had been in bed for three weeks and he was sick and tired of the hospital. First, they went home and inspected the freezer, which I'd filled with all the homemade roasts. The last phone call I had from Manny was that I'm crazy, I cooked for an army. Then, I'd bought him an electric cart, and Kenneth and Manny, with this electric cart, went Christmas shopping. They went on a crazy Christmas shopping spree — all the presents, decorations, food he hadn't tasted in a long time. After the shopping, they went back to the house they were staying in. Manny went to lie down because he was really pooped out from his first shopping trip. An hour later, after Kenneth had put all the shopping away, he went to look in on Manny and he had died during his afternoon nap.

"He died very peacefully. Kenneth had been with him and he'd had a ball. I could not have wished for a better, more appropriate death. Before I'd left, he had promised that he would give me a signal if what I'm teaching is correct and, within an hour, I got the signal. It was fantastic. I cannot mourn. I cannot feel sad. I'm happy that he's alive, he's well, continues to grow. If there is anything my children need, he can let me know and I can take care of it. You are more alive on the other side than you are here, minus all the pain and fear and agony and hardship."

In a sense, this is Elisabeth's secret. Even in the midst of one of the most confronting periods of her life, she sees hope, she finds cause, if not for celebration, for gratitude.

"Even when things are really, really, really bad, there is always something incredible happening that puts you back on your feet," she says. "Always. There is never a total storm and nightmare. There is always a glimpse of light where the sun breaks through or you see the stars in the heavens or look in the forest and see the animals peacefully living next to each other or you see a total stranger helping a needy homeless man who can hardly walk across the street or a child's smile or a flower opening up. I mean, there are millions of little blessings if you have eyes to see."

That every cloud has a silver lining would sound absurdly Pollyanna-ish were it not for the fact that Elisabeth knows the blackness of those clouds and has spent much of her life navigating them.

"My faith is tested continuously," she insists. "I don't think there is a week when I don't get the two-by-four. If you stand up, then you get another two-by-four and it's a neverending growth process. The whole of life is nothing but a struggle for spiritual evolution so that you can graduate. In a limited lifespan, the universe can appear very unfair but I have found that all the bad things that happen to you are really gifts from God and blessings to make you strong. Those people who have never gone through any windstorms are weak and uninteresting, have no guts, no *chutzpah*.

"Have I told you how my mother died? She had never learned to receive. For all her life, she only gave, and it's not balanced. Then she had a stroke and she existed in a hospital bed, unable to move an inch of her body or to say one word.

She existed that way for four years and I was mad at God. I was furious. Then, about twelve months after her death, I had to review my opinion. Suddenly it hit me like lightning: God is the most generous being. He allowed my mother to give and give and give and love and love and love for seventy-six years and only requested that she learn to receive for four.

"The most important thing I have learnt in my life is to hang in there. To know that, when tough things happen, God gives you credit for making it and for getting strong, rather than becoming weak and falling apart. The biggest gift God gave to us is free will. I mean, you can hang your neck on the next tree or you can stick it out and become stronger."

So who is this God in whom Elisabeth's faith will not be shaken. Is it a Christian God? Yes, she says, but not entirely.

"I think Jesus is a fantastic figure for humankind. It doesn't matter whether you call yourself a Christian or not, if you know what he came to teach and that he set an example of our potential, then you can strive towards that potential and you have a guideline of what you can do with your life. You don't just pay taxes and go shopping and cook and sleep and eat. There has to be some purpose in your struggle and the purpose has to be to grow in love, unconditional love, and that includes yourself, which is the hardest lesson for me to learn. Also to do some sort of service for your fellow men and women so, when you die, this place is a little bit better than before you entered."

The closest Elisabeth comes to describing her God is a memory from her childhood.

"As a young child," she explains, "I would often go into the forest next to our house and inside the forest was a big rock. Nobody could get to it unless they were a very skinny, tiny child. I would stand on that rock and make a prayer to the sun. So I was very connected to Mother Earth and, I guess, to indigenous people. When I talked to the sun and the forest and the animals and the kingdom of all living things, to me, that was part of God. The soul of you and me and every living thing is a particle of God that descends into the world. That is life."

MEANWHILE, BACK IN VIRGINIA, SNOW IS FALLING. THIS SOMEWHAT ECCENTRIC Swiss grandmother is wrapping and packing and planning for Christmas with Kenneth and Barbara in New York. In January, she will travel to South Africa to run workshops in Johannesburg, just weeks prior to the first democratic elections there. Elisabeth has never been afraid of hot-spots, political or otherwise, and she is determined her workshops will be attended equally by black and white.

We chat about the farm. "Oh, the baby llamas are so cute." About Kenneth. "His photography is going fabulously. After my workshops, we will go together to Kruger National Park." About Christmas and gifts, cooking and shopping. I almost begin to believe this voice crackling along wires from Virginia does belong to a typical Swiss grandmother. It's a fleeting impression.

"Are you connected to your guides and guardian and angels?" Elisabeth asks, just before we say goodbye. "You should talk to them tonight before you go to sleep. Ask for their names so you can get into a real dialogue with them. Then, if you have a big issue, you can ask at night for advice and, when you wake in the morning, you will have the answer. All people can do this and it will enhance their faith that they are in good hands. We are in good hands, you know … We are."

LESS THAN TWELVE MONTHS LATER, I AM AT MY WIT'S END. FOR MONTHS, I HAVE been trying to coerce Elisabeth into reading this chapter and approving it for publication. She has been back to Africa, she has spent time with her family, she has been dealing with the day to day conundrums of the association and the farm. Finally, as a last resort, I call her son, Kenneth, in Arizona. He promises, if I send him another copy, he'll sit her down and ensure she reads it.

I hear nothing for three weeks, then one morning, the phone rings. It's Ken. The office in Virginia has been broken into and, in what appears to be arson, Elisabeth's house has been burned to the ground. All her possessions, her papers, her keepsakes are in ashes and Elisabeth has suffered another stroke. He is leaving tomorrow to collect his mother and bring her south to stay with him.

I speak with Elisabeth again after she has settled in Arizona. She seems tired but philosophical about this most recent churning of her life's tumbler. She supposes, amongst other things, it's a lesson in letting go. She has just bought five acres of Arizona desert, which she loves. Three coyotes live outside her kitchen door. Doubtless they will soon be the best fed animals in the state. Her sister, Eva, is visiting from Switzerland. Her daughter, Barbara and her old friend, the Jungian analyst Greg Furth, will arrive for Christmas.

This time, she says, she really has retired. Should the world lure her back, it will not be for lectures or workshops. Those days are over. Perhaps, when the dust settles, she will think of some entirely new project on which to spend her days. For the moment, she's content watching desert sunsets, feeding coyotes and spending uncharacteristically relaxed time with family and friends.

Meanwhile, her work continues in hospitals and through dedicated individuals around the world. Patients facing the end of their lives today — whether in hospital wards, hospices or their family homes — meet with greater levels of support and understanding than was dreamed possible just thirty years ago. Even those who do not subscribe to Elisabeth's vision of an afterlife now have less cause to live in fear of death.

Oodgeroo of the Noonuccal Tribe

4

SAY IT LOUD

In the Dreamtime all the earth lay sleeping. Nothing grew. Nothing moved. Everything was quiet and still. The animals, birds and reptiles lay sleeping under the earth's crust.

Then one day the Rainbow Serpent awoke from her slumber and pushed her way through the earth's crust, moving the stones that lay in her way. When she emerged, she looked about her and then traveled over the land, going in all directions. She traveled far and wide, and when she grew tired she curled herself into a heap and slept. On the earth she left her winding tracks and the imprint of her sleeping body. When she had traveled all the earth, she returned to the place where she had first appeared and called to the frogs, "Come out!"

The frogs were very slow to come from below the earth's crust, for their bellies were heavy with water which they had stored in their sleep. The Rainbow Serpent tickled their stomachs, and when the frogs laughed, the water ran all over the earth to fill the tracks of the Rainbow Serpent's wanderings — and that is how the lakes and rivers were formed.

Then the grass began to grow, and trees sprang up, and so life began on earth.

All the animals, birds and reptiles awoke and followed the Rainbow Serpent, the Mother of Life, across the land. They were happy on earth, and each lived and hunted for food with its own tribe. The kangaroo, wallaby and emu tribes lived on the plains. The reptile tribes lived among the rocks and stones, and the bird tribes flew through the air and lived in the trees.

The Rainbow Serpent made laws that all were asked to obey, but some grew quarrelsome and were troublemakers. The Rainbow Serpent scolded them, saying, 'Those who keep my laws, I shall reward well. I shall give them a human form. They and their children and their children's children shall roam this earth forever. This shall be their land. Those who break my laws, I shall punish. They shall be turned to stone, never to walk the earth again.'

So the law-breakers were turned to stone and became mountains and hills, to stand forever and watch over the tribes hunting for food at their feet.

But those who kept her laws, she turned into humans, and gave each of them their own totem of the animal, bird or reptile from whence they came. So the tribes knew themselves by their own totems: the kangaroo, the emu, the carpet snake and many, many more. And in order that none should starve, she ruled that no one should eat of their own totem, but only of other totems. In this way there was food for all.

So the tribes lived together in the land given to them by the Mother of Life, the Rainbow Serpent, and they knew that the land would always be theirs, and that no one should ever take it from them.

"THE BEGINNING OF LIFE", FROM *STRADBROKE DREAMTIME*, BY OODGEROO

IT HAS BEEN A WEEK SINCE OODGEROO'S DEATH. TONIGHT I SEE HER WANDERING, much like the Rainbow Serpent, across her island. Walking long beaches, hearing crashing green waves, watching fish dart in and out of mangroves, following winding bush tracks, which, unlike modern roads, skirt around trees. I see her surveying her landscape, her charge, and taking stock. "Where's old wallaby today? ... Ah, there's bluetongue sunning himself by the pool ... Those trees are looking poorly. More straggly than last week. Perhaps it's the mining."

This might be pure romance on my part, but I think not. Oodgeroo's eyes lit up when she spoke of Minjerribah. "The whites," she laughed, "had the audacity to change its name to Stradbroke Island after the Earl of Stradbroke but Minjerribah means land of mosquitos and that's what it is."

Oodgeroo was born on this island of mosquitos just east of Brisbane and, despite a career that took her around Australia and the world as one of her country's greatest poets, activists and educators, Minjerribah remained her home and the keeper of her heart.

Oodgeroo's mother, the daughter of an inland Queensland Aboriginal woman and a Scotsman, named her Kathleen Jean Mary Walker. Her paternal grandfather was Asian, possibly from Sri Lanka, but her father's mother was of the Noonuccal tribe and her father's spirit was Noonuccal through and through.

Her parents struggled to span two cultures and their children were reared on a sometimes uneasy mix of Noonuccal and European education. As she grew older, her conversation was more liberally sprinkled with tales from her childhood — of a school system which used violence to ensure she wrote with her right hand when it was natural for her to use her left and of a father whose expeditions on the island and in the bay taught her that, if you respect and care for the natural world, it will in turn take care of you.

"We lived in two worlds but mainly in our own Aboriginal world because the whites never wanted us in theirs. We weren't allowed to dance on the same dance floor as the whites. We weren't allowed to sit with them in the picture show. I became conscious very early on that I was black and therefore a second-rate citizen. I was never allowed to forget my blackness, ever. My Aboriginality was classed as something that was pagan and that had to be wiped out."

At thirteen, Oodgeroo left school and went to work as a housekeeper in Brisbane, before deciding that the way forward was to get herself an education by any means she could. She joined the army, trained as a stenographer and gradually became more involved both in politics and in her art.

She was active in the Federal Council for the Advancement of Aborigines and Torres Strait Islanders in the 1960s, helping to bring about changes in the constitution which eventually gave Aboriginal people the vote. Her first volume of poems, *We Are Going*, was published in 1964. It sold out before it could be launched and was reprinted seven times in as many months. It was followed by a steady stream of collections of poetry, stories, essays and drawings.

In 1970, on the anniversary of Captain Cook's landing in Australia, she was awarded a Member of the British Empire. In 1987, in protest against the coming year's Bicentennial celebrations, she returned it and changed her name from Kath Walker to Oodgeroo, which, in her language, is the word for the paperbark tree. In the last years of her life, still faced with the horror of black deaths in custody, infant mortality rates in Aboriginal communities which rivalled those in many of the poorest nations on earth, and a constitution that claimed she did not exist, Oodgeroo continued to write, lecture and travel constantly. Her patience, her tolerance and her stamina were extraordinary.

I FIRST MET OODGEROO BACK IN 1991. A SMALL, WIRY, SEVENTY YEAR OLD WARRIOR of a woman, she was formidable. A thirty year old, white product of European-Australian guilt, I was uncomfortable. We stumbled through an hour and a half of conversation, Oodgeroo correcting my naive assumptions and answering my shopping list of questions in her own special no-nonsense, no-time-for-apologies, this-is-the-way-it-stands style. She made a point of glancing at my shorts and mentioning the unattractively anaemic appearance of unclad white legs. I can't say we warmed to each other.

At the time, she was living on twelve acres of bushland on Minjerribah in a house that she called her "Twentieth Century *gunyah* [rough bark hut]." Oodgeroo's home had no locks, no keys and the kitchen, in which she did much of her writing, was open to the elements. In part, this was because it was the way she liked it. It was also because she was virtually squatting. She had asked for the title to this small tract of her ancestors' land called Moongalba but the Queensland government had refused both her applications to lease and buy it. Finally they granted her "permissive occupancy", which meant they could demand the land be returned at any time and on her death it would revert to the Crown. So Oodgeroo saw no reason to build a permanent home there. Instead, she extended her caravan with a galvanized iron roof and awnings that rolled down in wet weather.

Oodgeroo was the custodian of Minjerribah, caring for the land in the spirit of the Noonuccals and sharing her knowledge with groups of children, black and white, who came to visit as part of a bold educational initiative she'd set up in the 1980s.

"I'm the protector of the land," she would often say. "I can't own the land. The land owns me. So my duty is to protect it, to look after it, to nurture it."

In return, the land nurtured her.

"I've got to have that contact with the Earth Mother," she said. "That's my balance. That's my sanity. Going back to the Earth Mother, communicating with her. I couldn't live with myself in the city. I'd just shrivel up and die or put a gun to my head. When I'm home, on the island, I garden and I go fishing. I dodge everyone. I'm anti-people and pro-conservation. I just communicate with the birds and the animals and the reptiles and wipe people out of my mind. You can get an over much of people and, you see, when I'm lecturing the seagulls and the pelicans and the hawks, they don't answer me back — I think that's lovely — and they don't ask questions."

WHEN NEXT I SAW OODGEROO IT WAS EARLY IN 1993. SHE HAD BEEN ILL, STRUCK by a virus that had kept her bedridden for days mid-way through a lecture tour. Perhaps the flu had sapped her energy for combat or perhaps she'd read the article that I'd painstakingly transcribed and sent for her approval after our last meeting. Either way, she had decided to like me.

We drank tea, we thumbed through books she wanted me to read, she spoke for hours of her life, goals, disappointments, beliefs, and we went driving through the backstreets of Sydney in search of a particular row of paperbark trees. When we finally spotted them, her gnarled, tired face broke into a grin and the sun peeked through clouds overhead. The trees took her back to her island and to the rich mix of ecology, science and spirituality she had imbibed there in her youth.

"There are times when I'm walking on that land and some unknown thing says to me, 'Stop right where you are. Come no further.' I obey those instincts. I turn around and go back. Then I go up the next day and there's no barrier. Something from the earth tells me. Perhaps there was a snake there — I don't know — but that instinct is important. Then there are times when I've made up my mind to go fishing and some instinct within me says, 'Not today.' Maybe Quandamooka, the sea spirit, is saying, 'Keep away from me today, I'll kick your teeth in.' I don't know but I obey the instinct. The senses of the Aboriginals are very much alive.

"People come to me and say, 'Isn't that a poisonous spider there?' And I say, 'Yes.' 'Are you going to kill it?' I say, 'No.' 'Will it bite me?' I say, 'If you're silly enough to put your finger in its mouth, yes it will. If you leave it well alone, it will leave you alone.' Their first instinct is to kill and I get mad with them because these are beautiful spiders, so pretty, and they're what the thrush needs to live on. You'll see the thrush flying at the web, picking the spider up and swallowing it. She doesn't get poisoned. I don't know why. Our elders learned from the ways of the birds and animals. Our approach to nature is spiritual and scientific."

By then we were sitting on the ground beneath the biggest, whitest paperbark tree and Oodgeroo was good naturedly taking my education in hand.

"Listen and learn from us," she chided. "First of all, let's listen and learn about conservation issues because, if we don't get them to stop this wholesale slaughter of all the living things on this earth, we won't get anywhere, we'll all go down the drain. That's number one. They've got to become conservation minded. They've got to stop digging holes in the land.

"The full bloods, they say to me, 'Kathy, white man will never be any good, he's always raping his Earth Mother,' and it's true. All we can do is not hate him and hope we can educate him. [Aboriginal writer] Jack Davis said to me, a long time ago, 'Kathy, I was thinking, maybe we're bad educators or maybe the white people are slow learners.' I never saw myself as a bad educator, ever.

"The young people in schools are getting it because they've been educated for it and that's good and let's hope those children will go home and educate their mums and dads. That's the philosophy that I cling to. After that, everything else will fall into place."

I mentioned that the environment and land rights movements have been uneasy allies in recent times.

"I've come out as a black, green conservationist for years," she declared, "but some of these groups are fighting to make park lands out of Aboriginal land. So, with all good intentions, they're making the same mistake they made two hundred years ago. That's got Aboriginal people right in the middle again and they're not going to win. They don't mean to do it but, if the greenies keep on doing this, we're in a no-win situation.

"Now I've been asked to go down to Tasmania to do a course with the wilderness people, explaining how we look after the land. I said, 'After two hundred years you ask me? Where were you two hundred years ago when my ancestors could have stopped you? Why didn't you talk to them then?'" She laughed and said sorry. "It's never too late, I suppose. So it's a matter of listening and learning again, from each other."

Aboriginal commitment to the land, Oodgeroo insisted, runs far deeper than anything the greenest of us have been able to muster in a couple of centuries.

"There has always been the Earth Mother," she explained. "We're not religious, we're spiritual. Always there's been spirituality around us. We've never recognised religion. We have that spirituality with the earth and something like ESP between ourselves. We've never lost that.

"That same spirituality was all over Australia. There were different names in different languages but, throughout all the tribes, the Earth Mother was there. We are all custodians of the Earth Mother and, all over Australia, you can see the tracks of her travels. Where she grew tired and went to sleep, there are lakes. You can see her in the rocks. At the beginning of life, the Earth Mother was asleep under the Earth, with all the Aboriginal tribes in her belly waiting to be born. When it was time, she pushed up the rocks, which is how Uluru came to be. All the rocks around there are where the Earth Mother pushed through to birth her babies."

The story of the Rainbow Serpent is almost as familiar as Genesis to most European Australians. What is not so generally understood is the complex web of spiritual interrelation and the deep sense of personal responsibility that springs from it.

"Every living thing has a spirit. That tree is my sister," she said, tousling the bark of the oodgeroo tree. "All the trees and all living things are our sisters and brothers — all living things — so we only kill to eat."

Naturally, Oodgeroo had a story to illustrate the point. Tales like this one kept school groups engrossed for hour after hour at Moongalba.

"I'll tell you what happened when our brother aimed the slingshot at the parrot and missed it. He was the best shot and he shouldn't have missed but he did, and we were all so relieved to see him miss that we rolled around on the ground laughing. Then, as if to join in with us, a kookaburra laughed at the same time. So, without even aiming, my brother turned around with his slingshot and said, 'Laugh at me would you?' And he broke the wing of the kookaburra.

"That stopped our laughter, of course, because we are forbidden to touch the kookaburra. We all gathered around saying, 'Oh, if Dad ever found out, what would happen?' Well, we didn't know it but Dad was collecting driftwood on the shore and he saw us huddled together and came straight over. He immediately knew what we'd done and he put the stricken bird out of its misery, then ordered us home.

"As we walked home, we were all trying to work out what he'd do. 'He's going to flog us,' I said. But my eldest brother, very frightened by this time, said, 'No he won't. The punishment's got to fit the crime. It's going to be worse than that.' So we had our tea in dead silence and Mum was just fiddling with her food, so we knew Dad and she had decided what was going to happen to us. In the Aboriginal world, if you do something wrong, the whole tribe takes responsibility, everyone gets punished.

"What he did was he made us bring in all our slingshots, all our tools and our punishment was that we had to eat the hated white man's food for three months. That's worse than a flogging, so the punishment did fit the crime. God, I used to hate it. We all did.

"Our black dog would sit and look at us as if to say, 'We should be hunting.

What are you sitting round here doing nothing for?' He was bored sick during those three months because the little humans had gone crazy and weren't hunting with him any more.

"Then, one day, out he went. He knew where the salmon sharks lived on the edge of the gutters at low tide and he flipped a shark onto the beach. Then he had to find a way of taking it home, which was about half a mile away. So he just took it a little way and then he panted and stopped and took it further. When he got it to the beach gate, he started howling and that had the desired effect because Mum came out to see what was wrong with the dog. She saw the shark and saw the drag mark and she said, 'After blackfella's food, are you? Don't blame me. We don't like that stinking mess that the white people call food.' He put his paw on it to say, 'This is mine,' and she said, 'Yes, I know. Come on, you can watch me cook it.' So she cooked it up for him.

"Of course, when the little humans came home, we could smell this fish. Mum put it in a dish for him and he kept running around her as if to say, 'I want to share it with them.' But she said, 'No, they're not allowed to have it. Three months isn't up yet.' We had tapioca. To this day, I hate tapioca."

Oodgeroo made the point that, while punishments were often harsh, Aboriginal law and Aboriginal education were unerringly practical and they worked. No one in her family, for instance, ever killed a kookaburra again and the lessons and stories of her youth were indelibly etched on her mind.

"Let me tell you about our initiations," she continued. "These were hands-on training for life.

"You've heard about boys' initiations at the *bora* ring [sacred ceremonial circle in which Aboriginal boys are inititated into the secrets of the tribe]. Girls had initiations too but the elders saw that, when a girl child was born, she was born at that level [Oodgeroo reaches high above her head] and when a boy child was born, he was born at that level [Oodgeroo's hand falls lower]. The gods weren't as kind to boys as they were to girls. Boys had the outer strength but not the inner strength. So, in order to get up to the same level as the girls, they went through initiation.

"The initiation was to teach them not to faint at the sight of blood. Girls don't, of course, because they have their menstruation period every month. It also taught them to bear pain because, if they're fifty miles away from home and they get speared or accidentally spear themselves, fainting at the sight of blood running down the side of their leg doesn't do a thing for them. What they've learned at the initiation in the *bora* ring gets them from there back home. They've learned how to bear excruciating pain.

"It also meant that, when the man saw the woman in labor, he could say, 'Oh, I've been there, I've done that,' and there was a stronger bond between the woman, the child and the man. It's only belatedly that modern man has been allowed to watch a woman give birth. The man goes through the initiation all over again when his woman is in labor. He's trying to help her out, trying to take the pain from her."

OODGEROO'S FRIEND, RHONDA, LIVES IN A TIDY HOUSE WITH A NEAT YARD AND A dog in Sydney's west. The suburb is called Riverwood. One assumes there was once a river and a wood. Now there is row after row of similarly neat boxes framed by squares of lawn. Oodgeroo watched them parade by the car window as I drove her back there in time for afternoon tea.

"Do you know what you should do?" she asked me. "You should go out to any of these suburbs and see how many people have met and talked to an Aboriginal. Very few. Some people go through life without ever seeing an Aboriginal. Do you know why? It's because, in the early days, Aboriginal people were kept out in the bush where they wouldn't offend mid-Victorian minds with their nakedness. That's something I could never understand about Christianity. They're ashamed of their naked bodies but didn't God make them that way? They're ashamed of the creation of God himself. Then, as for Adam and Eve. You were made from the rib bone of Adam." Oodgeroo laughed heartily. "And people swallow it. It's the best-selling book in the world."

Plainly puzzled by its contradictions, Christianity unfailingly brought out her dry sense of humor.

"I still can't understand the philosophy," she mused. "I can't understand the hypocrisy. They have the audacity to believe JC was a male. How do we know that? And the hypocrisy of the churches, when they separated us and said, 'You can pray to God but on that side of the church — whites only on this side.' Another thing I could never understand was why Roman Catholic priests were not allowed to marry. I'll believe in Catholicism when Roman Catholic priests are born without testicles."

I suggested that Aboriginal Australians were providing much of the life that was left within mainstream Christian churches but she was unequivocal:

"THIS ABORIGINAL DOESN'T GIVE ANYTHING TO THE CHURCH

— I want that in capital letters — but I know what you mean. They're still trying to forgive and forget and they think they need Christianity to hold onto, as a stumbling block or a leaning post or something.

"I've never felt that way about religion. It's a matter of choice, I suppose. I prefer the spirituality of my people to the religious gunk that goes on in churches. If churches were genuine about helping the Aboriginal people, they would give all the land that they get free of rates back to the Aborigines.

"Christianity was forced upon us. I used to say to my father, 'How did we get on without God before these white people came into our country?' He would say, 'Very well, thank you. We had the Earth Mother to protect us. She was always there.' Then I would say, 'Why don't we call her God?' He would say, 'Because there are no gods. God is in the mind.' He would say, 'Can you see the God?' I would say no. 'Can you see the Earth Mother?' I said yes. 'Question answered.'"

While Oodgeroo's faith in the efficiency of political revolution diminished over years as an activist, her belief in the wisdom of her ancestors only grew stronger. In 1972, she published a collection of stories she remembered from her childhood. *Stradbroke Dreamtime* was written for her grandchildren and for children all over Australia, black and white, young and old, who are searching for the ties that bind them to the land and to the past.

"We believe in the things we can see, not the things we can't see," Oodgeroo told me, as we made tea and watched the sky darken from Rhonda's kitchen window. "We can see Mirrabooka up there. We know his story. Mirrabooka was a man who was much loved by the tribes and he was Biami's right hand man. When the Earth Mother went back to Uluru to sleep, she handed responsibility for the tribes to Biami. Mirrabooka grew old and he asked to be given eternal life. He said: 'I never want to be far away from the tribes. I want to watch over them for eternity.' So Biami threw Mirrabooka up into the sky and put lights at his hands and his feet. When the whites came, they saw this beautiful cluster of stars and called it the Southern Cross but we know it's Mirrabooka watching over us.

"Then there is the legend of the Seven Sisters or the Milky Way. Scientists are only just discovering all sorts of things about the sky that we've understood for years. I don't know how our people learnt about it. I suppose, so many hours of darkness, looking up there and, in those days, there were no lights around to confuse the issue. The stars were bright and our ancestors could read the sky like the palm of their hand. These were the things we venerated."

NIGHT FELL SUDDENLY. MIRRABOOKA PEERED DOWN THROUGH STREETLIGHTS. Rhonda went to play netball. Oodgeroo lit another cigarette and began to talk of death. She claimed it didn't frighten her. I don't know whether that was entirely true. I do know that she was concerned, when she died, for the future of her land. The way she saw it, the government was just waiting for her to die to whip the land she lived on out from under Aboriginal people and that, she said, was just the motivation she needed to live forever.

"When we die," she told me, "we give our body back to the Earth Mother to help her live and we're also cuddled in the arms of the Earth Mother. We leave our part-time mother behind and go to our real mother. Death, to us, is a promotion because we're finished with this flesh and go to the spirit world.

"The Aboriginal way of burials is completely different from your European way. The digging of graves is done by loving hands. All the men will be around but each only has the shovel in his hand for five minutes before somebody else takes it from him. Nobody gets tired. Of course, when the Christians came, they stopped that. We had to be buried under God's guidance — a lot of good that did.

"Before my son died, he said, 'Mum, don't bury me like that.' So he was buried in the Aboriginal way. He said, 'Do not kill a flower because I have died.' So I just spread the word not to bring floral tributes. When people came to pay their respects, they brought pot plants. It's a lovely little park now. You can sit there and it's beautiful and calm and serene. The missing of him will always be in my heart but, you know, I believe he's in good hands — back with his Earth Mother."

Oodgeroo was not only a teacher, she was a serious student of her own culture. From time to time, she would travel to the far reaches of the continent to listen and learn from the old people who still clung to their ancient wisdom and tribal ways. One particular trip to the far north-west had an overwhelming impact on her. The elders gave her a sacred necklace of white shells — an extraordinary honor for a woman — and spoke to her about the cycles of death and rebirth.

"We believe in reincarnation," she later explained. "There are two ways you can come back. Tribal elders might recycle us back through a newborn baby. Our spirit would be taken into the baby. It wouldn't matter if it was a boy or a girl. I might come back as a boy next time. Or we could return as spirit totems. I might come back as a carpet snake. The spirit totem can't be killed. It just goes on and on living that way.

"When I was made a tribal elder on my visit to Western Australia, they said this was my fifth time around. I said, 'Why five?' And they said, 'With the knowledge you have and the compassion you have, you could not learn that in one, two, three, four generations. This is your fifth trip."

FOR MANY ABORIGINAL AUSTRALIANS, OODGEROO'S WRITING WAS A RALLY CRY, a source of hope and pride. She was revered as an elder not only by her own tribe but by Aboriginal people all over Australia. She managed to take Aboriginal concerns and Aboriginal consciousness into white living rooms and classrooms around the country and make people listen.

"My father said something to me when I was growing up," she once told me. "He said, 'It's no good you just being as good as the whites, you've got to be better than them.' I've ended up better than quite a lot of them. I took his advice very seriously."

Yet for all her bluster, all her anger and determination, Oodgeroo retained an extraordinary generosity to white Australia. She was not a racist. She resented attitudes and edicts but never people. Her poetry was fierce but never bitter.

"I'm glad you say that," she smiled, pouring more tea, "because most of the critics said the poems in We Are Going were very bitter. I didn't see bitterness in them either. They were hard hitting but not bitter.

"You see," she explained, "the Earth Mother has forbidden us to hate. I used to hate a long time ago. I was so angry. Then I met up with an old man in Western Australia. I said to him, 'Why don't you hate them? You're always forgiving them.' And he rebuked me by saying, 'Girl, you know it's forbidden us to hate. If you hate, you spit upon everything the Earth Mother has created for you.' He said, 'Besides, the first time you decide to hate those white people, that just might be the day they see the light.' So I threw the hatred out. I've always obeyed my elders. He said to me, 'Hate is a negative thing and hate eats you.' He said, 'You must, at all times, as taught by the Earth Mother, bring the best out in people because, if you bring the worst out in everyone, you bring the worst out in yourself.' It's a negative thing. Hatred is not part of our way of life. The Aboriginals do not hate. The young people might, until they get wiser and older and decide that hate is a burning thing within you that will destroy you as well as everyone else."

Moreover, right until the end and perhaps against the odds, Oodgeroo believed a better future for her people was possible.

"I have to be an optimist," she insisted. "I can't afford the luxury of pessimism. Within the next ten years, I am hopeful that they will recognize and give back to what they call 'Third World' people — I call them grassroots people — their identity and their dignity and their independence. We were all here long before the white men came and we did very well for ourselves, thank you very much. It was two hundred years ago that we realised just how violent was the white man and that sort of violence is something that we want no part of. It's a result of greed instead of need. I think they'd rob their own grandmother of the gold in her teeth before they buried her. That's the impression I get of the white people — not all the white people but the ones in power."

"Racism," she added, "is fear of the unknown. Racism is ignorance born of fear. A racist is a very frightened and very ignorant person."

NIGHT HAD CLOSED IN AROUND OUR LITTLE CAMPFIRE IN THE SUBURBS. OODGEROO had been speaking swiftly and directly. Now she fell silent. Sensing my initiation was drawing to an end, I asked her to speak for a moment, not for her people but as an artist, to explain her passion for writing and its importance to her as the constant thread that had run through the web of her life. Her answer was unexpected. It surprised and impressed and made me see that this small, wiry woman, with her caustic wit, dauntless energy and wise words, had never written in a voice that was merely her own.

"Nothing is important to me on a personal level," she explained. "I never think of me in that way. I think of me as a tool that writes things down, as [the Australian poet] Mary Gilmore once told me. It is important to this extent — I want to be able to get up in the mornings, I want to be able to look myself in the face, eye to eye, and say to myself, 'Did I do the best I could yesterday?' If the answer is yes, no worries. I need to make sure I'm doing the right thing by all living things, and I do try to uphold that philosophy — to do the best I can for all living things — be it a tree or a horse or a dog or a rock or a human being."

A FEW MONTHS AFTER WE LAST SPOKE, OODGEROO'S BODY WAS BURIED ON Minjerribah, near her son, in soil of dubious title, in the Aboriginal way. As she was lowered into the embrace of the Earth Mother, a pair of whales glided into the bay and swam close to the shore. This, like her precious string of shells, would have meant more to her than any number of honors or obituaries. This was the way Quandamooka marked Oodgeroo's passing.

Ina May Gaskin

5

A MIDWIFE'S TALE

INTERNATIONAL HOMEBIRTH CONFERENCES ARE SOCIAL AFFAIRS. EVEN TODAY, THE homebirth midwife in a small country town is either loved or reviled, sometimes both, but often isolated. Conference time is a vital opportunity to exchange knowledge, organize politically and swap yarns. It is at just such a conference that I first set eyes on Ina May Gaskin. Dressed in jeans and South American weavings, with long greying tresses pulled up in a bun at the back of her head, she is drinking tea with a posse of young midwives. Eyes wide, they savour her every word. Plainly she is the star here.

Later, standing on a podium, ignoring her notes, Ina May mesmerizes an auditorium full of women. She speaks about her days in the counterculture, traveling across America in a caravan of buses with her husband, who convened workshops on spirituality and philosophy. She speaks of a child, born on the journey, to a couple who were part of the traveling troupe. It was the first birth she'd witnessed outside a hospital and it changed her life. Finally the caravan came to rest in Tennessee, land was purchased and the group settled down to live an alternative lifestyle on the Farm. Among their priorities, in part because of the distance to the nearest hospital, was the development of a new approach to child-birth, one in which women were unequivocally in control. Their experiences over the first few years made up much of the substance of Ina May's groundbreaking book, *Spiritual Midwifery*.

Ina May is uncommonly beautiful, in a Georgia O'Keefeish way. I suspect it's the combination of her hair, which literally cascades when she sets it loose, and empathetic eyes. She is also possessed of a spirit unique to her generation. An eclectic array of influences — from Lao Tsu to the 1970s feminists, from Native Americans to Tibetan Buddhists to the matriarchal religions of pre-Christian Europe — meet in a cosmology which has no name but is all her own.

Moreover, she epitomizes the combination of pioneering practicality and unbridled optimism that once led hordes of the West's brightest youth into the countryside, to carve out utopian communities untouched by the excesses of twentieth century life and to map out ways of living which might be kinder to the earth and gentler to the soul. Many of these communities collapsed under the weight of shattered ideals, human fallibility, greed and frailty. The Farm did not.

THE FARM CONSISTS OF NEARLY TWO THOUSAND ACRES OF OAK AND HICKORY forest populated by deer, possums, raccoons, foxes, coyotes, wild turkeys and some two hundred and seventy settlers, among them Ina May's family and friends. Migratory birds stop by, drawn to the clear water and dense forest. Migratory midwives stop by too, to learn from the women here the secret of their uncanny experiences in childbirth.

Ina May sits at a table, overlooking the wooded Tennessee valley, drawing. She is copying an Australian Aboriginal painting of a Dreamtime woman giving birth. Only the sound of birdsong breaks the silence as she collects her thoughts and then begins to speak softly, in a warm American drawl, about the heyday of the counterculture.

"It all began for me," she explains, "with Monday night class, which was an ongoing spiritual seekers' discovery and discussion group. Stephen, my husband, started it up on the campus of San Francisco State College in the days when they had things called experimental colleges. It was one of those places where, if you felt you had something to say and people wanted to hear you, then the university provided a space and a forum. It went under different names. One time it was 'Magic, Einstein and God'. Another time it was 'Group Experiments in Unified Field Theory'. We studied the holy books of different religions. There were a lot of gurus in town from India. People started showing up from Tibet. There were all sorts of different disciplines that people hadn't known of before, like Tai Chi and yoga. So we studied and picked bits and pieces that we liked from the different religions, especially from the places where they all agreed. That was the philosophical, cosmological framework that this group shared. It had nothing to do with belonging to an organized religion.

"When Stephen and I first met, all this was happening around him. I hadn't heard of it at first. I learnt about it when I went to the class and, as I learnt more, I found it fitting right in with how I'd always believed things should be. I just hadn't known you could implement it. I saw that people's behavior could change, that people could straighten up and do right and, if you had a whole bunch of people who tried to do that at the same time, it was positively exciting."

Monday night class began with a handful of inquisitive students in 1966. Within four years, it had become a mainstay of San Francisco campus life. Then, in the fall of 1970, a chance speaking engagement led Stephen and Ina May on an archetypal 1970s odyssey across the nation.

"All these preachers came to San Francisco for a conference and heard Stephen talk. Some of them approached him afterwards and asked if he'd be willing to speak to people in their towns. He said, sure, but that meant recessing his classes, at which fifteen hundred people were turning up every week. So a lot of them, when the recess was announced, put their hands up and said, 'We want to come too.' Stephen didn't think about it, he just said yes, and the implications were enormous. That's how the caravan started.

"Suddenly, it was like this whole school of fish started swimming — looking for places to live and good engines and combing Northern California for vehicles and thinking about crossing America in winter at a time when counterculture people tended to be scared of the rest of the country.

"People passionately wanted to change America. It was the time of the Vietnam War. People's friends and brothers were being killed and a lot of men were trying to figure out how not to go to Vietnam. It looked like there was going to be a war between the generations. Young people were being shot by National Guards on college campuses, so you really didn't know how bad it was going to get. We were all talking peace and trust and understanding but it felt very bad.

"So people cashed in their savings, quit their jobs, those who were on welfare got off it and we headed out of town. It was a huge mass effort of people working together. Lots of fun and excitement. We came through Tennessee maybe four months into the trip. It was a very cold winter. People had to stop and get work in order to have money to buy fuel and there was a farmer who was very impressed that young, long-haired types wanted to work. It didn't fit the picture that the media had been putting out, that we were shiftless, aimless, dirty, lazy. I think he had a long-haired son himself, so he liked these young people who came and offered to work. He was so friendly and fatherly that, when we went back to San Francisco and felt like the scene was over there and that what we were doing was far more interesting and important, we remembered him. We decided we'd go buy land some place and the first choice was Tennessee. That was mainly because of the connection with that one farmer."

It was while she was on the caravan, somewhere between San Francisco and Tennessee, that Ina May witnessed her first natural childbirth.

"The couple had asked my husband to attend the birth," she recalls, "because he was a Korean War veteran and they figured he'd be the best person to be there. It sounds strange but there was a real logic to it because it meant he would have more nerve and he wouldn't get rattled. He probably would have been good but there was a group of people waiting for him to speak, so I said, 'Look, you speak and I'll go to the birth.' I had a feeling that I might know something. It's hard to explain but it was there. I'd never known what I wanted to do when I grew up but I started to get a feeling on that day.

"So I went into this tiny school bus. The father was getting ready to catch the baby and I was looking at the mother. I didn't know her well. I'd never thought about being there when she had her baby but there she was and she looked beautiful. I couldn't take my eyes off her. I had never been told that women are beautiful when they give birth. Since then, I've felt that, if a woman doesn't look beautiful when she's giving birth, then someone's probably not treating her right or she's scared and somebody's not giving her enough comfort because most women look wildly beautiful when they're giving birth. She did and now I realise that the reason she kept wanting to look at me was that you want to be treated as a goddess when you're giving birth and that's what I was doing. You want to be admired.

"That was the first step. Afterwards, I began gradually to move into midwifery. I felt, for the first time in my life, that I knew what I was suited for. I knew finally what I was going to be. Even though I was a mother before and I'd done some things — I'd been in the Peace Corps, traveled the world, studied — still, I don't think it was until that first homebirth that I knew what I was suited to doing. Somehow I felt complete."

When the caravan drew to a halt, Ina May and Stephen moved briefly back to San Francisco and there, she began to take the first tentative steps towards what would become her life's work. Even before she had left on the caravan, she had heard of women who were beginning to take control of their birth process. Now, these women's experiences played strongly on her mind.

"I heard fantastic stories," she smiles. "There was one in particular. In those days, in San Francisco, there was never a man present at the birth of his child. It just wasn't allowed. Then news spread about a couple who came into the labor ward handcuffed together. They became famous throughout the whole Bay area. They changed the policy of the hospital. One couple figured out how to have some power.

"Another woman had a temper tantrum at full dilation. She just said she was not going to have the baby unless her husband was there, and she got her way. Then there was a journalist who wrote a story and she made me think too. She'd had two medicated births that were really awful and she was having her third child, which was going to be her last, and she was determined that they weren't going to abuse her again. She was almost having the baby when along came the nurse with the gas mask and she just hauled it off and socked her in the face.

"It was incredible to hear those stories. When you come to a moment of truth like that and there's a single act of boldness and daring, you're changed forever. You're a different kind of person to deal with and you'll be a different kind of parent."

What struck Ina May about these stories was how markedly they differed from the birth of her own first child in a hospital some years before.

"I wasn't raised as a fearful person," she insists. "I had a brother two years older and I quickly noticed that males had more power, so I decided that I wasn't really female, I wasn't going to accept that. I refused to wear dresses, I played sport, I just didn't want to go along with what being a girl was then. I remember thinking about childbirth when I was a teenager. I remember thinking, 'Well, men go to war, women have babies — it's some kind of testing thing, it tries you in some way.'

"Yet, when it was time for me to actually confront childbirth, I came out the other side plagued by irrational fears. After the birth, they wouldn't let me have my daughter for a while and, when I was allowed to hold her, I didn't feel this outpouring of emotion and I knew there was something missing. Everyone seemed to want me to behave in a certain way but it wouldn't come out of me and I didn't know how to play act.

"Then, when it was time to take her home, I thought, 'Well, don't I get a course in what to do?' They remove you from your instincts, then they expect you to take responsibility and feel comfortable with motherhood in total isolation. Nobody I knew was a mother and I was hundreds of miles away from mine. It was overwhelming.

"I did okay, in the sense that I figured out how to breastfeed her and which end to put the diaper on, but emotionally it was awful. I'd been told that she wasn't anybody, that she didn't know me from anyone else, that she was stupid and that she couldn't see. That's what they told you in those days. So I wasn't one to just start yakking at somebody who didn't know whether I was talking to her or not. It's amazing to me how, when you tell people things like that, they totally miss the obvious.

"I remember, one day, my husband was driving and I was sitting with my daughter on my lap. The car window was open just a fraction but I had this fear that somehow she would get out the window and under the car wheels. I was terrified of my daughter. She would cry in some public place and I couldn't stop her. I didn't know what she wanted. I used to open the door of the fridge and pick things up — 'Do you want this? Do you want this? Do you want this?' Isn't that bizarre? That was me: college graduate, Masters degree, Mom, but I didn't know how to act. They took it away from me. My experience is that moms don't have those problems when they're treated right. You don't have irrational fears. If you're scared of something, it's of crazy men who start wars and then you direct your energy towards stopping things like that."

Recollections of her first birth, and these stories indicating that there might be another way, sparked discussion between Ina May and Stephen and a band of interested friends, as they packed up their lives in San Francisco and traveled back towards Tennessee. By the time the first buses rolled off asphalt and onto the dirt track that led into their small slice of America, it had been decided that this would be no anarchic free love commune, that the Farm would pioneer a new sovereignty for women and that women would be wholly in control of women's business — all this at a time when the women's movement still wore training wheels.

"I have to give my husband credit here," Ina May concedes. "He really put himself behind it and said, 'Women should get to figure out how birth is done. What would men know about it?' He actually did have some insights and was very helpful but that was a good first principle.

"We could see that, if we followed the sexually free ethic of the counterculture, we would have a lot of single mothers and a lot of babies. So we began by making a rule that, if you were traveling with us and if you were sleeping together, you were considered engaged. If you became pregnant, we would think of you as married. That was our way of saying, we need commitment here, and the interesting thing was that we made that announcement to the group and some of the more disreputable men just left voluntarily. We didn't miss them. Then, when we established our presence on the land, we had to behave according to a certain ethic and we wanted to maintain that safety for women. Rape was never a problem. When there were a lot of marches in the United States — 'Take Back the Night' and so on — we didn't have to do that on the Farm because we'd already laid the groundwork."

Like women everywhere, those on the Farm were as concerned with not having unwanted children as they were with having appropriate births when the time was right. That's how their early experiments in natural birth control began.

"I was taught in high school, in the Mid-West in the late 1950s, that oral sex was okay. Now that's unusual," Ina May laughs. "I was told this by a high school teacher and, you know, when you tell a whole room full of virgins that sort of thing, you're going to change their lives. So I taught that in my community. This was the early era of the pill and how else were we going to do birth control? I mean, we weren't going to just have endless babies — we didn't want to be like the Amish down the road — but you had to figure out how to stop it.

"So one woman went to the library and did a lot of research and figured out how to determine when a woman would be fertile and how long the sperm could live. She figured out how to use the basal body temperature and check the cervical mucus and compare your last cycle so you knew what your pattern was. Then we did a lot of talking. We talked about sex and fertility and all this stuff a lot. She became quite an expert and, because she lived with me, I heard all these stories. So, when somebody got pregnant, I knew why. I knew that certain women became irrationally horny when they were fertile — it didn't matter whether they wanted kids or not — and the husband then had to take responsibility and be the strong one. At other times, it was the man who needed talking to. Sometimes there were a few days or weeks when women couldn't be sure if they were fertile or not and, if they just cut off having any sort of relations, they would fight, so that's where oral sex came in.

"Then you had to undo all this teaching they'd been given. Someone from a Catholic background had been taught that, if you had oral sex, you'd die. Even now, I get reactions when I talk about it. I was speaking to a group and one woman said, 'Do you mean what I think you mean?' I said, 'Yeah.' She said, 'Oh, what do you do with it?' I said, 'Well, you swallow it, it's protein.' You can't talk about that too much because people freak out but it worked well on the Farm because it helped with birth control.

"We only had a few women with unplanned pregnancies. Once, the man ejaculated and the woman sat in it and she became pregnant. Then, I know a couple of women who got pregnant without taking their jeans off. One Canadian girl, at fifteen, was wheeled into the delivery room yelling, 'Mom, Mom, I'm a virgin.' So then you explain to the kids how it happens. All you need is wet contacting wet and the sperm have a way to swim. Kids need to know these things and kids want to know these things but the grown-ups are too inhibited to talk about them."

Ultimately, of course, some of the women on the Farm chose to begin families. They gave birth at home with their partners and Ina May who, now certain of her vocation, drew around her a small team of midwives. For all of them, mothers and midwives alike, it was a steep learning curve, but it was not long before the safety and ease with which children were being born on the Farm began to attract attention right across North America.

"What we discovered on the Farm," Ina May explains, "is that, when you put enough women together and the men behave in a supportive, rather than a dominant fashion, you create a very powerful situation. We were pretty isolated, we didn't have a lot of books and there was no television. We had a lot of college graduates among us but that was no help when it came to childbirth and breastfeeding because they didn't teach you anything at college that would help with that. So there we were and I was filled with respect and awe for how perfectly women's bodies work.

"Our beginner's mind was just what was needed at that time because there was nothing in America that made birth seem like something that ought to be able to happen. You needed machines, you needed men, you needed stirrups, you had to be flat on your back and tied down and they had to cut you and stitch you and all these things had to happen to get a baby out. It seemed like the hardest thing in the world.

"So, with the births on the Farm, just because we were poor and didn't want to go to the hospital unnecessarily, we started thinking up things that we didn't know anybody else had discovered. For instance, I remember distinctly the first birth during which I dreamed up that this woman needed to pull on something from above. I got her husband to string up something good and sturdy and she pulled on it and we got that baby out. She wouldn't have had the strength to do it sitting on the bed or standing without holding onto something.

"I can remember when having a woman dance made her able to have her baby. She was ramrod stiff and wouldn't wiggle her pelvis at all. So we put on some music and got her to dance and down came the baby. I had a woman sing once. She was somebody who couldn't stand to hit a wrong note and that helped her quit resisting the birth because she was focusing her energy and attention on something else.

"Then there's shaking. A lot of people don't know that, if you take a woman who's having a lot of trouble giving birth, having a lot of pain, and you get hold of her bottom or the large muscles on her thighs and you just shake them, it makes her feel good and she'll relax.

"My husband used to shake me like that and it's a nice, relaxing feeling. So our relationship in touch has inspired a lot of what I've applied to women. We knew that nipple stimulation encouraged uterine contractions before I ever read any books on it. I just knew it from messing about. I knew it because I felt it. If you don't have any inhibitions about touch, it works. That was one advantage to being in the counterculture. We had our rules about who slept with who and about commitment but, in other ways, we were pretty free."

Months and years passed. With trial and error, experiment and intuition, the Farm midwives built up a vast body of knowledge, becoming a voice of authority at the vanguard of the burgeoning homebirth movement. Members of the medical establishment began to take reluctant notice. Ina May kept meticulous records and it became evident that rates of medical intervention in Farm births (including those where complications necessitated a transfer to hospital) were a fraction of those in hospitals around the country. Cesarean section rates on the Farm were as low as 1.46%, compared with an American hospital sample rate of 16.46%. Assisted delivery rates on the Farm were 2.11%, compared with 26.6% in American hospitals. Infant mortality and postnatal complications were also uncannily low. All this, the midwives insisted, was the result of creating an environment in which women were supported, respected and encouraged to understand how their bodies worked.

"The same went for breastfeeding," Ina May recalls. "We just assumed it was going to work. If our bodies were so good at having babies, why would they stop working when it came time to feed the child?

"About our twentieth birth was the tiniest baby that I've ever assisted into the world. This baby weighed two pounds, ten and a half ounces, and fortunately was born in August, when it's very hot. The baby was born in a bus, so the dad just got into the driver's seat and drove into town and that was when I made my first contact with my mentor, Dr Williams.

"Dr Williams had sixteen years of experience helping at births in the local Amish community of a thousand people. They refused to go to the hospital for good reason — you can't get there in a horse and buggy in less than five hours. If you give birth every year and a half and you have as many as a dozen or fifteen children — that's the average — then you're not going to make it to the hospital. Dr Williams helped them and he noticed that they had better statistics than the women in the hospital — less infection, less post-partum complications, less hemorrhage — despite the number of kids they had and the frequency with which they gave birth. So he was there to help me too.

"Well, this little baby was the first patient from our community in the local hospital and they called her the littlest hippy. There we were, living out on this huge expanse of land, with no electricity, no running water, no refrigeration and I knew she'd need to be breastfed when she got out of the hospital. I hadn't ever read a book about breastfeeding — I'd just breastfed one child — and I knew we had to keep the mother's milk going by emptying the breasts all the time. So we organized for the mothers in the neighbourhood to bring their babies over and say to them, 'Okay, this is your first job, go to it.' They couldn't get up in the middle of the night to bring their babies over, obviously, so then her husband helped out — he gained a little weight — or she expressed her milk and we made ice cream. We found that everything worked better if we had a good laugh about it because then the milk flowed well."

AT THIS POINT, I SHOULD MENTION THAT TALKING WITH INA MAY ABOUT GOD IS rather like trying to pin down a shadow. Her God is, or is part of, her every word and deed, sunsets and snowstorms, the most majestic wolf and insignificant caterpillar on the Farm. Her spirituality and politics are inseparable. Birth is an epiphany, birth control a chance to tap deep pools of women's strength. Metaphysics and matter are one. Life is sacred. Her God is everywhere and nowhere at once.

Ina May's intermittent childhood exposure to religion left her far from impressed.

"My grandmother was religious," she recollects, "and tried hard to impart some of that but I couldn't get the Trinity, I couldn't understand original sin or the curse of Eve. I was fascinated by the Adoration of the Infant, this special child, but the special child was the one who was conceived without sex. That was troublesome too — that the only sacred woman was the one who was a virgin. I don't like to be asked to be twenty impossible things before breakfast in order to be considered spiritual. The Bible is no help at all. The only person who behaved decently towards women was killed."

Ina May did, however, retain a sense of spirit, which finally had its germination in Monday night class and began to bud as her work in midwifery progressed. Gradually, she came to understand that the secret to the Farm's success was not purely in the mechanics of natural childbirth. Birth, she realized, is a natural process for which women's bodies are perfectly equipped. It is also, she became convinced, a spiritual experience through which women realize a new strength and power and during which a veil is lifted between our mortality and our sacredness.

"Women talked about having spiritual experiences when they had their babies on the Farm," Ina May explains. "Having a baby was a spiritual quest for us, an initiation into a certain level of womanhood. It wasn't like being trapped. It wasn't like, 'Oh no, you're falling into the trap and you're going to just live for a man.' It was a spiritual journey and you learned things as you made that transition. You learned something of value that made you stronger.

"Let me give you an example. It was six weeks after the birth of my second child — a great big ten pound baby and my first to be born at home. I was sitting outside and there was a baseball game going on. I was full of milk but I had such a feeling of accomplishment after that birth that I decided to go and play and the first time I swung the bat, I hit a home run. I was never a baseball player as a kid — I really disliked it — so I knew that home run was connected with the birth. I had this feeling of, 'I can do anything.' I realized that all those old men who wrote the text books on childbirth didn't know what they were talking about. It made me think, 'All the world is screwed up and maybe I know something about how it ought to be and I think I'm going to be vocal about it and I'm not going to act like all this is sane and I'm insane because I know it's the other way around, even if I seem to be in a minority."

Ina May's research into spiritual midwifery was a matter of collecting clues as she stumbled upon them, keeping them filed in the back of her mind and waiting until there were enough of them that they would tell a story. The first clue came while she was still in California, though it would be many years before the extent of its implications became clear.

"I hadn't even heard of homebirth at the time," she says. "It hadn't dawned on me that my parents and grandparents and every one of my ancestors had been born at home. I just didn't think of it because everybody I knew was going to hospital. It was unspoken. I knew a woman who'd had a hospital birth much like mine and had determined to have her second baby at home, out in the country in California. I spoke to her after that second birth and she said the most wonderful thing: aside from the fact that it hadn't hurt nearly as much as the hospital birth, she said that, when she looked outside towards the end of her labor, she noticed the neighbor's cows had walked several hundred yards up the road and were gathered around the window.

"That told me something even then — that there's an energy present at a birth. How else would the cows have known? So, I thought, when we see pictures of Jesus in the manger — the Adoration of the Child — perhaps we're seeing something of what happens at every birth. That one attracted particular notice but what if that happens all the time? That's what I was going on and that's what I'm still going on."

To sceptics, Ina May admits, this sounds absurd but she has felt the energy of birth too often to simply dismiss it.

"There's a saying," she explains, "that you have to be in a state of grace to receive grace and I think that's true. If there are negative emotions, you can't tell that something subtle and spiritual and sacred is happening. Your negative emotions blank it out and they can make that spirituality imperceptible, even to other people. That's why so many births happen in hospitals and, you know, you don't see animals flocking there.

"This energy is perceptible and I think there's a lot that's been missed because we haven't lived in such a way that we notice it. In fact, that knowledge has been discredited. Once women's storytelling networks broke down, we were told, 'That's an old wives' tale, don't listen to it.' We've had a real rupture in culture. If you move away from having a foundation of women being the source of knowledge about childbirth, then you're on the wrong track, you're shutting off the source. Women want dignity and respect and women want to be treated like goddesses when they're having babies and then they'll have amazing powers. I think these powers are coming back to women."

Ina May is not alone in her belief that women's spirituality, sexuality and power are irrevocably entwined. A synchronous historical meeting of the women's movement and the New Age has led to a burgeoning business in cauldrons, books of spells and all manner of old religion paraphernalia. Right across the world, women are charting their menstrual cycles, meeting at full moons and scouring history books for traces of ancient matriarchal religions.

Ina May's work is unique because it is an experiment in applied women's spirituality and because it yields results. It begins with the premise that women's bodies bring forth life and are sacred, a premise unknown in the West since spiritual and political power shifted into the hands of a celibate male hierarchy with the Judeo-Christian era. The philosophy by which she lives, and on which she instinctively bases her work, is about honoring life, sexuality, fertility, nature, things which are warm, which are green, which grow. She also assumes that women are not children and are capable of taking control of those areas of life which primarily affect them. Ina May is no born-again goddess worshipper but her work springs from a stream of unabashedly female spirituality which is ageless.

In following this stream, she has delved deep into European history, looking for times when it flowed strongly as a powerful force in the dominant culture and for others when it was forced underground, winding its way through subterranean caverns. Interestingly, through even the most oppressive epochs, a woman-centered spirituality has survived.

Much of Ina May's inspiration has also been drawn from non-European cultures, a number of which, she says, have nurtured this stream of women's culture without the hiatus it has suffered in the West. Her home is a gallery of keepsakes from her journeys. There are Indonesian fabrics, South American carvings, Aboriginal prints from Arnhem Land in the Central Australian desert.

She knows the history and significance of each one. In recounting the turning points in her life and the development of her philosophy and cosmology, the influence of indigenous cultures appears again and again.

"I've worked in Guatemala and some other places," she says and I remember the weavings she wore on the first day we met. "I love the sense of humor I find there and it's neat to be around people who have intact cultures, to feel the strength of that. It's quite something. It makes me think about what we've lost, how one recovers it and replaces those connections and that sense of continuity. I'm sure it can happen but it's going to require an intelligence and a flexibility that we haven't seen for a long time. There will need to be a lot of storytelling and art and music and dance and a lot of good things, like people having babies at home and women getting into government and making people be nice."

Like Oodgeroo, Ina May believes the West could listen and learn from indigenous cultures. "We've worked out how to put people on the moon," she says, "but there are other societies which have a far healthier grasp on the fundamentals of human life."

"Not many years after we began our community," she recalls, "we had visitors who came from the Six Nations. They were the people who gave the first instruction to European settlers who arrived in America in the seventeenth century. Were it not for them, our people wouldn't have survived that first century.

"They came to our community because they'd read about us in *Mother Earth News* and they were interested in how we had reclaimed sovereignty. That's an interesting word, sovereignty. What they meant by it, they said, was that we'd managed to regain control of some of our important life passages, like birth and death and education too. They were interested in knowing how we had done that and we said, 'By having midwives in charge of childbirth.'

"When you have a midwife in charge of childbirth, you quit being so afraid of death. You see that death could also happen at home and you don't need to have some corporation making money from you. In the United States, death is a time when the vultures come. They infer that you didn't love the person who died if you won't have them embalmed, buy a Cadillac coffin, buy them a whole new wardrobe and get this Hollywood make-up job done. People are truly coerced into that and sometimes go deeply into debt.

"So that got me thinking and a lot of the philosophy that I live by has developed out of what those representatives from the Six Nations said. It's a philosophy that revolves around life and death and finding appropriate behavior for these times of passage when people are vulnerable, when people go through spiritual and emotional changes. I believe it matters how we are born and how we die. It matters who's with us. These are the sacred times. Not the times when people go to church and say prayers. The real sacred times involve people's behavior around birth and death and illness. Do you help or do you not? Do you mess people over so you can have more or do you know that you're related to everybody and try to make sure that it goes around and that everybody's included?"

Her conversations with the Native Americans confirmed what Ina May had suspected for some time: that it is not only at birth but at all these times of transition that a threshold between the spiritual and temporal worlds appears. That's why indigenous cultures shroud these times in elaborate ritual. It is when we are at our most vulnerable that we are most likely to bridge the chasm between the spiritual and the temporal and in such moments, fraught with danger, we are offered our greatest potential for growth. Ina May believes the systems that are in place to deal with these times of change are telling indicators of a society's health. Another reliable sign is the distribution of power.

"Following our meeting," she hurries on, "we started training midwives who were Native Americans and, in getting to know them, I found out about their form of government. The government of the Six Nations was studied by the founding fathers of the United States. They admired the way the Six Nations had lived in peace for hundreds of years and they wanted to know how they'd achieved that.

"This is the basic structure of their government: only men can serve as chiefs but only women can choose them. Now that's interesting. If only women can choose them, then you have the grandmothers, who have watched these guys since they were little kids, and the other women, who share all the knowledge about them, making the decision. So you're not going to get a rapist as a chief, you're not going to get somebody who'll run off to war easily. The other part, recognizing that power can corrupt, is that the women can pull down a chief if he becomes a drunk or in some way irresponsible. I think that's better than a presidential election every four years. This one's even better: only women have the power to declare war but only men fight it. So blood isn't shed for silly reasons or for oil."

Ina May believes that religious and secular power structures have brought European society perilously close to its own near death experience. In times of vulnerability, compassion is replaced by competition. In the political arena, Atlas still holds up the world, which might be in better shape if he shared his burden.

"Now we're coming to a point," she says, "where we can see that Western culture has been on a track leading straight to destruction. We're at the precipice going, 'Is there any way we can make a deal here and get it better?' Here's the way I think about it: there's not a chance that men can sort this out on their own, with the women just hanging back, watching and trusting that they're going to get it right. 'We'll look after the kids and you guys figure it all out.' Not likely.

"The Oriental philosophy says there's the yang and the yin and there's supposed to be a balance. There has to be some way of achieving male/female balance. The Six Nations government is one way. In our community, we've tried to do it in other ways. I want us to dream some more about ways we could organize ourselves so that women would have more power. I'm not saying we're going to do this overnight but, if women voted in greater numbers and ran for office, maybe we could get some of these things we've talked about today discussed at top level.

"This has implications, not just for women, but for everyone. The way we treat women reflects the way we treat the earth. Women are the earth in a really deep sense. We can see the manifestations of that imbalance all around us. The same can be said of our attitudes to birth. They affect everybody. Birth is the beginning of life. It affects how the rest of it goes on. We are all born of women and first impressions are lasting ones on children. So how do our birth practices affect society, what kind of people do we get from this and how does that fit in with the survival of the species? These are the subjects that ought to be discussed in governments, not just in our living rooms."

Stephen comes in from the shed where he's been turning wood that Ina May brought back from her trip to Australia. He smells of eucalyptus. He stakes out a space at the far end of the room and begins to chop vegetables for the evening meal.

"Things are out of balance," Ina May resumes, though they're obviously not around here. "When we're talking about the difference between men and women, we're talking about half the world and the other half. To be out of it with so many of your relatives is bound to throw everything off economically, politically, socially, spiritually. Just as I'm not comfortable with a male-dominated parliament, so I'm not comfortable with a cosmology that isn't nice and balanced. I don't want to relate to a male ideal deity. If there's going to be anything of gender at all about it, it had better be both.

"I don't really think about a supreme being in a personal sense. I mean, I wouldn't leave out any of creation. I've never liked the religious idea, whether it's in Buddhism or Hinduism or Christianity, that says, 'This is God but that is not God, this is spiritual, that is not spiritual, there are good people and there are bad people and we care about these but not about these.' I think a healthy spirituality is about coming together. It's not about being individualistic or number one.

"Rather than a supreme being, I probably think of the collective spirit of everything. I find it hard to put words to it but it's certainly not a European person, male, with a beard. You could use different metaphors at different times but I don't like to cut it down. It's like butterflies — they're better when they're flying around than when they're pinned to a board. Words try to contain something that's uncontainable, unfathomable. What I'm trying to say is that words fall short and I'm comfortable with falling short on this."

Ina May stands, stretches her lanky frame and helps Stephen with dinner. I make my way back to nearby Summertown. As the car speeds over potholes and winds its way through wooded hills, I make two decisions. One is that, next time someone tells me, "This is just an old wives' tale," I'm going to sit up and listen. The other is that, if I ever have a child, I swear it will be born in Summertown, Tennessee.

I think too of Ina May's parting words to me on the subject of faith.

"On the Farm," she said, "we've never had a name for our religion but, if there's anything that it stands for, it's for clean air and healthy babies and the principle that, if the most vulnerable are in good shape, everybody else is too. That is the idea around which everything else has evolved."

Professor Paul Davies

6

IF GOD WERE A PHYSICIST

I SHOULD EXPLAIN, UP FRONT, THAT I AM ONE AMONG THE MULTITUDE WHO HAVE been stricken with an unnatural fear of numbers. I trace it back to somewhere around age eight. The rest of third grade, under Miss Game's keen tutelage, made the jump from the five times table to the six. I remained behind, watching my classmates vanish before me into a realm which would henceforth remain mysterious, separated from the real world by a chasm so great that, try as I might, I would never cross it. To be honest, I didn't try very hard and it was not until many years later that I began to glimpse what I had missed.

The new physics was at the height of fashion when I reached my early twenties. I struggled through the prerequisite works of Fritjof Capra, attempted to grasp relativity and was dazzled by chaos. Having emerged from my education as near as possible to innumerate, none of this was easy. I wished Miss Game had explained, before I'd lost interest, that maths was about more than counting apples and oranges. I wished someone had explained that physics, like French or English, was a language which had evolved to express beauty and meaning, that it was, in fact, a key with the potential to unlock the secrets of universe.

I say all this so you will understand that I have a romantic vision of physics and will appreciate the trepidation with which I view my first meeting with Paul Davies. You will also understand why we don't get right down to the business of divinity but begin by discussing the difficulties inherent in explaining even rudimentary scientific concepts to ignorant enthusiasts such as me. It is something of a hobbyhorse for the professor and my spiel about Miss Game and Fritjof Capra elicits immediate sympathy.

"There's something terribly wrong with our education system," he concurs. "The experience of maths and science is not captured in standard school teaching. It's such a pity. I don't know whether it's the way the teachers are trained — so they go into teaching already less than inspired by what it is they're going to teach — or whether it's that we're so locked into the syllabus and passing exams that we fail to educate.

"I feel that people are shut off from science and particularly from mathematics. Actually, it's worse than that. It's not just that people don't know the mathematics, it's that they have a fear of mathematics, a psychosis about it. That's tragic because the language of nature is mathematical."

Paul Davies is a member of that most mysterious of all fraternities. He is a physicist. Born and bred in Britain, he has held academic appointments at the Universities of London, Cambridge and Newcastle-upon-Tyne. Currently he is Professor of Natural Philosophy at the University of Adelaide in South Australia. He moved there, to escape Thatcher's Britain, in 1990, with his wife (who, he says, once had an Australian boyfriend and has since been fascinated with all things Australian) and his two children (who, at the time, were eight and twelve and "thought the move a great adventure").

Paul Davies is also an author and communicator of international repute. He has published more than a hundred specialist papers, several textbooks and over twenty popular books, including *God and the New Physics* (1984), *The Cosmic Blueprint* (1989), *The Mind of God* (1993) and *The Last Three Minutes* (1995). In 1991, he was awarded the Eureka Prize for the promotion of science. He is possessed of an agile mind, a roaming imagination and a rare ability to translate complex scientific ideas into the language of the laity.

"One of the problems involved with trying to get articles to the public on the concepts that inspire us, as scientists, is this enormous gulf," he continues, whilst making tea with an attention to detail that is unmistakably British. (Never before have I seen someone warm the pot before adding water to hotel tea bags.)

"I used to despair," he says. "I used to think of the years and years of work that go into understanding this concept and that concept. How can people who haven't been exposed to mathematics ever truly understand what's going on? The answer is that they can only glimpse part of it."

We are sitting around a table in his room in an old hotel set on a cobbled courtyard in the backstreets of Sydney's Kings Cross. Its stone facade and maze of dark corridors look like just the place in which a science professor ought to be holed up. Paul Davies is a small framed man with quick, decisive gestures and a somewhat academic sense of humour.

"Before coming to Australia, I used to be a lecturer in mathematics at Kings College London," he laughs. "People would ask what I did and I'd say, 'Well, I'm a mathematics lecturer.' I don't know what they thought. Perhaps they expected me to be ever so good at doing sums. Like, 'You must really be able to work out your mortgage payments fast,' as though mathematics was just awfully difficult arithmetic. When they found out I was hopeless at arithmetic, they were absolutely baffled and asked, 'What is it you actually do?' How could I begin to explain?

"So there is this enormous gulf but I passionately believe that we've got to make some attempt to explain what we're doing as scientists because, firstly, it's thrilling and tells us a lot about human beings and our place in the great scheme and, secondly, it's important for society because science impinges a lot on everyday life and people need to make informed decisions."

Paul Davies leads a schizophrenic professional life. On the one hand, he spends much of his time "scribbling equations on pieces of paper," trying to solve the latest technical problems in physics. His primary work is in an area known as quantum gravity and, he says, there are a number of problems connected with black holes that particularly interest him.

On the other hand, he writes. He retreats to a small farm in the Adelaide hills, bought expressly for this purpose. He remains there, for days at a time, addressing such fundamental human questions as the existence of divinity and the meaning of life from the perspective of science.

Indeed, in *The Mind of God*, he takes on the unenviable task of explaining the scientific rationale behind his belief that there is some God-like force at work in nature. What's more, his arguments stick. Even hardened atheists emerge from reading it, if not convinced, at least challenged.

So, what is a hard-nosed scientist doing on the trail of God?

Paul Davies is the first to admit that he did not enter a career in science because he was particularly keen on manipulating figures. He came to physics via a far more circuitous and philosophical route, which explains his uncanny knack for seeking out its mysteries and articulating them clearly, yet with all their magic and allure intact.

"I'm not a religious person in any conventional sense," he begins. "I never was. I was brought up in north London in a family that called itself Anglican. My parents went to church two or three times a year and I used to get dragged along but never found it terribly inspiring. I've not been seriously influenced by the church or my parents or the Bible and I don't have very much time for institutional religion.

"However, from an early age, I was preoccupied with what we might call the meaning of existence and I can remember, at the age of fourteen or fifteen, that I would go to church and argue with the curates about things like free will and determinism and so on."

Paul stopped attending church altogether in his mid-teens and "apart from weddings and funerals and meeting members of the clergy, which I'm always happy to do," he has not witnessed a church service since. At about that time, he began reading science fiction ("which was," he admits, "an impoverished form of theology") and thinking about purpose and meaning in terms of science.

"When I was sixteen or seventeen, I read a book called *Honest to God* by Bishop John Robinson, who was the Bishop of Woolwich. He created a bit of a stir because he was trying to drag the concept of God at least into the twentieth century, if not the twenty-first. I was impressed that an Anglican bishop could argue for such a radical view of God, which seemed not a lot different from what we might call the god of the physicists. At the same time, I was reading a lot of Fred Hoyle's books — both his science fiction and his popularisation of astronomy and cosmology. I thought that these two people wrote and thought in much the same way.

"So, gradually, I came to feel that doing physics, with a view to applying it to cosmology, was going to be the most revealing spiritual journey. It seemed that, if you were interested in the very deepest issues, then physics was the way to go because it was the founding discipline of science. I explain it this way: if biologists get stuck, they'll often go to a chemist for help and if chemists get stuck, they'll often go to a physicist for help, but if a physicist gets stuck, there's nowhere to go except theology."

Paul Davies' work as a scientist has not diminished his interest in those fundamental issues which so absorbed him as a boy. On the contrary, the more he has come to understand the laws of the physical universe, the more he has seen them as clues to the greatest mystery of all.

"I share with most of my scientific colleagues," he says, "a feeling that there is something going on in nature, that the world seems amazingly ingenious, in some ways contrived. It's so beautiful, it's put together with such delicacy and there are so many felicitous qualities about it when you look at it at a fundamental level, that I can't accept it all as brute fact, as something that just happens to be or has no explanation or is essentially absurd. It seems all too good for that."

Which is not to say that he has a simple answer nor even that a simple answer is possible.

"I don't know what's going on and I don't quite know where we fit into it," he admits, "but I do not believe that our existence, as human beings, is trivial. I'm not saying we're literally made in God's image but I do think that the emergence of life and consciousness, somewhere and somewhen in the universe, is a fact of the deepest significance.

"It's a hard message to get across because people want to take extreme positions. On the one hand, they'll say, 'There is no purpose in the universe, life is pointless, we're just an accident, let's give up in despair.' The other point of view is, 'We are the pinnacle of God's creation and the center of the universe.'

"I'm not saying either of those. What I'm saying is that I think the universe has something like a purpose or a meaning and that we human beings have a part to play in that. We have a place in this scheme. It's not a central place, by any means, but it's not an insignificant place either. One of the great disservices that has been done by science over the last three hundred years is that it's given the impression that human beings are trivial, marginal to the great scheme. I think post-modern science and mathematics restore a certain amount of dignity to human beings because we now feel we have a part to play. It's a modest part but it's one which imparts purpose to our lives. That is the message at the moment."

It's a message that's been a long time coming but a message, Paul believes, that was inevitable. A myriad of clues scattered about in the workings of the universe have led him and other scientists to construe an underlying meaning, perhaps even an underlying consciousness. What's more, Paul says, it was natural for scientists to embark upon this route because, at its core, science is a spiritual pursuit.

"I come at what looks like a religious, certainly a spiritual view of the world," he explains, "through my scientific work. Indeed, there is an aspect to the work of all the very best scientists and mathematicians which, I believe, might be termed spiritual.

"Roger Penrose is one of Britain's finest mathematicians and his book, *The Emperor's New Mind*, is very much about his own spiritual voyage. He may not want to use that word but that's what it's about: his deep sense of inspiration, his sense of discovery. He catalogues some examples, taken from earlier in history, of mathematicians who stumbled across results which were totally unexpected, results which sometimes they were able to grasp all in one go.

"Normally, when you do mathematics at school, you go through a series of steps and you get to the answer — it's a long and painful process — but these great mathematicians can somehow reach into a mental realm and grasp the result ready-made, without even proving it."

Paul reels off names, at breakneck speed, of scientists and mathematicians whose greatest work has been the product of sudden and inexplicable inspiration. Among the most famous is the Indian mathematician, Ramanujan. Despite little formal education, he wrote complicated mathematical results which later took some of the world's finest mathematicians many years to prove.

Paul proposes that these great minds have tapped into something akin to Plato's mathematical realm, where the laws of physics and mathematics exist independently, accessible by a process which more closely resembles mystical revelation than rational thought.

"Many of my colleagues have spoken in what I would say are mystical terms," he insists, "although they don't like the word mysticism because it sounds like the opposite of science. Nevertheless, this type of sudden inspiration, sudden discovery, sudden sense of 'Aahhh, that's how it fits together,' is very much akin to a mystical experience. I'm talking about the finest mathematicians, not the run of the mill people who use mathematics as a tool for advancing their trade.

I'm talking about people, right at the cutting edge, who are discovering new mathematical forms. These people are engaged in a type of spiritual exercise and they will write in those terms if they are honest."

However, Paul lays claim to no mystical experiences himself.

"I can't say I've ever had anything remotely like the experiences that, for example, Roger Penrose and Fred Hoyle have reported, where a blinding light comes out of nowhere and suddenly everything falls into place. I've never had anything of that sort happen to me, I'm afraid. Though there's still time."

Nonetheless, his vision of mathematics is unabashedly spiritual. It is a passion with him and he speaks of it with the unbridled enthusiasm of the devoutly religious.

"Many people feel that maths is in some way sterile and that, if you reduce nature to mere mathematics, you somehow demystify it or rob it of its spirituality. I think it's exactly the opposite," he asserts. "Through mathematics, you see the linkages and the subtlety and the beauty of it all. The Greeks knew this.

"The Greeks believed that the whole world was built out of mathematics. Everything was a manifestation of geometry and harmony. They found something deeply inspiring about the mathematisation of nature.

"Mathematics was created by human beings but it's something beyond ourselves, something that I believe is out there in nature. So it takes on a life of its own and it becomes a voyage of discovery. You get the impression of an unknown territory of mathematical forms and properties that are out there in an abstract realm and that you're uncovering this as you go. The joy of doing it is very much like the joy of discovering an unknown land."

It's seductive, this notion that mathematical forms have an existence independent of the human mind, that they would exist whether or not there was a consciousness capable of apprehending them. This is the sort of talk that fuels my novice's fascination with physics and I drink in the professor's every word, envisaging Elysian fields in which Euclid's geometric forms hover a foot or so above rolling green hills and Plato and Socrates stroll, in flowing white robes, having just emerged from Raphael's "School of Athens."

Paul Davies' vision of a mathematical realm is, naturally, more prosaic. It is, nonetheless, infused with an element of romance.

"People talk about a mindscape or a mathematical landscape but I can't envisage myself literally visiting such a place and seeing formulae lying around," he smiles, obviously used to beginners' literal interpretations of his ideas. "I suppose, I cart around some vague, wishy-washy image of what I see as this Platonic realm. It's just not one of those things that can be easily conveyed. It's like someone who had never been in love asking you to describe it. It's a little bit difficult."

Paul oscillates, he says, between a conviction that this realm is "a concretely existing thing" and a suspicion that it is actually "just the best description we can find for a mysterious and abstract process that we don't fully understand." Either way, it is a notion that is fundamental to both his scientific work and his writing and there are times when he is convinced that, not just mathematics, but great ideas, great pieces of music, great leaps forward in human knowledge and the arts might all be inspired by contact with this other world.

"There are many instances in the history of the creative process," he confesses, "whether in the sciences or the arts, which have the hallmarks of what we might call a revelation or even a mystical experience, by which I mean a holistic apprehension of an entire concept in one go.

"Of course, there are scientists who say this is simply a result of the subconscious mind working quietly away, putting the whole thing together and delivering the package ready-made to the conscious but that seems somehow too neat an explanation to me.

"We don't understand the human mind. We certainly don't understand the creative process very well. It may be that, at the end of the day, it will have a very mundane explanation but I think, at this present stage of our knowledge, it must remain one of the more mysterious aspects of human creativity."

Those members of the scientific community who are of a more reductionist bent find Paul Davies' musings hard to swallow. They are, however, in the minority. As comfortable discussing theology, art and literature as he is with leptons and quarks, Paul insists that the popular vision of scientists as white-frocked robots is as far as possible from the truth.

Indeed, he traces his scientific lineage back to the ancient Greeks and explains that, since its inception, science has walked hand in hand with metaphysics, theology and humanity's quest to understand its place in the physical and spiritual worlds. He draws inspiration from the earliest scientists, whose aim was to decode God's handiwork and who believed that scientific discovery unveiled thoughts in the mind of God.

Science, as a matter of historical fact, grew from Western European culture as an offshoot of theology. The influences upon its development were twofold.

On the one hand, there was Greek philosophy, with its emphasis on rational thought and reason and humanity's potential to understand the world through logic and mathematics. On the other, there was the Judaic tradition, which informed both Christianity and Islam. Its focus was a rational, law-giving deity who had ordered the universe according to a definite set of principles. So the twin pillars upon which science was built both enshrined this notion of a pre-existing rational order which, through the application of logic, humanity could come to understand.

"Of course, we don't talk like that these days," Paul laughs, "and most scientists would say they're atheists but nevertheless they do, unwittingly, share with their early forebears an essentially theological view of nature. To be a scientist, you have to believe that there is a real, existing order in nature, that it's not just something we impose on nature by our own processes. Indeed, without a strong notion of an underlying law-like order in nature, I don't think you can even approach the concept of science as we understand it."

No less important, Paul insists, is the belief that this law-like order is comprehensible. The early scientists believed that human beings were created in God's image and shared a common spark of rationality with their designer. Thus, it appeared perfectly natural to them that the laws of nature should be written in a language that was within human ingenuity's grasp.

Today, such leaps of faith come to us far less easily, yet our ability to comprehend the language of nature is perhaps the greatest of those felicitous circumstances with which Paul Davies' world view is thickly populated. It is so fundamental to us that we tend to take it for granted but is it not an extraordinary coincidence that the laws of nature are inherently mathematical and that a consciousness has evolved in the universe with just the right circuitry to unravel them?

The professor ponders this as he unties a small parcel of chocolates that has been sitting at the center of the table. The tension in the room is palpable. I feel as though we have been winding our way through a philosophic maze, with its center always around the next corner.

"To be a scientist," he continues, "you have to believe that this real, existent order is intelligible to us, at least in principle, and that we can come to know it through this curious process that we call the scientific method. It's the sort of thing we all take for granted doing science but, when you think about it, it's a peculiar activity for human beings to be engaged in. You set up laboratories and do these funny experiments, whether in a test tube or an atom smasher. Then there's a whole lot of mathematics and finally out pops a result that is meaningful in some sense.

"It's a very strange, arcane procedure, yet we do feel that it tells us something about reality and I don't think you'd do it if you didn't have this essentially theological point of view that you were dealing with utterly dependable and absolute universal laws."

These laws of nature are indeed universal, existing beyond both space and time and this, for Paul, provides a vital clue in the quest for a God who can coexist alongside our knowledge of science.

"The traditional God," he explains, "is a two-faced God. One face is what I call the Greek god or the Platonic god — this abstract, timeless, all powerful being, who underpins the world and its natural order. This god is outside of time, this god is remote and inaccessible, it has an austere splendor. Then we have the personal god of popular religion, the guardian angel type of god, the old man in the sky or now maybe it's the old woman in the sky. It's somebody or something, a person who is just out of sight, just out of reach and greater than a human being but almost recognisably human. This is the god of petitionary prayer."

Now, from the point of view of a scientist, and even from a theological perspective, these two notions of god coexist uneasily. The latter god, for instance, could be described as contingent, which means that it could have been different, that the reasons why it is the way it is depend on something beyond itself. The former god, on the other hand, is said to be necessary, in that it contains the reasons for its existence within itself and would remain unchanged, even if everything else was otherwise.

This difference becomes strikingly obvious when we examine the relationships that these gods have with time. The first god is clearly a timeless being, transcending time altogether. The second god, however, exists within the stream of time. This god is enmeshed in the real world. It is, as Paul says, "a god who is going to suffer, who is going to react to events, who is going to communicate and act within time."

"If you ask people who don't think too much about theology for their image of God," he continues, "it's very much the contingent, within-time god. If you ask them who made this god or where this god came from, they feel uneasy because there's clearly a problem."

This is an area of theological debate which, Paul says, physics has helped significantly to clarify. Up until this century, there was a general belief that space and time, like God, were necessary entities. Thus it was possible for God to be both necessary and enmeshed in space and time. That is no longer the case. Scientists can now stretch time in their laboratories. Time is clearly intimately bound up with the physical world and it is malleable. In other words, the reasons for its existence do not depend purely on itself. So, we can't have it both ways. If we want a necessary god, if we want to attribute the physical world to the activities of a deity who transcends that world, then we must find a god who exists beyond, not only matter, but also time.

"If physics leads us to any image of a god or a meaning or a purpose or an underpinning of the world," Paul says, "it must be in this timeless, abstract realm and this is both good and bad news. The bad news is that it doesn't help us if we're looking for a guardian angel but maybe it's time we grew up and divested ourselves of that image. Maybe we have to confront the fact that there isn't somebody just out of sight, just out of reach, who will fix things up when they go wrong.

"I like to think of something a bit more remote, a bit grander and, in some ways, a bit more inspiring. I think of a timeless underpinning, a timeless purposefulness behind existence. A number of theologians have come to this same conclusion. They understand that we have clung to a juvenile view of God and that we may have come far enough now to outgrow it and face the reality of our place in the universe. It is still a beautiful universe and still, I believe, a purposeful universe."

Popular notions of God have taken a battering, over the years, from the ebb and flow of scientific opinion. Paul speaks of the "God of the gaps" and claims religion might not have spent so long on the back foot if it had charted its own course from the outset. Wherever science has left a question mark, he chuckles, some affiliation of God botherers has come along and claimed responsibility for God. When a new scientific discovery has ruled out divine intervention as an explanation, the God botherers have moved along and found another gap. A more successful approach, Paul believes, is to seek out the most rational place for a rational God to be hiding.

"A lot of people who worry about theology," he says, "tend to worry overmuch about the origin of things. If you start talking God, people always say things like, 'Something must have started it all off,' or 'There must have been something around to make the big bang go bang.' They focus on the originating events, as though the best evidence for God or purpose is in the pressing of a button, the deistic view where God starts the whole show on the road and sits back to watch.

"I think that view of God went out of favor among professional theologians rather a long time ago. Of course, many ordinary people still feel that is God's most important function — as the creator who started it all going — but that's not the place to look for a truly plausible God. The place to look, in my opinion, is in the laws of physics themselves."

In fact, Paul believes, these laws possess many of the qualities which have traditionally been assigned to God. They are omnipotent, universal, absolute, unchanging, utterly dependable and perhaps even transcendent, in that they exist beyond the visible, physical universe with which we're familiar. "There is," he concludes, "something super-cosmic about them." They are both the grandest and the most fundamental things we know.

"If we have an explanatory scheme, layer upon layer, each dependant upon the one beneath, then for the physicist," Paul explains, "the bottom level of reality is these laws. They are the ultimate reality, in a sense. One of the curious things about quantum physics is that it shows us that, what appears to be real and concrete, isn't necessarily real and concrete at all. The physical world has a shadowy half-reality and the only dependable reality is in the realm of these underlying, abstract, mathematical laws."

Paul Davies is not asking us to replace our notions of God with the laws of physics. However, his descriptions of the two are almost interchangeable. The more he speaks of these laws, the more it becomes evident that, in a scientific world view, they have taken on not only deistic qualities, but also many of the functions which were once reserved for God, in terms of ordering, maintaining and directing the universe.

The professor gets to his feet to make more tea. The laws of physics allow the water to boil, allow him to walk to the kitchen without drifting into space, allow the hotel to stand upright and the moon to rise over rooftops nearby. Paul tries to communicate a little of the awe he feels when confronted with such everyday miracles.

"If you want to tangle with the physicist's view of God," he says, returning to the table and setting the pot aside to brew, "you've got to stare into those laws and ask, 'Could they have been otherwise and what is their logical structure and where have they come from and is there anything special about them?' It's my opinion that there is something very special about them, that they could have been otherwise and that, if they'd been anything other than what they are, the world would be far less interesting than it is and probably wouldn't have us in it.

"That, for me, is the great inspiration: it's the ingenuity and the mathematical beauty of this set of laws upon which this enormous edifice, which we call nature, is built. It's built upon the very elegant, very slim theatre of such laws. You might think nature is infinitely complex. How could we ever describe it in terms of a few mathematical equations? However, the truth of the matter is that the complexities are in the states. The laws themselves are actually simple. They're not beyond human ingenuity's grasp."

If Paul is correct, we are now confronted with a God whose nature is expressed in the laws of physics and who steers the universe through those laws. We can also see that at least one consciousness — though there may be others — has evolved an ability to decode those laws and understand much about its origins. Yet, even if there is a designer and even if we and the universe are so ingeniously designed that we can read its code, still one puzzle remains.

"Why," I ask Paul, "has this designer created a scheme in which we can decode everything about the universe except its designer? Have we simply reached a hurdle in our understanding which we might ultimately cross or is the designer hiding from us?"

"I can only say that I don't know," he concedes. "The fact that we understand as much as we do is a deep mystery and, to me, it's strongly suggestive of something like a purpose. Why do we have the ability to unravel the cosmic code, when this ability has no obvious survival value? I don't know how it has evolved and I doubt that we will ever have the complete picture."

There are those, Stephen Hawking among them, who believe that an end to theoretical physics is in sight and that, some day soon, there will be a "theory of everything" which will describe all of nature in perfect detail and nothing more need ever be said. Paul, however, takes a more pragmatic view.

"There is," he says, "a sort millenarianism abroad and it's infecting science. I have to say it is far from clear whether we will ever be in a position to say that we've gone all the way bar that last step and that we will ever have this marvellous theory of everything. When physicists talk about a theory of everything, what they mean is not literally a theory that would explain why your eyes are blue or what I'm going to say next. They don't go into that level of detail. What they mean is really a unified set of laws which describe certain classes of phenomena but not the individual details.

"There are few scientists — even physicists, who are often considered the most arrogant of the lot — who would actually claim that we can know it all. Even if physics is completed as an exercise — even if Stephen Hawking is right and the end of theoretical physics is in sight and, by the time we reach the grave, the formula will be there and we can wear it on a tee-shirt — it still won't explain things like consciousness and human behavior and love and political expediency and other aspects of complex systems. I feel there must be an unending hierarchy of complexity. There will always be more things to explain out there."

"Moreover," Paul continues, "there is a logical limitation on parts ever understanding the whole."

He is referring to Gödel's Theorem, which deals with "undecidable propositions". In effect, it proves that the very nature of logic prevents us from solving certain mathematical and philosophical questions through rational inquiry alone.

"It is," he says, "the most profound thing that we know because it tells us what we can't know, even in principle."

Paul believes the existence of a designer might well be one of those unsolvable questions. Science can take us just so far. It can provide us with clues and directions — and it has provided Paul with enough of these to convince him that the evidence is weighted in favor of the existence of some sort of God — but it will never provide conclusive evidence. It simply does not possess the tools with which we can meet our maker face to face. There will be no scientific proof of a designer.

For the pure rationalists among us, here ends the search for God. It ends with an ingeniously designed universe, teeming with coincidences and alluding to the existence of a consciousness behind it all but falling short of raising the curtain and exposing that consciousness to its creation.

For those of us who are not married to the logical method, however, Paul proposes another route.

"There is a loophole," he says. "Maybe mystical knowledge can transcend this limitation and we can come to know the ultimate or absolute through mystical revelation. Not being a mystic myself and never having had any sort of mystical experience, I'm loath to go that route. Yet, I do believe that, however far science can take us and however marvellously we feel we can describe the natural phenomena around us, these ultimate questions of existence cannot be fully grasped through the scientific method or the logical principle method alone. As I like to say, "there's a mystery at the end of the universe" and I simply leave open whether that mystery is forever mysterious or whether there's some way of bridging that final tantalizing gulf."

THE SKY IS DARKENING AND A GRAY BLANKET ABOVE IS BEGINNING TO SPIT RAIN but the manager has insisted we see her roof garden, so we make our way up in a rattling old elevator and peer through the fire door at red geraniums and wooden benches and terrace roofs, all shining and wet. On the western horizon, a slit of bright orange runs from north to south and fingers of sunlight creep through, painting a sky which might hang in the Vatican. We discuss our good fortune, in that the laws of physics allow for sunsets.

Paul looks at his watch. In half an hour he must be across town at the Australian Broadcasting Corporation, to participate in a panel discussion on national radio. Paul Davies has spent as much of his time speaking with artists and theologians as he has with scientists in recent years. The "science/religion interface", he says, is the subject of growing media attention and he is called upon, with increasing frequency, to address conferences and speak, alongside theologians, to the press.

"I don't know how productive it is from the point of view of religion," he muses, as the car speeds through dark city streets. "The reason I do it is because I'm fascinated by these deep questions and it seems to me that the natural people to talk to are theologians. I always find it rewarding but whether they find it as rewarding to talk to a scientist and whether they feel that they can go back to their congregations and re-invigorate them, I just don't know."

The reason he doubts the impact of these meetings is that the two-faced God, he believes, has spawned a two-faced clergy. People often ask whether he finds a gulf of understanding between members of the clergy and himself. Behind closed doors, he says, the answer is no. At a public gathering, however, common ground is more difficult to find.

"I think most of the Christian clergy, certainly if they've thought seriously about these things, will accept the scientific picture of the world, lock, stock and barrel," he asserts. "They will accept that science is the right way to describe the natural world and they're usually comfortable with an image of God of the sort I explained earlier. Serious theologians have long been aware of scientific developments and go ninety-nine percent of the way with the scientists.

"I've always said that the biggest gulf is not between the scientists and theologians but between the theologians and the ordinary members of their congregation, many of whom are living in the eighteenth century with their image of God."

Paul has challenged senior members of the clergy to "come clean" with their congregations and explain that the theological agenda has changed.

"You don't believe in Adam and Eve," he tells them, "you accept the big bang, you don't think it was necessary to have God directly interfering with the evolution of the universe, you believe that the laws of physics can take care of it. You should say all this and explain that it's time to get away from that old fashioned image of God."

The response, Paul says, normally runs something like this: "They take it in, then say, 'Oh but our parishioners just aren't ready for it yet.'"

Nor has public response been encouraging when members of the clergy have gone public with their personal beliefs. Paul mentions the former Bishop of Durham, David Jenkins, whose attempts to communicate modern Anglican thought were greeted with almost universal outrage.

"Margaret Thatcher described him as a cuckoo," Paul recollects, "and people made out he was a devil in disguise, simply because he tried to drag Anglicanism into the twentieth century.

"This seems to me to be the issue. When will the ministers of religion come clean and say, 'The church abandoned the fairy story view of religion one hundred and fifty years ago and accepted the scientific world view'? Maybe this isn't quite so comforting — it's not such a sentimental view of religion — but at least it's honest."

So, where does this leave religion and, more specifically, where does it leave Judaism, Islam and Christianity, whose Western God was, figuratively and perhaps even literally, the prime mover behind science? It leaves much of the flock thoroughly bewildered. We read, in the morning papers, about discoveries of new black holes and supernovas. We even hear of some of the more accessible developments in particle physics. We have an uneasy suspicion that our Saturday or Sunday service God doesn't quite fit the bill anymore but our rabbis and priests and ministers seem uncertain what variety of God they should propose in its place. We can no longer wholeheartedly believe the propaganda but where else can we turn?

According to Paul, the reluctance of theologians to communicate their beliefs beyond their own kind has led to a critical division amongst Western theists and the two camps, he says, are drawing apart with increasing speed.

"The people who want to turn away from the facts," he says, "hide in crackpot religions, fringe religions, fundamentalism and so on. Whereas, those who have the guts to face up to the world as revealed through science, investigate these new radical reinterpretations, as presented by people like the former Bishop of Durham."

There is, of course, one more place to which the flock is deserting, aside from fundamentalism, and that is science. This raises the spectre of the scientist/ priest, a notion with which Paul feels most uncomfortable.

"They think we are the high priests of a new religion," he confesses, with a worried brow. "A lot of people feel that way about physics. They get very mystical about it. Often, they ask, 'What can physics tell us about right and wrong, good and evil in the universe?' I say, 'Well, we look out into the wider world and we see powerful and violent processes going on and sometimes good comes out of them and sometimes evil comes out of them and nature is neutral in that respect.' With something like chaos, which we see all around us, if it causes metal fatigue and a plane crashes, that's bad news, but if it helps the immune system fight disease then it's good news. We don't find good and evil in nature. They are categories of human behavior and you don't go to physicists for moral advice. I can give my opinions, for what they're worth, but they're no better or worse than yours."

For all its trials, Paul does not believe the end of religion is nigh, largely because he sees no other institution that is equipped to take its place.

"I think religion plays a fundamental role in society," he admits. "We understand from anthropologists that religion goes back as far as they can make any sense of the human past. It is extremely deep-rooted. People have always wanted something like it. Although religion purports to be an explanation of the world, for most people, it's function is a moral, almost a social one. I believe that's still an important function and it's one that science alone is unable to adequately fulfil."

Paul does, however, believe Western religion is in a state of crisis, that it struggles on, at present, in a vacuum and that it must inevitably evolve or something new will be created in its place.

He speaks of a post-Christian age, "in which we might be able to take a hard-nosed view of the world without abandoning the significance of our humanity or the wonder of the universe." It's an idea that appeals to him and he hopes that his work, in some small way, will contribute to the movement of popular thought in that direction.

"Perhaps it will evolve into something that might even be called post-religion," he speculates. "I'm thinking of a framework of ideas, a view of ourselves and our place in the world that will enable people to lead their lives with dignity but that won't be based upon a set of unverifiable myths or dogma or looking back to the past for received wisdom.

"I do think people need to feel they're part of something bigger and that there's a meaning or purpose to their lives. So we need to find a middle path. We need to show people that we live in a wonderful universe, that it's a rich and interesting universe, that we are an integral part of it, that what we're doing in our lives is, in a limited sense, useful and purposeful. We need to show people that we're part of this magnificent scheme and, therefore, we don't despair but we're not God's agents in the old fashioned sense, we're not central to God's plan and we don't need to go around killing each other in the name of God."

We pull over by the curb at a brightly lit corner in Ultimo. The rain has eased. Passing cars splash the pavement. The professor's watch is ticking. He will be on air in half an hour. A thoroughly rational religion seems a worthy aim but, I postulate, surely we're fundamentally romantic creatures. Even if a no-frills post-Christian framework is created, won't people naturally color it with their individual biases and dreams and notions of what the universe should be?

"Inevitably it will be colored," Paul concedes, "but I think that's a better way to go than looking at some ancient book and saying, 'Well, they knew it all two thousand years ago.' The great thing about science is that it's forward looking, not backward looking. It's not dogmatic. It's prepared to change as we discover new things. So, I don't see religion going away but I believe that a faith which has a good scientific grounding is better than one that is based on a lot of crackpot doctrine."

A Londoner is never caught without an umbrella. Paul Davies steps onto the pavement and unfurls his, waving energetically as he makes his way through puddles to the ABC.

THE RAIN CLEARS OVERNIGHT AND FRIDAY DAWNS WITH A WIDE BLUE SKY AND shafts of light reflecting almost too brightly off Sydney harbor. I make my way to the Botanical Gardens. Flying foxes hang from the Moreton Bay figs. The professor has staked his claim on a park bench beneath a jacaranda tree with a view of the water. He's chuckling merrily to himself and leafing through a Douglas Adams book.

The book, it turns out, was a gift from the author, with whom Paul shared a stage in London some weeks back. He has read all Adams' books, from A HITCHHIKER'S GUIDE TO THE GALAXY on, and claims they're more amusing by far for those with a background in physics.

"I even told him my pet theory as to why I think the answer to life, the universe and everything is forty-two," Paul laughs. "It's just a simple thing. You see, computers can only run algorithms and, if you think of the simplest algorithm for a question involving words, it would be to associate numbers with letters. So, A might be one and B might be two and C might be three and so on. If you put 'Big Bang' in and add up all the numbers, you get forty-two."

Adams was, by all accounts, impressed and the pair then moved on to a spirited discussion of extra-terrestrial intelligence, a subject dear to both their hearts.

Indeed, most of Paul Davies' favorite topics of conversation are controversial. He enjoys the challenge of new ideas and he appreciates a worthy opponent in debate. Dinner time around the Davies' family table must be broadcastable.

111

"We do often have discussions on these sorts of topics," Paul admits, with religion among a number of recurring themes.

"I think it's important that parents don't indoctrinate their kids into any particular line. When they were little, I'd say to them, 'Look, this is something you have to make your own judgment about. I don't want to force a set of beliefs on you. Ideas like God are difficult for children to understand and you really have to wait until you're old enough to grasp abstract concepts before you'll know what people mean when they're talking about God.'

"If they ask me about religious conflict, I suppose it's obvious that I'm disapproving of the warfare between factions but, if they wanted to join a religious group, I wouldn't stand in their way. I feel that's their right, though I wouldn't enrol them on their behalf. If they ask me whether I think there is life after death, then I say, 'It would be nice if there was but this isn't something I can say yes or no to and you might want to make up your own mind.'"

Speaking for himself, Paul suggests he'll be pleasantly surprised if he wakes up one day to find he has a soul which has survived his body.

"The word soul has been corrupted," he explains. "It's actually a Greek concept but it also appears vaguely in the Bible as the breath of life. There was never any intention of a schism between the body and the soul. The soul was simply meant to describe some aspect of the living body."

Not particularly predisposed towards dualism, Paul finds the notion of soul a conundrum.

"I find the word useful metaphorically," he says. "I use it to describe those aspects of ourselves which are closest to our innermost feelings, our innermost personality, the source of inspiration, that which makes us human and so on.

"I certainly don't like the idea that the soul is some extra stuff, that it is an entity with an almost physical efficacy, as Descartes wanted. The soul can't push and pull atoms around and of course, if it can't move matter, then it can't affect the brain, so it can't affect our thoughts. Likewise, I suppose, our thoughts cannot affect it. So, in as much as we can make sense of the soul or the spiritual dimension of human beings, it's got to be within the physical description of the brain and the brain processes and thought processes that go with it."

Which does not mean that, in his extravagantly optimistic moments, Paul Davies does not wonder whether some part of him could still survive death.

"Supposing, here, we equate mind and soul for a moment, in contradistinction to brain and body," he suggests. "Then, we think of them, not as two sides of a coin but as different levels of description. A good analogy is that the mind or soul is like software and the brain or body is like hardware.

"Imagine there is a computer chugging away and you ask, 'What is it doing?' The electrical engineer will tell you that these circuits are firing and those electrical pulses are moving through these conductors and so on. The mathematician will tell you it's computing, say, a square root. These two descriptions are entirely compatible. They're complimentary descriptions at different levels of the same complex phenomenon. That is the best way I can describe my view of body and soul.

"The best hope we have for survival of the soul is that, just as, when my computer blows a fuse, I can run the software on another machine, so it's not inconceivable that some aspects of our mental life could be run on another machine, another body, another system. It doesn't hold out much hope for survival after death but it's not logically impossible."

A less fantastic scenario might run something like this: Paul writes a book, I read it and, in that act, some of Paul's software is transferred to my program. If I pass this information on, Paul achieves a precarious immortality.

"That's right," he smiles. "We have to distinguish between the plot and characters of a novel and the physical words on the page. We don't say that a book is nothing but a collection of words. So we have to recognize that there are different levels of description in the world and the more abstract levels, which are supported by, but not reducible to, these lower levels, are every bit as real as the lower levels.

"Whether the world is contrived so felicitously as to preserve the upper level that we might call the soul or the mind, I don't know. It seems too good to be true. On the other hand, I sometimes console myself with saying that it seems almost too good to be true that we're here in the first place. The world is so marvellous and unexpected and incredibly contrived that I suppose you could even believe it could contrive to save souls."

Paul Davies considers himself blessed with a scientific world view. When he says that the universe is a magnificent place, it is not just because the harbor is sparkling particularly brightly today, it is because he knows that the universe is magnificent, right down to the nuts and bolts of it. When he says that humanity is not a mere accident and that he believes the universe has conspired to have us in it, he knows, better than you and I will ever know, what a precise act of balancing and juggling is necessary to create consciousness and life.

On the other hand, his scientific world view precludes from him the existence of a god to whom he might pray and who might answer his prayers. Accepting that science deems this personal god an improbability involves both struggle and courage. Even now, there are times when he feels tempted to fall back on some notion of a personal god.

"Oh, I feel very tempted," he admits, "but it's difficult for me to square that with what I feel would be a good universe. I find it hard to imagine a truly good god just interceding on behalf of somebody who happened to call. I find it hard to accept as a scientist — that God would meddle and tinker and move matter around, violating the laws of physics — and it seems to me a childish notion of God. So, whilst I can see the temptation and the comfort in thinking there is a guardian angel type of God, I find it difficult to be honest with myself and suppose that there is such a being."

Yet the God that Paul has come to believe in and the universe which that God sustains is, to him, more extraordinary, more inspiring than the dogma and mythology and fairy tales.

"You see," he says finally, "I don't believe life is unique to the earth. To me, the central message of *The Mind of God* is that the emergence of life and consciousness are things that are written into the laws of nature. This is why I find it all so inspiring. We have come out of nature without any miracles. The miracle is nature itself, that it can give rise to the complexity and the life and the consciousness, and then consciousness develops to the point where we can actually uncover these laws. It's an incredible story."

Paul tucks his book under his arm and gets to his feet. As we walk along the foreshore to the road, I venture one last question.

"If you did discover the mind of God," I want to know, "what would you ask It?"

"How to quantize a gravitational field," the professor replies in an instant, "or the purpose of the universe as a whole. That's what I'm groping towards in my scientific work. That's what fascinates me."

IN MARCH 1995, JUST A COUPLE OF MONTHS AFTER OUR MEETING, PAUL DAVIES wins the world's largest annual award, the Templeton Prize for Progress in Religion. In doing so, he joins a distinguished league of former recipients, including Aleksandr Solzhenitsyn, Charles Birch and Mother Teresa. In the statement which Paul reads to the media in New York, he quotes the astronomer Sir James Jeans: "God is a pure mathematician," he says.

PHOTO BY GIOVANNA TRENOWETH

Rev. Dorothy McRae-McMahon

7

SINGING TO THE ENEMY

IT'S TEN O'CLOCK ON A COLD SUNDAY MORNING IN JUNE 1990. SYDNEY IS ALL gray silence except for the shifting feet of the homeless and the lonely sound of wind blowing litter along deserted asphalt pavements. The desolation of the empty city is broken by the pealing bells of St Mary's and St Andrew's.

In the shadow of the monorail, squeezed between tatty shops, the Pitt Street Uniting Church is humming. Parishioners blow clouds of steam into the air, rub hands for warmth, greet one another cheerfully.

To the right of the nave, a candle wrapped in barbed wire (the symbol of Amnesty International) sheds light on a board crammed with notices about human rights. At the far end of the church, another candle burns permanently as a call for world peace. The congregation moves into the body of the church, filling almost every seat. Shuffling of feet, shuffling of papers, then the deep droning and swelling of a didgeridoo and everyone stands.

"We believe in God who brought us forth from the earth, our mother," the parishioners chant, "who supplies our needs with fruits from the earth, who moves us to love the earth …".

"God who listens," prays the liturgist, "God who empowers and saves us, we pray for the struggle to end Aboriginal deaths in custody, for an end to prejudice and discrimination."

"Thanks be to God for the hope that we may live for better things," pray the parishioners, "for justice for Aboriginal people, for release from exploitation and greed.

"Thanks be to God," prays the congregation, "for the gift of peoples of different dreamings and colors and cultures — to love, to care, to share lives with."

I AM NOT A CHRISTIAN. NOT SINCE CHILDHOOD HAVE I, FOR A MINUTE, CONSIDERED myself one. Yet I sit here on a hard wooden pew, shoulder to shoulder with the faithful, blowing on gloved fingers, shivering, singing hymns. I am intrigued by this parish's minister. Her name is Dorothy McRae-McMahon. She is best known for the harassment she was subjected to, some years back, by National Action, a loose collective of racist thugs. She is a vocal exponent of human rights, supportive of the peace, environment and women's movements and she welcomes gay and lesbian parishioners without a hint of punitive church dogma. I have an interview arranged with her next week.

The service unfolds with an admirable attention to politically correct detail which underscores a genuine commitment to change.

Parishioners, one after another, move to the front of the church to speak or sing. Conspicuous by her absence is Dorothy McRae-McMahon. Towards the end of the service, she rises briefly to offer a handful of carefully chosen words but, for the most part, she sits quietly, another of the faithful in the pews. She is the minister here, and a well-known figure in the church and wider community, but this is emphatically not her service. The overriding impression is that this church and all that goes on here belongs to the people it was built to serve.

When finally I meet Dorothy it is in her small, dark, wood-and-book-lined office. She is a warm, attractive, middle-aged woman, with softly graying hair, a gentle manner and an enthusiasm that is contagious. She offers me tea and a seat cushioned with well worn upholstery. Her soothing manner alleviates some of the discomfort I feel as a heathen in this antechamber to the house of God.

I shift in my seat, I look at my questions, I wonder where to begin. I have begun to realize that I am looking for a home. I have chanted in Hindu temples, meditated with Buddhists, seen spirits in my lounge room and auras like the

Northern Lights. Each time I have dipped a toe into one of these metaphysical pools, I have found deeper conviction and greater strength but always a subtle after-taste that is culturally alien.

So here I sit with a Uniting Church minister. I have returned to the religion of my childhood. Dorothy smiles welcomingly. Perhaps this is simply ministerial manner or perhaps she senses I am measuring my cosmology against her every word, that I want her to hand me a faith that feels like my own.

So we begin by discussing the service, her commitment to human rights and the environment. Here we meet, here doctrine is unlikely to come between us, here there is common ground.

"I think," Dorothy explains, "the Christian community has a responsibility to release Western society from a view which is related to the first chapter of Genesis, which talks about human beings having dominion over the earth. I think what's meant there is a sense of responsibility for the earth, but I don't think that's the way we've seen it. I think we've seen it as ruling the earth and it's high time we gave a lead to the community to release it from that.

"It's time we tapped in much more richly to the spirituality of Aboriginal people, who understand the God who goes down deeply into the earth and who is their mother. I think we have a lot of work to do theologically and the church must certainly help people to work towards a more sustainable form of living.

"The church is being forced to respond to a rapidly changing, crisis-ridden, alienated society, where many of our assumptions are beginning to be challenged. The way we had aligned Western capitalist society with the church is now being questioned. You wouldn't find that thought in every parish but it's here. We thought we were heading in such a wonderful, progressive direction and inviting the Third World to one day discover this great upward path, but now we know that a lot of the values and aspirations we've had lead into the desert. We can see that we are not only destroying ourselves but that we're also going to destroy the earth if we proceed, and that what we call progress is not necessarily progress at all. If we could pause and listen to other cultures and to the poor, then we might understand a lot more about the nature of reality and the nature of God."

This is what I came to hear: that this life is as important as the afterlife; that this world is sacred; that missionaries no longer want to strip belief, language and culture from indigenous peoples around the globe; that Hindus and Buddhists and Muslims and indeed atheists won't burn in hell; that you don't have to be reactionary to be a Christian.

Dorothy is meeting change with the doors to her church wide open. "All sorts of things are rocking," she insists. "We're in a time of flux and I don't feel afraid of that sort of transition to new things." Some of these changes, she feels, result from the influence of 'Third World' churches. Others are coming about as women take their place more clearly in religious leadership and spiritual life. The image, for example, of God as an old man on a white cloud, wielding lightning bolts and bestowing blessings, is well on the way out.

"My feeling," she explains, "about the perception that God is as female as God is male, and therefore that God is discovered as strongly in the female as in the male, is that it's something that's always been there, even in scripture. It's been a very thin stream because it's been conveyed and interpreted through male models and male leadership — it's come out of a patriarchal tradition — but it is there."

"Acknowledging the femaleness of God," she believes, "will release a sense of wholeness into the church. It's rather like the wholeness that God claimed for us in creation. I always think that's the model. God created us in His or Her own image, and that was to be a wholeness. I'm not talking about whether you're married or not. I'm talking about how, in the whole of creation, that engagement of male and female is creative. One on its own is sterile, together it's creative, and it can be within a person or between people or in a group of people. In the end, that's what conceives life, brings it into birth and frees it to live. Therefore, to acknowledge that in God is simply to name what, astonishingly, is there in the first chapter of Genesis. Within God is male and female and we are made in that image."

Sitting in her draughty office on a blustery winter's day, it is difficult not to be caught up in all this talk of revolution. Dorothy envisages enormous change — social change, moral change, theological change. She is articulating for me a dream of what her religion could be, what she seems certain it will be. While her confidence is due more to her faith in people than her faith in institutions, she believes Christianity can survive such great upheaval.

"I have a sense of safety about it all," she smiles. "I believe there is an underpinning of immovable, broad truth. For instance, if you explore the femaleness of God and live out of that, what it gives expression to in people's lives is something that is free and strong and healing. Jesus said, 'By their fruits, you will know them.' He took that risk. He didn't say, 'If they believe this, they're my followers.' I believe that you can, in fact, trust people's perception of truth. There's something in the human spirit which recognizes what is authentic and good and beautiful and true. Even if they don't particularly want to live out of that, it's something people know."

Dorothy's vision is of a church which allows its congregation to use that capacity, a church which encourages questions rather than dishing out pronouncements. If it would just loosen up, she insists, Christianity might find it has more to offer secular society than either party has hitherto noticed. She has a wonderful story to illustrate this point — a story which probably says as much about Dorothy as it does about the Christian church.

"I was talking on women's spirituality at a secular meeting a couple of weeks ago," she explains, "and a woman who works with child incest victims approached me and asked me to work with her on rituals of healing and affirmation for the children."

These would not be specifically Christian rituals but it was the type of opportunity to be of service to the broader community that Dorothy would never pass up. Her ideas for the rituals speak for themselves.

"I would ask the children to bring an image of themselves, some object to remind them of who they are. I would ask them to put their objects in the center and say, 'That is like me.' Then perhaps those children could look at each other and, if they knew each other, name what they had seen as beautiful in each other. So we'd start off with a sense of mutual affirmation. Then we might get a bowl of tears — of salt water — and say, 'These are our tears and why do we weep?' Just in a sentence, they could name their weeping, and then pour those tears out so the bowl was empty. Then we could say, 'Let's remember a moment when we have felt strong and clear,' and the children would remember and name the moments. After that, we could do something that involved sharing. The Eucharist is the most profound human symbol and it's been in many cultures, not just Christian ones. The Incas used to do it, they'd share a common cup. I would probably have something which also involved brokenness — feeling our own brokenness and sharing that brokenness — and a symbol which restored it. Then I'd have each child take away a common cup, which had been passed around, to remind them of that moment."

Dorothy created a similar ritual for the women of Bulli, south of Sydney, when a rapist was wreaking terror in their town, and women all around Australia threw in their support.

"A beautiful patchwork quilt was made and sent from a national women's conference in Melbourne, with a message that said, 'We are all part of this patchwork'. Aboriginal women from Redfern made paper flowers with messages on them and each of the Bulli women was given a flower.

"There are ways of catching up energy and love and community and hope and beaming it in on people, so they feel surrounded and supported by love. You can hold hands and feel the energy that travels from one to the other and the cloud of healing that's in the center."

All this is part of Christian worship but Dorothy is not concerned that it should always be named in Christian terms. One of the treasures of her religion, she believes, is its powerful sense of healing through ritual — ritual which can be framed to respect individual spirituality and offered to the wider community by the church.

"It's about eternal truth," she insists, towards the end of the afternoon, "and you can set it free of its bondages of language and dogma and get at that kernel underneath. That's what it's about and people recognize it. We name it in Christian terms but, if the core is truth, it doesn't really matter how it's said."

IT IS EASTER SUNDAY 1992. I AM SITTING IN AN OUTDOOR AMPHITHEATRE SWARMING with tourists trying to remember the sense of purpose I imbibed that day from Dorothy's cosmology. I am midway through three days of meditation with a charismatic Indian guru. I am sitting in a public space unabashedly crying. Tourists want to take my picture. Somehow, over the past day or so, my world has tumbled down. I have chanted in a dark auditorium for hours without ceasing. This ought to lead to enlightenment but my head is spinning with every twentieth century horror — war in the Middle East, AIDS, cancer, rape, murder, child abuse. I have lost the thread of purpose. I cannot find a god.

I look to the city across the harbor. Hidden behind towers of glass is Dorothy's church. Right now, it will be packed with true believers. I want to march over there and rattle the doors. I want to ask what sort of creature this god of hers is. I want to ask her how to hang onto a notion as elusive as a compassionate god. I want to ask her how she justifies this mess and misery and still believes.

I don't, of course. I chant some more and meditate some more and gradually, over a month or so, the desolation passes. I do not, however, forget my questions and I don't forget Dorothy McRae-McMahon.

IT IS A FRIDAY AFTERNOON IN NOVEMBER 1992. IN TWO DAYS, DOROTHY WILL SAY goodbye to her eclectic urban parish and move on to a national position as Director for Mission within the Uniting Church. She is at once filled with the excitement of meeting a new challenge and a sense of loss at being wrenched from a community which has seen her through some of her greatest achievements and her darkest hours. In the silence of the weekday church, the abyss between the old and new in which she now stands is almost tangible. It is a time of looking back, gathering up the experiences of her ten years here, recognizing the place to which they have brought her and preparing to ride on their back into futures unknown.

Our conversation is filled with a sense of history. I want to know where this woman's unshakeable belief in a God so good, so just, it deserves to be real, has sprung from. So we travel as far back as Dorothy can remember. There we find a tiny girl, the eldest of five children born into the family of a minister, and we uncover Dorothy's first conscious understanding of her God.

"I had a strong sense of God when I was a child," she smiles, watching memories appear fleetingly in the space between us. "I can remember, almost pre-verbally, the sense of company, of safe presence, which, as a fairly lonely child, was comforting to me. I didn't name that 'God' but that's what grew into my God as I was able to name it and I always felt there was something between myself and other people that was good.

"That was probably my first sense of God. Then that matured into my naming of it as a loving and gracious company for me in my life and that stayed with me and was affirmed by my parents quite strongly until I was about sixteen. My family were highly responsible people. I mean, they felt responsible for all the pains and the injustices in the world. They believed in struggling with those. They were quite radical people. So my God always had high expectations of me.

"Then, in my mid-teens, I connected with some very fundamentalist people, through my peers, and got into the hellfire and damnation mode and met a punishing God, just briefly. It was awful because I was very shy and I went to one of those meetings where we had the big altar call to come forward and witness to our faith. I had a strong sense that I wanted to relate to this God but I was too shy to go forward, so I assumed that I then had to earn the favor of this punishing God who would be most unhappy that I hadn't witnessed to my faith.

"That feeling of having to earn my salvation stayed with me for ten years. I remember my mother saying, 'Are you sure this is Christianity, Dorothy? It's so miserable.' I mean, one of the ways I tried to earn God's favor was by not wearing make-up and not going to films and not dancing and, of course, not drinking and gambling — that went without saying. Anything pleasurable, I thought, offended this God. It came to me at a very impressionable period of my life and, while some of it dropped away, even so, I went on doing good works to the point of drivenness for the next ten years, hoping to earn the favor of a rather hard God."

Dorothy's hellfire and brimstone days ended as abruptly as they'd begun. Sitting one day in church, she heard the minister say, "I am come that you might have life and have it more abundantly."

"I thought, 'I'm not having abundant life, this is terrible,'" she laughs. "I suddenly realized God was saying that life is a gift, which was a major shift for me. So I lived with that God fairly comfortably and in a more relaxed fashion for some years."

Meanwhile, the world was swiftly shifting on its axis, engulfed by a tide of social and political change. Dorothy too was swept up in the spirit of the 1960s. She became active in the peace movement and the movement against the White Australia policy: a set of principles which restricted immigration and reflected the ultra-conservative, Eurocentric ethics which dominated Australian society at the time.

"I began to gain confidence in myself," Dorothy recalls. "I became a political activist, I joined a political party and I marched to ban the bomb. My God, at that time, was in solidarity with the poor and fighting with me for justice. It was again a pretty hard God, not a punishing one but one which drove me very strongly. It did not allow me to do much playing or many light-hearted things — that was self-indulgent because the world had to be changed — and this God was with me in that, my word. I was very grim, determined. I regarded people who were not involved in these movements as not on the right track at all. So I was fairly self-righteous as well as very committed."

With the dawn of the 1970s came another far-reaching movement for change and again Dorothy's God was challenged, perhaps more vigorously than before.

"It was in the early days of my connection with the women's movement," she recalls with a wry smile, "that someone called God 'She' and I was deeply offended. I challenged this person and I was challenged, in return, to explain why I was so upset by the thought of a female God. I realized then that, if I was offended, it was because my own self-esteem was very low. I had been fighting for other people but not for myself. I went through an agonizing period, then, of coming to terms with that. I was part of the consciousness-raising groups of the 1970s and began to work with a God who might be as female as male and therefore a God who might be imagined living within me, rather than a God who was external. This phase was me, as a woman, struggling with other women to understand what it meant to believe that we were made in the image of God."

In direct proportion to her increasing self-confidence and feminist consciousness came a growing disquiet about her role in politics, and particularly in the Australian Labor Party, with which Dorothy eventually severed ties. Strangely, despite her knowledge that it suffered many of the same patriarchal woes afflicting politics, it was also the time at which Dorothy determined to cement her relationship with the church and take the steps which would finally lead to her ordination.

"I wasn't fighting for my rights as a woman when I chose to become a minister," she insists, "although that was certainly a consequence of what I was doing. It was more a matter of respecting the things which were within me. I was fascinated by the expression of grief, of anger, of hope, of joy through rituals which mark our journey. I also became deeply interested in the whole concept of God and faith."

Yet when one of the flock elects to join the shepherds, she explains, God does not gaze beatifically from a cloud, shower blessings and announce that life will be a breeze from here on in. Far from it. Her time of training for the ministry was as difficult as any she'd experienced, and filled with a very different set of challenges.

"In the next phase of my life, I went through quite a destructive time," she admits, "where I engaged in a lot of personal power as one of the token women on about seventeen committees. In the early days of the women's movement, there were not a lot of articulate women and I had learnt to be articulate from my political days. I found myself rising in the system, particularly in the church. I told myself that nothing was changing — that I was still fighting for powerless people like myself — when, in fact, I was beginning to accrue a great deal of power. I went through two years of very painful dismantling of that power, of realizing who I had become and how far I'd traveled from a relationship with God."

DOROTHY STOPS FOR BREATH AND LOOKS ABOUT HER, MENTALLY TAKING LEAVE OF these old chairs and desks and shelves that have been the landscape in which she's played much of her life since 1983. She took up the position of minister here immediately after her ordination.

"In these ten years," she smiles as her gaze turns back to me, "I've moved into relationship with another understanding of God — a God who is still within and without but whose main hope for me is that I might be truly human. To be truly human is to be able to laugh and play, to recreate myself, to balance my life, to leave changing the world to everyone, not just me. Certainly I have a responsibility in that but I also have a responsibility to model fullness of life, which has to do with fun, with developing relationships properly and honoring them, with feasting and partying and lying in the sun and a very corporate understanding of how life is lived.

"I've learnt that the journey is what it's about, rather than what you achieve. I've learnt that the with-ness of God is what it's about, and the with-ness of each other, the company. I've learnt that God is not too troubled about sins, that God is really about calling us away from death — the choices that lead to our own death — and that those choices are the ones which move us away from justice, away from peace, away from grace, away from love and compassion, away from freedom. So my religion is not about doing or not doing naughty, immoral things. It's about choosing life and sometimes, as I make those choices, I'll make mistakes, but that's okay. Through the journey, I'll see things more clearly, and next time perhaps I'll make another choice. It's a rigorous, painful, joyful journey and life is very tough but that's okay. You get stronger as you go if you head into it with some sort of courage. It's better to make the decisions and move than to sit and reflect on them forever and never move, because that is a choice for death."

Dorothy is conscious that time provides perspective which, in turn, illuminates the meaning or purpose behind a life. This afternoon, she has taken time to follow the threads out of which she has woven her faith. Now she sits back, sips her tea and describes the current state of the tapestry. The clearest impression is of a calm certainty that the best possible God she can imagine does indeed exist.

"The God who I experience now is respectful of my struggle, respectful of my humanness, respectful of my strength and energy and very healing," she explains. "The God that I understand now invites me to go beyond where I thought I could go — not in a driven, straining way — but, if I'm prepared to move towards the edges of where I think I can go — in courage, in hope, in love, in dreaming — if I push out towards that, I find the fence falls down and there's an even wider thing that I can do, a greater thing that I can be, a deeper moment that I can have, and always in company with other people.

"So it's that God who gives a sense of meaning, of purpose, of energy. It's a very gentle God who grieves with me, suffers with me, understands with me what's happening, honors me when I make even small steps forward, is kind to me when I step backwards. There is no judgment in this God — none at all — only invitation and company. There's always the sense of a God who, if I'm about to enter anything tough, has been there before me and is safely traveling ahead. It's that sort of God and, although I name that God as best revealed for me in Jesus Christ, I also know that's a language for profound truth. I know many people who have arrived at that truth through different means and I respect that. I find it in cultures all around the world, in people of other faiths. Anybody who is genuinely seeking for meaning and truth, in the end, arrives at some of the same patterns and some of the same understandings and we can recognize each other."

I am at once in awe and envy of Dorothy's conviction. My notions of divinity, like hers, have shifted and changed over the years. The difference is that I can't help wondering whether this is a sign of God's fondness for gradual revelation or an indication that there is no God, aside from the one we each create in our own image.

"I think we have some part in creating those images," Dorothy smiles with sympathy, "but I do have a very strong sense of a transcendent God — a God who is other than me and other than anybody. I can only describe it as a presence which calls me beyond. I feel as though it's other than me because I don't feel I have within me, as a human being, the capacity to produce that entirely from within myself. It has to do with amazing moments of awareness of other, magic moments of awe and mystery, sacred, holy moments where I'm aware of a surrounding presence which permeates my being but which is not entirely of me.

"I find that sometimes in great music, sometimes in the bush. There are people who have a sort of aura around them. You could say that God is within them. Usually I experience that sense of space around people who have suffered, lived at great cost. I want to stand back from them in respect. Now maybe that's coming from them or maybe they've lived so closely with this God that God shines out very powerfully from them.

"It moves and shifts but there's something about the experience of spirit which is more energetic than I am, more lively, more faithful, more strong, more powerful, more free, that's set loose from me, dancing around in the universe. I don't personify God very much these days but that doesn't mean that God is not intensely personal for me, something that can be reached towards."

"Dorothy," I interject, and I go on to talk about last Easter, about the sense of purposelessness, about the difficulty I've had — that most of us have — reconciling a compassionate God with the misery we see around us.

Dorothy pauses a moment before answering.

"I was just reflecting that I have come full circle to my childhood again. The difference is that I'm no longer innocent. So my claiming of the presence of this God is now filtered through very tough questions, very hard experiences, tragedies, injustices in my life, many of which have no answers, no explanations. I don't see this God as having set up a universe which has all this wonderful justice built into it. There's a terrible brokenness in the way we are set up, which is probably necessary. If it was all neat — if we were good, we were rewarded and if we were bad, we were punished — then we'd all be good, wouldn't we? There has to be something far more random about it and I've learnt that doesn't matter and I don't need to have the answers to all those questions.

"So my claiming of this good and love, which I still believe is at the center of everything, has now journeyed through a very rough life and has come round again to my childhood understanding of this surrounding grace and presence which simply travels with me. However, it's at some cost that I now claim that as my truth, rather than the innocence of childhood.

"It can be hard to come back to that. If you go through a tough life, God is challenged very significantly and you have to choose whether you think nothing is at the center of everything or evil is at the center of everything or chaos or love. I now freely choose to believe that love is at the center of everything and that life is ultimately stronger than death, but that's very ultimate and there are a lot of things that stand between me and that experience."

I find none of this particularly reassuring. "So, there is no reason?" I ask. "It's not possible for you to say, 'I know this to be true because …'."

"I don't look at life and find it all neatly laid out there for me," she responds. "It's very much me saying, 'This is what I'm going to live out of and I'll see how it works.' All I can say is that it does work. That doesn't mean life becomes other than tough for me but it means life has a sense of growing energy and strength and peacefulness. It comes from facing life always believing that the things that would kill you off are not as strong as this life-giving center. So you can be rocked and battered and dumped and smashed around, as you would be in the surf, but there's an exhilarating celebration in breasting into it and going on, picking oneself up again and gathering one's friends and one's faith and saying, 'I'm intact somehow. I am a survivor and I survive well.'

"I might go through all sorts of shouting and rage and pain in the middle of it but it's a bit like the prophet Habakkuk. That's my favorite book in the Bible. It's a very little book. The Chaldeans came to slay the Hebrew people again and Habakkuk said to God, 'What are you doing? All this injustice, the evil people are prospering.' The answer to him was, 'The righteous shall live by faith.' In other words, there are no signs. So what he did — which is what I've tried to do — was, in the face of that, he stood up and sang a funeral dirge to announce the death of the enemy. I'll paraphrase and abbreviate it a bit but what he sang was essentially, 'The fig tree will not blossom, the vine will not bear fruit but I will exalt in the name of the Lord who carries my feet into the high places.' That's the end of his book and that's how I feel and I know what he means."

Anyone who has tried to sing such a song in the face of the enemy will know it's a tough call.

"Sure it's tough," says Dorothy, "and I don't always sing it. Sometimes I think, 'What the hell is happening here? What are you doing, God?' Yet the beauty of it is that the confident relationship with God means you can do that. You can rage and shout at God, as the psalmists did, and know God is weeping with you and there are other people to hold onto you and, if your faith runs low and your hope runs low, theirs lifts you up and on you go. I've found that is a great way to live and a rigorous way to live."

The afternoon is fading into evening. Dorothy stands to switch on a light and looks at me quizzically, wondering whether, in the absence of hard evidence, she is nonetheless explaining her case.

"Can I describe an experience I had which, for me, was very powerful?" She sinks back into her chair and begins to recount a time at which her faith was sorely challenged.

"I went through a major crisis in my life earlier this year and everything came to a crunch on a Saturday, the day before I had to preach. It's very difficult being a clergy person and I thought, 'Oh, God, how will I preach the next day?'

Anyway, we use a lectionary where all the passages are set each Sunday and the passage for that Sunday was about Jesus being one with God and calling us to be one with God and, if we did that, we would experience the glory. I thought, 'Oh, how can I preach on that?'

"So I was lying on my bed, crying my heart out, and all of a sudden I had an insight, which said, 'Well, you can choose. You can choose to be one with me or not. I will travel with you in every part of your life and you can choose whether you will let me be with you, but I'm there.' So that was the first part and I was very comforted by that.

"The next part was the vivid bit. The word that was troubling me was 'glory'. I mean, glory is a very strange word. It's not one we use, really. So I went out in my car and I drove back into my driveway and an inner voice said to me, 'Now look at the vine leaves on your house and you will see the glory.' It was autumn and there, across the front of my house, were these blood-red vine leaves with the sun shining behind them. Then the inner voice said, 'The glory always lies between the dying and the rising.' I looked at the blood-red of the leaves and I thought, 'Yes, glory has a lot of blood about it, a lot of bleeding.' The insight was that it is not in the rising that the glory lies but in the struggle in between. That is the glory, if you will stay there, stay there in the center of that pain and hold and go through to life. That is a vivid symbol for me forever of what it's all about.

"The beauty of it was that I could come to church the next day and say to the people, 'I'm going through a major crisis. The sermon will be short. These are the two insights that I had. Here are the vine leaves and I'll put them on the table and I'll sit down and cry.' It was alright and everyone respected that. So I've been moving with people in whom I have that level of trust and I'm going to miss them terribly. That was a really deep understanding for me of what it's all about. It's unjust, it's very tough, it's very painful and yet it's okay."

So this great faith is not built from nothing. It has been fired in the kiln of life and polished with moments of clarity, even grace. Dorothy opens the storehouse of her memories and begins quietly to recount those times in which her courage and her belief have been most deeply tested.

"Undoubtedly a very big moment in my life was when our first son was irretrievably brain damaged by his polio vaccination. That raises the whole question of innocent suffering, which really is the toughest question of all. That was one of those moments like Habakkuk. In the end, I came through saying, 'Well, this is not going to change but I will still believe that there is a God of love and that this God weeps with me as I weep for our son and that we will survive.' That was a very central moment. He was our eldest son and he was only two when this happened, so it was about 1960.

"One of the other really big moments for me was when I decided to end my marriage. That was about six years ago. I'm not a person who gives up easily or fails in anything at all easily. I'm very determined. It's a problem as well as an advantage because it makes one very tough on oneself and also fairly tough on other people, although I think I'm gentler with other people than I am with myself.

"This time, I just had to say, 'No, this is not going to work, I'm going to have to end it.' I had to say, 'I am no longer able to sustain something that I vowed to sustain.' I had to say, before my God and my friends, 'I have nothing, I am dependent on your grace.' Not that I thought it was a dreadfully wicked thing to do. On the contrary, sometimes you can do no other than end things. Even so, I had to let myself be known to have not succeeded in something, to have failed. I'd been married for thirty-two years and had four children. Then, to make the decision to hurt somebody. I wanted a family for my children, I wanted to have family Christmas with them. For me, that was a very big thing to do."

Dorothy has emerged, like Habakkuk, with a strength that can sing in the face of danger, an acceptance that faith implies mystery and unanswered questions and a conviction that her God nonetheless hears and is by her side.

"When I look at the bigger picture," she continues, "I don't for a minute think that God plans wars or violence. That's part of our freedom and it's a terrible part. We're free to plan all manner of holocausts for ourselves but even beyond that, there are brokennesses that we have no control over, I think, and random things that happen to people."

Does that mean this compassionate God creates a universe which is somehow chaotic?

"I don't think it's chaotic but I think it's random. Who can say why tragedy hits one group of people or one person more than others? It has nothing to do with the goodness or otherwise of their life. I mean, sometimes it does and you know if it does but that's not the thing that worries us, is it? It's when things happen to us that we think are quite out of proportion to the sort of life that we're living that it shatters us and, if you really think that's being beamed at you by a punishing God, you're in a lot of trouble and it can be a dreadful journey.

"The alternative is to think, 'No, that's the wildness of creation. It's not going to be neat and it can't be neat. If it was, we would choose a relationship with God because of what it would bring us.' Life is not about lying under a palm tree being happy. It's actually about growing and changing and struggling to survive and finding that we can, as long as we do it together. It's about being together. We're not meant, I think, to find the resources within ourselves to cope with all of life. The prayer, if you like, is about the joining of our corporate energies and healing with the energy of God and then waiting respectfully.

"There will be different answers to that prayer. I have seen miraculous physical healings. That can happen. On the other hand, which is the greater miracle? Is it the healing or is it the fact that the woman who took the photograph on my wall, who is going blind from diabetes and is a very young woman, lives her life with courage, in spite of not being healed, and still lives with guts and faith and hope and energy and all sorts of wonderful givings to people? That's a miracle — that a person like that survives richly and powerfully.

"Also I watch people die of AIDS and I watch them live more vividly in three months than some people live in eighty years. So I learn that life is not about time, it's about moments. It's not about length, it's about eternal things. I learn that those people can live with passion and with peacefulness and live victoriously to the end of their days, which may be brief.

"Therefore, all these things are not quite what we think they are. We have this view of life, that to be successful is to achieve personal things, to live long without too much pain, and I think that's nonsense. I don't think that is life. I think a lot of that is death, it's an illusion."

Dorothy looks up to measure my reaction. Many of us, I suggest, are seduced by the easy option.

"I am too," she laughs. "I like to be happy. I don't mean that I'm a masochist and I enjoy suffering. I don't, and I don't actually think God chooses suffering for us in the direct sense. People say, 'Oh this is sent to test us.' I don't agree. I think that all sorts of things happen that God weeps over. It's not the will of God that we do dreadful things to each other and that awful things happen to us. The point is that God can take many things that we think will kill us off and transform them into life-giving things and strength and power and freedom."

The noisy rabble of five o'clock commuters drifts in from the street. Dorothy's God, I think, would take the subway.

"It's enlightening, inspiring and hopeful," she continues. "It's a passionate presence that calls me on to the edges of everything, pushes me out into new frontiers of living. It's an adventurous God, an exciting God, never boring. Boredom would be hell for me. Lying on a cloud playing a harp would be hell. I think I'd rather burn. Even sitting adoring at the feet of God would be boring. I just can't imagine that's what heaven is like."

WHEN NEXT I SEE DOROTHY, SHE IS WALKING IN AN ECUMENICAL PROCESSION with the Archbishop of Cape Town through the streets of Sydney. An old fundamentalist man in a drab grey suit hollers obscenities from a balcony. An African choir chants and sways inside St James' Church, from whose doors a standing-room crowd overflows, all intent on celebrating the fall of apartheid and South Africa's impending democracy. Dorothy, whose church once impressed me with its candle wrapped in wire, wears a smile that lights up the evening sky. We speak of the hope that is tangible around us and of quantum leaps in Uniting Church policy since last we met. I congratulate her on her church's relatively new stance on abortion.

"Over recent years," she explains, "there has been a lot of consulting across the parishes and presbyteries. We realized the church has tended to say that there is one issue: at the point where a woman chooses whether or not she will have an abortion, she chooses between life and death for a fetus. Now the church sees that as far too simplistic because there is a whole train of events which mean that a woman can or cannot sustain the life within her. That train of events might be to do with unemployment, with the breakdown of contraception, with lack of support for the woman in her life in lots of ways. It could be lack of housing, it could be all manner of things that contributed, in our community, to that woman being unable to go ahead with producing a new life.

"Therefore, when we said it was a woman's right to choose, we were assuming that the person most able to determine whether life could be sustained was the woman. Only she, in consultation with other people, as far as she has support around her, can judge whether that life is viable."

This is not the 'God is great and I have all the answers' ministerial patter I remember from my childhood. It is an enormous thing for a church to concede it might not be the most qualified body, in this instance, to form judgments.

"It is a breakthrough," Dorothy grins, "and it was by a very large majority.

People are becoming more realistic, more honest and more merciful. They could see it isn't simply a matter of saying murder or not murder. Good heavens, that's a frightful way of looking at it. They could see that the ethical dilemmas are similar to those in war. There is no clear right and wrong. There are all sorts of clashing values and, depending on circumstances, you make that decision, with agony. Do you defend yourself or do you let yourself be killed? Neither of those is a good thing ethically. Yet that's the dilemma we're faced with sometimes in war. Will we fight for justice or will we let ourselves be killed off in South Africa by the dogs and the guns and all the rest? How do you decide? Alan Bosak, who is a South African leader, said that only those who stand knee-deep in the blood of the people can make that decision. That, I think, is what we were saying in relation to abortion — that it is the same process of doing ethics, that it is complex, that only those who stand knee-deep in the lifeblood of that woman have the right to make the decision and that is to be respected. It isn't as simple as saying, 'abortion on demand,' nor is it as simple as saying, 'abortion is murder.' Both positions are extreme. In the middle is the agonizing struggle of a woman to understand what she must do, and it's very rarely done lightly."

Standing here in a city square, listening to African music drift out through the doors of an Anglican church, it is easy to feel the forces of change at work around us. The abortion issue is one drop in the bucket, the ordination of women is another, the influence of indigenous cultures yet another. I wonder whether all these changes suggest the church is coming to reflect God more accurately or whether, once again, we are remaking God in the image of our evolving ethics, aspirations and social mores? Dorothy naturally prefers the former scenario.

"I think we're seeing that God is much bigger than the church," she says, "and that the deepest things in life, which we name as God, have been struggling to be evident through all of time. They've come through in the experiences and stories of people in every generation. I mean, the Bible itself is made up of hundreds and hundreds of witnesses to people's experience of what they name as God and there's no reason why we should confine it to that. Truth is truth. We shouldn't be afraid of that. Just because it's not put in our formulas doesn't mean that we have to be oppressive about it.

"If you look at the reality of people, then you know who is linked with truth. Look at those who are living creatively, life-givingly, in costly solidarity with all who struggle or are victims, who search with great authenticity for what is true and real and honest and just and peaceful and who are seeing the ideal of life as a great harmony. When you have that big vision, then the way you name it becomes less significant.

"If I hold to my Christian faith, it's because I am deeply helped by a God who is embedded in our history. That's why I'm also involved in political activities. To me, if we are not seeing all history as our business and also needing to be brought into that harmony — political systems, economic systems, ideologies, social systems — unless that's our business, then we're on a very narrow front, a very funny, personal thing which has little to do with the great dream. The great dream, for me, is about all things working together for good, for everything and everybody. It doesn't mean it's a paradise. It simply means we are for each other and we are for the creation and for freedom and for the maximum amount of adventurous, free living. That's the agenda. How it happens and in what name it happens and in what language it happens is not as important as that it happens."

We smile. It's unlikely I'll ever become a church-going Christian. Despite my admiration for Dorothy, Sunday services (even the best of them) leave me with an aftertaste of saccharine that harks back to my childhood. Nonetheless, we understand each other.

"With you, it's always a positive agenda," I offer. "It's never a 'thou shalt not' agenda at all."

"It's always an invitation," Dorothy replies. "I'm a very hopeful person. Hope is hard to kill off in me for long."

PHOTO COURTESY OF THE JEWISH NEWS, SYDNEY, AUSTRALIA

Rabbi Harold Kushner

8

WITH WINGS
AS EAGLES

HAROLD KUSHNER IS A TALL, GRAY-HAIRED MAN WITH THOUGHTFUL EYES, SOFT features and a mouth that hints at generosity. When he opens his mouth, out streams a lively patter that's developed naturally over more than thirty years at center-stage in Saturday services.

He grew up in Brooklyn, New York, in a conservative Jewish family, in a predominantly Jewish neighborhood. His parents, he says, "were serious but flexible". The Kushner home was kosher and, most Saturdays, his family, like others in Brooklyn, turned out at synagogue. "We didn't act out of fear that we might break some rule as many of the Orthodox did."

He went to public school in New York and graduated to Columbia University. Growing up, he was interested in the religion of his forebears but not for a minute did he consider making it a career. "A lot of my friends were Jewish," he remembers, "our neighbors were Jewish and they did much the same things we did. So, there wasn't any sense that you were making a bold statement." Then, at nineteen, in his junior year of college, it occurred to him quite out of the blue, to become a rabbi.

"There was a combination of reasons," he recalls. "Partly, I thought that the demands of the job were a good fit for the things I was good at and the things I enjoyed doing. Partly, I admired my rabbi and partly, I think, it was a way of following my father, who was a businessman but also an active leader of the synagogue. I knew I had no head for business, so going into synagogue life was a way of endorsing his values."

Harold Kushner spent a year studying in Israel and graduated from the Jewish Theological Seminary in New York City. He entered into the spirit of the 1960s, marching with Martin Luther King, campaigning for integrated housing and exploring the common ground between the civil rights movement of the time and the concern for justice at the core of his Jewish faith.

"There has always been a very strong Jewish commitment to social justice," he says now. "When you look at life through Jewish spectacles you're reminded to see the beauty, the complexity, the intricacy of the world, the regularity of sunrise and sunset and the change of seasons. You're instructed to take this world seriously.

"I remember one of my professors saying that Plato and Aristotle would have laughed at the prophet Isaiah. They would have said to him, 'Why are you so concerned about one widow being cheated, one orphan being oppressed? Worry about the definition of justice and the details will take care of themselves.' The Jewish impetus was always that defining justice was a waste of time if it didn't ensure that no widows were cheated.

"So, taking this world seriously, a sense of commitment to social justice, an obligation to see the image of God in every human being that I confront — these are ways in which I look at the world differently because of my Jewish background."

He began also, around this time, to think more critically about the symbols and ceremonies of Judaism. With the completion of his theological studies, he found himself called upon to explain and justify his religion to congregants who lacked both his knowledge and commitment. Their questions prodded him to look deeper and the explanations he found served to further affirm his faith.

"One of the unique aspects of Judaism," he says, "is that it believes that everything God created is potentially holy. It does not draw a sharp distinction between the sacred and the secular, between the religious and the worldly."

He was struck by the fact that, at its core, his was not a dualistic faith. Thus, he explains, there are laws about food, about sexuality, about speech, about finance —

about all manner of areas which one does not ordinarily consider spiritual — and these laws exist in order to elevate the day to day business of living beyond the profane.

"Judaism," he realized, "shows us how to respond to life. How to respond to the day changing to night and the sun coming up again, how to respond to the change of the seasons, how to recognize the potential holiness in all these things. When we do that, we exercise our own God-like capacity. We do something that God can do, which is to sanctify the ordinary."

In retrospect, he believes, another cornerstone of the 1960s was the steady stream of Americans who deserted both Judaism and Christianity in search of enlightenment on Eastern shores. He watches now, with interest, as many of them return.

"A lot of people who had given up on religion," he suspects, "are coming back but they're not coming back to brand name religion. They're coming back to an eclectic religion. They will call themselves Christians, Anglicans, Catholics, Jews, whatever it may be, but they will pick and choose among the doctrines of their own faith and they will not be at all embarrassed to bring in elements of Buddhism or the Mormon church or whatever they've found that speaks to them. There are Jews who meditate and Jews who believe in karma and Jews who practice yoga and I think that's relatively unprecedented."

None of this, today, troubles Harold Kushner, just as none of it ruffled his commitment to his own conservative Jewish faith at the time. There will be borrowings, he concedes, as there have always been, but those who speak of a movement towards a single world religion are, to his way of thinking, ill-informed. A variety of religions, he believes, will always be required by the variety of human experiences.

Back in the early 1960s, Harold Kushner's faith was strong and his life was near idyllic. He met, fell in love with and married Suzette, a young dental hygienist, and in 1963, their first child, Aaron was born. He was bright, cheerful and thoroughly adored. According to his father, he was able to identify a dozen species of dinosaur by his second birthday. In 1966, the family packed up and moved to Boston. Harold had been offered a position at a suburban synagogue there, Suzette was pregnant again and the leafy streets of Boston seemed the perfect environment in which to raise a young family.

The day his daughter, Ariel, was born, Harold Kushner's life was changed forever. He and Suzette had been concerned about Aaron for some time. He was small for his age, gained weight only with difficulty and had begun losing his hair at just twelve months old. On moving to Boston, the couple had met a local pediatrician who specialized in children's growth disorders and had introduced him to Aaron. Now, two months later, this pediatrician came to visit the couple in hospital, within hours of their daughter's birth. Their son, he told them, was suffering from a rare condition known as progeria or "rapid aging". He would never grow to more than three feet tall, would never recover his hair, would gradually come to resemble a tiny, elderly man and would die in his early teens. Harold Kushner was devastated.

"Everything I had grown up believing about God and the world did not fit the facts," he recalls. "I knew I could not go on affirming that kind of world view but I had not yet come up with anything to replace it. It was a difficult time. I could think of nothing but that our son had an incurable disease and what was God's role in that?"

Between November 1966 and January 1967, Rabbi Kushner traveled to hell and back. He wrestled with his God. He watched everything he had held as solid and secure go tumbling into a deep personal and theological abyss. He wondered whether he could keep working as a rabbi. He wondered whether he could maintain his Jewish faith.

Then, just as swiftly, came resolution. In two short months, Harold Kushner entirely redefined his notions of God and faith and later wrote a book about the process, called *When Bad Things Happen to Good People*, which became an international best-seller. This resolution did not cure Aaron of his illness, nor did it eliminate the pain through which all his family would journey in the years to come. It did, however, make the passage easier, both for the Kushners and for millions of others — Jews and gentiles alike — who have read his book and flocked to synagogues and auditoriums to hear him speak.

Rabbi Kushner's question, during those months of torment, was a variation of the question I tried so hard to articulate to Dorothy McRae-McMahon. "Why do bad things happen to good people? Why has illness struck my innocent child? If there is a God who is good and just, how has this God come to create a world which is so generously endowed with injustice and pain?" There is no more universal theological question yet, in Western religions, there are few satisfying answers. Harold Kushner set out to find an answer that was satisfactory, at least for himself, and in so doing, struck a chord with millions around the world.

ALMOST THIRTY YEARS HAVE PASSED SINCE THAT AFTERNOON WHEN HAROLD Kushner's world was torn asunder. This evening, he sits, bent over an old wooden desk, in the far corner of a cavernous suburban synagogue in Sydney. A queue of nearly a hundred people snakes its way across the room. Each man and woman in the queue clutches a copy of one of his books which they hope, eventually, he will sign. Forty minutes pass. The rabbi, who has already given an extensive lecture tonight, is visibly tired. Ninety minutes pass. He promises he will remain until every book is signed.

He is the author of a handful of books now (including the Christopher Medal winning, *When All You've Ever Wanted Isn't Enough* and his most recent work, *To Life!*) yet most everyone in this queue clutches a well-thumbed copy of *When Bad Things Happen to Good People*. This was the subject on which he spoke tonight and the promise which drew hundreds here.

"This is the crucial religious question," he explained earlier this evening. "When it is left unanswered, it festers in the soul, it corrupts faith, it causes people to leave faith. When it is answered badly, it breeds cynicism and mistrust. When it works, when people are able to find consolation and solace in the teachings of their religion, at a time when they need it most, then that religion will be a source of sustenance for the rest of their lives. How shall we understand the sufferings of good people? There is no more important question we can ask."

Every person in this room would agree with him and most came along tonight expecting an answer. Many have lost or are losing a loved one. Some are, themselves, battling terminal illness. Others are simply baffled by what they perceive as a conundrum in their faith and the Jewish consciousness still burns fiercely with memories of the great injustice of the holocaust. The fact that Rabbi Kushner has faced his own crisis of belief and survived offers them hope.

Fourteen years after the publication of *When Bad Things Happen to Good People*, Rabbi Kushner is still bemused by the resounding chord his book has struck. He has identified two primary reasons for its reception:

"First," he offers, "the book confronts a question which, sooner or later, we all have to ask: if there is a God in this world and if God is good and just, why do bad things happen to good people? The longer you live, the more people you know and love, the more inevitable it is that you will have to ask that question. You will see the wrong people sick and the wrong people dying and the wrong people unemployed and the wrong people divorced and the wrong people rejected and you will look at them and you will say, 'I don't understand it. Why do these things happen at all and, if they must happen, why do they happen to a person of such innocence and goodness?'

"You will go home at night and turn on the news and — although the Australian news, I've learned, is a bit better than the news in the United States — early on in the program, there's likely to be the story of a murder, of an automobile accident, of a plane crash, of some sort of disaster in which people are suffering. You will pick up your newspaper tomorrow morning and there, in the first few pages, you will see a similar story and you will say, 'Why do these things keep happening?'

"That's the first reason, I think, for the reception my book has earned. The second is that, when we ask this question, we discover that most of the answers we're given simply do not work."

For Rabbi Kushner, that is the crux of the matter. It is the issue which, when his son was diagnosed, very nearly cost him his faith.

"My son lived his entire life with physical and psychological pain and he died the day after his fourteenth birthday," he recounts, his voice soft and measured, his eyes gazing steadily ahead. "That was hard. What was harder was that I, as a congregational rabbi, tried to make sense of what the doctors told us by saying to myself the same words that I had been saying to members of my congregation. All those years I thought I was helping people, all those years I thought I was making people feel better but when I tried those words on myself, I was not comforted. When friends and colleagues in the clergy found out how sick our son was and sat with us to cry with us and try to help us, their words were not comforting either.

"They would say to me, 'God is putting your family to this test because you're so strong in your faith and you can handle it. You'll be an inspiration to others.' All I could think of was, 'I wish I was less religious. Let God test somebody else and give us a healthy child.' People said, 'God is doing this to you so you will become a more sensitive person and write this book which will help thousands of people afterwards.' I imagined the response if a defence attorney for a human murderer was to get up in court and say, 'Look at all the good my client has accomplished by killing that child. All over the country, people are much more vigilant about where their children go when they leave the house and all over this continent, people are grateful that their children are alive and well because my client hasn't got his hands on them.'

"That would never be taken seriously in a court of law. Why do we say the same thing about God? We say that God would torture and kill an innocent person so that other people will grow spiritually as a result. I have never accepted the idea that God allows retarded children to be born so that the woman next door will realize how lucky she is that her kids are normal. Why does God strike somebody blind or crippled? So we can have the opportunity to drop a coin in their tin cup as they beg? I cannot take seriously a God who would do those things."

Thoughts like these consumed Harold Kushner and in 1966, as winter settled over Boston, he hit rock bottom. He was battling, night and day, to come to an understanding of God's role in human suffering, in his family's personal suffering. He thought of nothing else.

He set three demands on any resolution he might come to. The first was that it should help him come to terms with his son's illness. The second was that it should shed light on the holocaust. The third was that it should not leave him with a God who was "a moral monster", that it should reveal a God who he could continue to worship and admire. Yet nothing in his training and nothing in the explanations supplied by well-meaning colleagues and friends would fit the bill.

"Then one day," he says, "I realized why all the conventional religious answers didn't comfort me. You know why? Because they weren't supposed to. They were not intended to make me feel better. They were intended to defend and justify God. I would like to think that, if we could ask God for an opinion, God would say, 'Don't worry about me and my reputation. I can take care of myself. Your job is to bring healing and comfort to my bleeding children on earth.' Nobody who sat with us was wise enough to do that."

A turning point finally presented itself when Harold Kushner sat down one evening with the Old Testament Book of Job. It was a book with which he thought he was familiar. He had studied it in his rabbinic training, he had written papers on it, taken seminars on it. He had, at one point, even taught the Book of Job. Yet, in the past, he had read it only as a student of scripture.

"Now," he recalls, "I was reading it as Job. Now, I was the man who raised his hand to heaven and said, 'Why me and why my family?' Now I found things in the Book of Job that I had never seen before. I found things that I'm not sure the author put there but I found them and I found them satisfying."

Job, says Rabbi Kushner, is a "once upon a time story". It is the story of an implausibly righteous man whose world is perfectly ordered, harmonious and fulfilling. Then, very suddenly and for no reason he can fathom, calamity strikes. His business is destroyed, his children are killed and Job himself is afflicted with a terrible illness. Here, Rabbi Kushner takes up the story:

"Three friends drop by to try to bring him comfort. They say to him, 'Cheer up, Job, nobody ever suffered unless there was a good reason for it.' Job says, 'You know, it's a funny thing but I don't find that a cheering message.' Then, for thirty-five chapters of the most brilliant philosophic poetry ever written, the argument goes back and forth between Job and the three friends."

Not surprisingly, the story of Job was, at that time, a particularly poignant one for Harold Kushner. For days, he read and reread it. It occurred to him that there were three ideas which each of the characters in the book wanted to believe. Firstly, they wanted to believe that God was all-powerful, the creator, the prime mover, indisputably in control. Next, Job and his friends wanted to believe that God was absolutely good, compassionate and just. Finally, they wanted to believe that Job was a righteous man.

Around these three points, he noted, the Book of Job's central debate swung. For as long as Job was healthy, happy and successful, it was possible to affirm all three of them. God could be powerful, God could be good and Job could be a righteous man. However, as soon as Job's world began to rock, it became impossible to assert more than two simultaneously. The problem for Job and his friends — and for Rabbi Kushner — was which of the three they should jettison.

"For the friends who visit Job," he explains, "it is very simple. It is so important for them to affirm what they were taught in Sunday school — God is good, God is powerful — that the only possible answer is to deny statement number three, that Job is a good man. He can't be a good man. If he were, why would a righteous God be doing these terrible things to him?

"So they say to Job, 'Well, you had us fooled but you couldn't fool God. You must have done something so outrageous that God has to punish you in this extreme way.' They say to their friend, 'Now listen, we have studied Sigmund Freud, we understand about repression, we realize you have done something your conscious mind is so ashamed of that you can't face up to it and, as long as you keep denying it, you're going to be a terrible person. This is God's way of forcing you to confront your sinfulness. Now, if you would stop complaining and get down on your knees and admit what a terrible person you are, then God could stop teaching you this lesson.' Isn't that kind? They call that comfort."

In the words of the three friends, Harold Kushner recognized not only the advice he was receiving from colleagues but also his own words to congregants. He read the subtext behind those words with horror.

"Do you recognize the process at work here?" he asks. "Job's friends are doing what we have learned to call blaming the victim. They're making sense of the world's pain by saying there must be a good reason for it. If the Jews of Germany had not been so conspicuously successful and affluent, maybe Hitler would not have chosen them as his target. Or we say to the woman who was attacked and assaulted on the streets at night, 'Why were you walking alone? You should have known better. Why were you dressed like that? What did you do to provoke this crime?'

"I remember the story of a young woman in my congregation in Massachusetts. She'd been married for five or six years and suddenly, one Saturday morning, her husband told her he was leaving. It was totally out of the blue. He said he found her boring, the women he met at work were more interesting, he didn't want to live with her any more and would she please get out of the house for two hours so he could pack and leave and they could go their separate ways. Crushed, rejected, she drove to her parents' home and told them what had happened. Her parents said, 'What did you do wrong? Did you nag him too much? Did you spend too much of his money? Were you unresponsive in bed? What did you do to cause this to happen?' Finally, she threw down her teacup and said, 'Will you stop blaming me. I didn't do anything. He did it to me.'"

Job's friends fell into the same trap. In order to make sense of the world, they needed to rationalize Job's suffering. They could not live with a world in which random, senseless events could tear people's lives asunder. They could not live with a God who had created such a world. The obvious path out of their bind was to insist that Job had done something to provoke all that had befallen him. Job, however, would not accept their verdict. Nor, ultimately, would Rabbi Kushner.

"Job is not prepared to purchase the world's innocence at the cost of his own," he explains. "His answer is to deny statement number two, that God is good. Job says, 'God is completely powerful and I am completely righteous and those statements have nothing to do with one another. What, God owes me something because I'm an honest man?' Continually in the book, Job says things like, 'Would that there were an umpire between us,' meaning, 'I wish somebody were powerful enough to make God play by the rules but God is so completely powerful that he doesn't have to play by the rules. He is beyond rules. He can be arbitrary, he can be unfair. Who's going to stop him?' Job says, 'If God's actions were limited by considerations of justice and fairness, he would be a limited God, wouldn't he? If God had to give us what we deserve, wouldn't that be a limitation on his power?'"

Job believes God is so completely powerful that we humans, regardless of our righteousness, have no ability to control what God does with this world. Job believes that God can be neither coerced nor constrained by human morality and notions of fairness. Rabbi Kushner, while sympathizing with Job's dilemma, thinks otherwise.

"I don't think Job's is a good answer at all," he muses. "For one thing, if God is above such petty limitations as justice, who wrote all those words in scripture? 'Justice shall you pursue', 'Do justly and love mercy and walk humbly with your God.' More importantly, if God is so powerful that limitations of justice and fairness cannot constrain him, where do we learn to be just? Where do we get the instinctive response, when we read about political corruption and crime, to say that it's wrong? Who teaches us, when we see a television report about children starving in Africa, to reach out with charity, unless that's God's justice and God's compassion flowing through us? Is it conceivable that we human beings would be more decent than God, that we would be just and compassionate and God would be above all such considerations?

"My Orthodox Jewish friends, if I still have any, are always saying to me, 'You know, Kushner, if you can't understand why God does certain things, maybe the problem is with you, not with God. Isn't it possible that God does things for reasons our human minds cannot fathom?' I say to them, 'Yes, of course, it's possible.' Yes, God can do things I can't understand — my plumber does things I can't understand and when my daughter was a teenager, she did things every day I couldn't understand — but you know, that's not what we're talking about.

"A toddler falls into the swimming pool and drowns because the babysitter turned around to answer the phone. What's so hard to understand about that? We know exactly what happened but we don't like it. A wing falls off an airplane, the plane crashes and forty people die. We understand what happens but we don't like it. It's not that it's too hard for us to comprehend. It's not that God's ways are too wondrous for us mortals. The question is, will God permit himself to do things which he has told us are wrong?"

Job's friends solve their dilemma by denying the third statement, that Job is a good man. For Job, the solution is to deny statement number two, that God is good. Our embattled rabbi, at this point, quotes Sherlock Holmes: "When you have eliminated the impossible," he says, "whatever remains, however unlikely, must be the truth."

"The conclusion I came to," he explains, "and I came to it very reluctantly, because I was raised on the same Bible stories and the same Sunday school classes as you, was to challenge statement number one, that everything that happens in the world, God wants to happen. What kind of God would want cancer? What kind of God would want multiple sclerosis? What kind of God would want earthquakes and plane crashes and house fires? What kind of God would want any of these things to happen?"

Not a God around whom Harold Kushner was willing to base his faith. So, on a cold night early in 1967, Harold Kushner jettisoned his belief in an all-powerful God. He had examined every possibility he could find and had settled on the only one that would fit with his knowledge of the world and leave him something in which to believe. That decision has been affirmed by the response of his readers and congregants ever since.

"After my book came out," he says, "I received a letter from a Lutheran minister in a small town in the American west, who told me the following story: he'd presided over a funeral, one Saturday afternoon, for a twenty-eight year old man in his congregation. The young man, who had died in an automobile accident, had been scheduled to be married in his church that same Saturday. He'd gone out on Wednesday night, with a few friends, to celebrate his forthcoming marriage. They'd left the restaurant at about ten o'clock and were run off the road by a drunk driver. Everyone else was all right. The bridegroom was killed.

"In the same church, on the same day, almost at the same hour for which they had scheduled the wedding, they conducted the young man's funeral. They buried him in the churchyard. Then, the minister went back to his study and the man's fiancee was waiting for him there. She said to him, 'Pastor, if one more person tells me it was God's will, I'm going to scream. Why are they teaching me to hate God?'

"I think that's what we do when we insist on explaining that God has his reasons why the young mother is crippled, why the young father was struck down with a heart attack, why the child was born deformed, why the plane crashed, why the earth quaked. We teach people either to hate themselves for deserving it or to hate God for doing it to them when they don't deserve it."

By choosing a God of limited power, Harold Kushner has come to believe, we need hate no one. "I would rather affirm God's goodness," he says, "while compromising his power. I would rather believe in a God who sees things happening that he does not want to happen but cannot stop them. I think goodness is of more religious value than power." Around this central tenet, he rebuilt his faith.

According to Rabbi Kushner, the primary reason why bad things happen to good people is that laws of nature do not differentiate between a good person and a bad one.

"A falling rock," he says, "is morally blind. It is simply obeying laws of gravity. It has no way of knowing who's underneath and whether that person deserves to be hit in the head by a rock. Viruses, speeding bullets, out of control automobiles, fires — they treat us all alike.

"This is not only Harold Kushner talking. This is traditional Judaism," he adds and refers to a passage in the Talmud which he paraphrases as follows: "If a man steals seeds from his neighbour and plants them, justice would require that those seeds not germinate. Why should that man profit from his theft? However, nature is not just and stolen seeds grow." Life is full of such instances. Nature is amoral, he insists, and God does not interfere with laws of nature.

"I believe," the rabbi continues, "that God created the natural world. This world is so complex, so intricate, so stunningly beautiful, that it cannot simply have just happened. It must have come from the mind of God. Yet I believe that, when God created the natural world, he withheld from it one blessing that he only shared with you and me, and that is the ability to know the difference between right and wrong. Human beings have that ability. Falling rocks and viruses don't. You go into a home where there is a contagious disease and you run the risk of catching that disease, irrespective of why you're there. You can be a doctor or you can be a burglar — germs can't tell the difference. So, no matter how nice we are, we are just as vulnerable to illness, to accident, to injury as anyone else. That's the first source of suffering and unfairness that God cannot prevent."

The second, according to Rabbi Kushner, is the notoriously thorny notion of free will. Fundamental to his religious faith is the idea that human beings are responsible for their own behavior and that we live in a universe which values freedom above even the life of a fourteen year old boy.

"We write the script of our lives," he says. "We choose whether we want to be decent people or cruel, deceitful people and we suffer the consequences. If a thief goes into a late night grocery store to hold up the cash register and, on the way out, shoots the clerk, don't ask why God didn't protect that clerk. Don't blame God. Blame the thief. He's the one who did it.

"In my book, I quote a woman who was a teenager in Berlin during the war. Her name is Dorothy Soelle. She is a German Lutheran theologian and she asks the question, 'Where was God at Auschwitz?' Her answer is that God was at the side of the victims, suffering and grieving with them, not on the side of the murderers. She believes that to suggest, by word or hint, that what the Nazis did to

Jewish men, women and children could possibly have been the will of God is to offer us a God so cruel that no decent person should ever worship him."

Rabbi Kushner throws in his lot with Dorothy Soelle.

"For me," he says, "the holocaust is not a theological issue. For me, it's a psychological issue. How could people have done such things to each other? How could human beings have so totally misused the freedom that God gave us? At the very outset, God said he would give us that freedom so we could choose good over evil, and he would not take it away, no matter how dangerous we were to his creatures. As the Talmud puts it, when a human being chooses to do something good when he didn't have to, God looks down and says, 'For this moment alone, it was worth creating my world.'"

AFTER FOURTEEN YEARS OF WRITING AND SPEAKING ON THE SUBJECT, HAROLD Kushner's thoughts now tumble from his lips in neat, considered bundles. He accepts speaking engagements both to deliver a message of consolation and hope and to receive it. Even now, he says, he needs to hear his own message as much as anyone.

"It's important," he explains, in a momentary lapse from measured rabbinical manner, "for me to experience, once again, the news that God did not strike my son down, God did not send the illness that caused his death, just as God did not will the holocaust. Once it happened and God could not keep it from happening, he showed me how to take this experience and redeem it from being a meaningless statistic and forge it into an instrument of salvation for many."

I wonder whether this God of his has not been fashioned to fit the circumstances of his life too neatly. I find it vaguely dissatisfying, this notion of a God, crying out against human misery, yet unable to intervene because, in designing the laws of the universe, it has written itself into a bind. I suggest as much to Rabbi Kushner, who is swift in his reply.

"I don't believe in a God who is an absentee landlord. I don't believe in a God who created the world, gave it a push to start it off, then sat back to watch what would happen and every now and then, looks down, shakes his head and says, 'What a pity. I really hoped it would work out better.' That's not what I believe at all. I believe in a God who is actively present in our lives even when we suffer, who is perhaps actively present in our lives especially when we suffer."

Harold Kushner sees God at work in our lives in a number of tangible ways. To begin with, his God has provided the world with natural law and order. Even what appears to be anarchy and chaos, he feels sure, is part of an intelligible plan.

"The things that happen to people in God's world," he believes, "may not make sense morally but they make sense physically, biologically. I don't understand why one person gets cancer and another doesn't but I am absolutely convinced that, somewhere, there is a reason and one of these days, we'll find out what that reason is. I am convinced that, if we cared enough about why people die of cancer, we would spend as much money on cancer research as we spend on cigarettes to make us sick in the first place, and then we would uncover that reason. If we were prepared to pay the best of medical researchers what we are happy to pay the best of soccer players, I think we would find an answer and reduce the amount of undeserved suffering in God's world."

He quotes Ernest Jones, Sigmund Freud's biographer, who recounts a telling event from Freud's student days. In the corridors of the Vienna hospital in which he was studying, Freud, one afternoon, came across a pathologist who had just completed an autopsy on a patient with bone cancer. The pathologist, according to Jones, held up a cancer-ridden bone and said that, if he ever came face to face with God, he would pull out the bone and ask why such a thing was permitted to happen in God's world. Freud reportedly answered, 'If I ever come face to face with God, I'll ask him why he didn't give me the intelligence to find a cure for it.'

"When I was growing up in Brooklyn," Harold Kushner recalls, "my mother wouldn't let me go swimming in the summer. Every summer, there would be a polio epidemic and you would pray that you'd get through the summer without your children being sick or crippled or worse. Do you know what happened? We were so outraged at the prospect of little children being crippled for life that we gave our dimes and our dollars until, finally, somebody broke the code, found out what caused polio and how to prevent it. Instead of raising our hands to heaven and saying, 'God, why do you let these things happen?' we applied our God-given intelligence to the problem, until we solved it, just as we will one day solve the problems of cancer and AIDS and heart disease."

So the rabbi's God has provided us with natural laws, which are comprehensible, as well as rational thought and an intellectual propensity towards cracking codes, following leads and learning to understand and manipulate the world around us. In other words, while God's hands might be tied in the face of natural laws and human freedom to wreak havoc, God has ensured we have the wherewithal to help ourselves. This is the second way in which Rabbi Kushner sees God at work in human life. God works through people.

"My favorite line in my book," he admits, "is not mine but one I quote from a nineteenth century Hassidic rabbi: 'Human beings are God's language.' When you have been hurt by life and you cry out to God, how does God respond? God responds by sending you people. God comes to you in the incarnation of caring, loving friends and neighbors, doctors who will sit at your bedside through the night, nurses who will stop at nothing to make you feel better, friends who will come and do whatever they can to ease your pain. We need people. We need to know that we are cared about."

Rabbi Kushner has a story to illustrate:

"There was a little boy whose mother sent him on an errand and it took him a long time to come home. When he finally got back, his mother said, 'Hey, where were you? I was worried about you.' The boy said, 'Oh, there was a child down the street who was crying because his tricycle was broken and I felt bad so I stopped to help him.' Then the mother says, 'You don't know anything about fixing tricycles,' and the boy replies, 'No, of course not. I stopped and I helped him cry.'

"I'll tell you something," the rabbi smiles, "he was right. There will be times when you will face situations in which you desperately want to help and you will think there is nothing you can do but there is always something you can do, even if it's just to sit with somebody and help them cry. If you don't do that, you're leaving them to cry alone and nobody deserves that."

He likes to tell another story. It's about an experiment conducted, some years ago, at the University of Wisconsin in the USA. A candidate for a doctorate in psychology aimed to measure how long people could sit with their bare feet dangling in buckets of iced water. "For this, you get a Ph.D," Harold Kushner laughs, and goes on to explain why the findings of this little-known study have remained a beacon in his world view to this day.

"The psychologist learnt that, when there was another person in the room, her subjects could keep their feet in the water for twice as long as when they were alone. Isn't that absolutely fascinating? The presence of another caring person doubles the amount of pain you can endure. So, if you have a friend who is going through a hard time and you feel helpless because you don't know what to say — as if the price of admission to helping a friend is to say something so clever that nobody's thought of it before — don't worry. You don't have to say anything. Just be there and, by your presence, indicate that you care."

In practical terms, this might well be the most important lesson of Harold Kushner's life. Not only did it provide the basic tools with which he survived the life and death of his son, it radically altered his approach to his vocation.

"When I was a young, inexperienced rabbi," he recalls with a hint of embarrassment, "I would sometimes receive a message that someone had died in the congregation and I would rush over to her house and try to make her family feel better. I would walk in and the people would jump on me and say, 'Why would God do this to such a nice person?' I thought they were asking me a question about God and that was great because I knew about that — I'd taken courses in it. So, I would give them a ten-minute summary of my senior theology course from rabbinical school and when I'd finished and their eyes had glazed over, I'd say to them, 'Now, I understand this is a little complicated. Maybe you didn't follow it the first time. Would you like me to repeat it?' They would say, 'Rabbi, please, we've suffered enough.'

"After a while I learned that, when somebody says, 'Why did God do this?' they don't want me to answer with theology. 'Why me?' is not a question. It sounds like a question but it's not. 'Why me?' is a cry of pain and you respond to it, not by explaining why it happened but by easing the pain. If you don't know what to say, I'll give you a very quick course. You say, 'I'm sorry, I feel bad for you,' and then keep your mouth shut and hug and hold hands. You will do more good with your silent, comforting presence than with the most learned theological explanation. Somewhere down the road, there will be a place for theology — for explaining God's role in this — but at that moment, the person who says, 'Why me?' doesn't want explanation, she wants consolation."

For his work in this area, Harold Kushner could justify a little pride. As Elisabeth Kübler-Ross has brought revolution to the medical profession's approach to bereavement, so his work has reverberated through the clergy, changing attitudes among his Jewish colleagues and in the Christian community beyond.

"In the fourteen years since my book was published," he notes, "I have seen a difference in the way clergymen respond to people in need. They don't explain and they don't minimize and they don't dismiss. They keep their mouths shut and they hold hands and I would like to think I've had some influence on that."

Ask the rabbi whose work this is, however, and he is quick to point out that much of it is not his own.

"It happens often," he says. "I'm sitting at my desk, trying to write the next chapter of a book. I'm stumped. I'm trying to say something important but I don't know how to say it. Then, all of a sudden, I understand exactly what I need to say. Where did this idea come from? How did it get inside my mind? For me, that's a manifestation of God."

Moments like these confirm and reconfirm Harold Kushner's faith day after day.

"I can believe in God after what's happened to my family," he explains, "and to the families of so many other people I care deeply about. I can believe in God, not because of all the stuff I learnt in college but because I am always seeing ordinary people doing extraordinary things. I am seeing people come up with reserves of courage and love and resilience and wisdom that they didn't know they had — reserves they knew they did not have until the day they needed them — and they can't explain where they got them from. The only answer I can think of is that they got them from God."

Back in the spring of 1981, just before his book was published, Harold Kushner announced to his family that his new goal was to get into shape because he intended to run in a popular five-mile race at Cape Cod that summer. "It's such a popular race that everyone in town has to choose whether they want to watch it or participate in it, except for me," he jokes, "because, the way I run, I can do both at the same time."

To encourage her dad, his daughter, Ariel, printed up a tee-shirt for him. On the back, she carefully inscribed the words of Isaiah 40:31: "Those who trust in the Lord will have their strength renewed. They shall mount up with wings as eagles. They shall run and not grow weary."

"It didn't help," he admits. "That is to say, it didn't help me run the race but it's helped me ever since. That's the cornerstone of what I believe. God does not send us the tragedy. God sends us the strength to survive the tragedy because that's what you do with a tragedy. You don't explain it, you don't justify it, you survive it. The only response to a tragedy is to survive it.

"I think of a particular family in my congregation. It's now more than twenty-five years since they gave birth to a severely brain-damaged child and against the advice of doctors and relatives, they took the child home and tried to raise him. Every morning, month after month, year after year, they would wake him up and help him get dressed because he never learnt how to dress himself. They would feed him breakfast because he never learnt how to feed himself. They would play with him and sing songs to him and as he grew older, they would look for settings where he could meet with other similarly handicapped young people.

"I look at that family and I say to myself, 'I thought I knew them before the child was born and I never would have guessed they had a twenty-five year supply of love and courage and humor.' Is it possible they did or is it more likely that, when they used up whatever they had, they turned to God and God gave them more so they could keep on caring for that child?

"I try to imagine my response, if somebody had said to my wife and myself, on New Year's Day 1963, 'Before this year is out, you will have a child with the following physical problems and this is what it will mean to him and this is what it will mean to you and to your marriage and to your family. Can you handle it?' I know that my wife and I would have said, 'Please, don't test us, we know our limits.' However, we were not asked and Aaron came into our lives without our being cleared and somehow, somewhere, we found the strength and the grace to love him and to raise him and one day, to lose him and to survive that and I cannot understand how we did it, unless I go back to that verse that my daughter printed on my tee-shirt."

HAROLD KUSHNER IS A GOOD MAN, A COMPASSIONATE MAN, A THOUGHTFUL MAN. His theology is not a complex one. Academics around the world have written to him in droves to explain the gaps they find in his philosophy. Their letters do not trouble him at all.

"Ordinary clergymen, congregants, members of communities have been very grateful for my work, while academics," he admits, "have picked it apart. They seem to miss the point — that it's making a lot of people feel better about their problems, that it's helping them to heal and that it's doing this with religion.

"I was unprepared for the response I received from the non-Jewish community. I thought I'd written a book which most people would ignore and which religious Christians would be upset by. I remember, my publisher sent me to Houston, Texas, on a publicity tour and, as the plane landed, I said to myself, 'Why am I coming here? This is fundamentalist Christian Bible-belt country. Nobody wants to hear my message here.' I went on a radio talk show and Baptist ministers started calling in, thanking me for writing the book which they could now give to people who had a problem. Congregants called in and said it was so wonderful to be reminded that God was not trying to punish us. I began to feel that maybe my book wasn't so radical, maybe people wouldn't be quite so upset about it."

Harold Kushner does not frame his arguments in academic-speak. He writes as an ordinary man, a man of faith like Job, who, in a time of crisis, was forced to reassess all that he held dear, that he had been taught, that he believed in. Out of that struggle came a homegrown theology which made sense to him and which continues to make sense to his readers, many of whom find that life throws them moral and philosophical dilemmas for which their traditional religious upbringing has left them wholly unprepared. That this perspective of his helps people to survive the pain of life is, to him, the barometer against which it should be measured. That there remain questions which it will not answer is less important than that it offers hope.

"Why do good people suffer in God's world?" he asks again. "The answer is, I don't know why and if I knew why, I wouldn't tell you because, if I told you, I'd be making the same mistake that all those people made with me so many years ago — taking something which fundamentally doesn't make sense and trying to make sense of it.

"You know something? 'Why?' is the wrong question. People come to me because they've read my book, because they know what we've been through, and they say to me, 'Rabbi, why? Why my mother? Why my child? Why my husband?' I say to them, 'I understand where you're coming from — I've been there and I've asked that question too — but it's the wrong question." 'Why?' focuses on the past. 'Why?' too often deteriorates into 'What did I do wrong? Whose fault was it? Who should have been paying attention, doing something different? Which side of the family carries the defective gene?' 'Why?' becomes a search for somebody to blame.

"The lamentable thing is, no matter how smart you are, no matter how pious you are, you cannot change the past. 'Why?' focuses on the past. So I tell people, 'Turn your back on what happened, not to forget it — God forbid, you won't forget it — but to measure how far you've come. Instead of asking the wrong question — 'Why did it happen?' — ask the right question — 'What do we do now? How do we go on? Where do we find the strength and the grace to survive what has befallen us?' The word 'answer' has two levels of meaning in English. An answer can be an explanation — make sense of it, tell me why it happened — or an answer can be a response. The answer to tragedy is not to explain but to respond, to survive."

After he had read the Book of Job, the next book to which our rabbi was drawn in his search for a path forward was a play by Archibald MacLeish, called J.B. It is a play loosely based around the life of Job and for much of it, while setting the action in the present, MacLeish remains relatively true to the biblical account. Towards the end, however, he makes a radical departure, and this twist appeared to Harold Kushner, back in 1967, with the force of revelation.

"Remember how the Book of Job ends?" he asks. "God appears and says, 'Job, time to let you in on the secret. This was all a game. I wanted to see if you would be upset with me if I killed your children. I wanted to see if you would be angry if I took away everything you had. Job, you're great, you passed the test. Here's your reward — more health, more wealth, more kids. You're better off than you were before.'

"MacLeish responded to that ending the way I suspect many of us do: 'Who wants a God like that? Who wants a God who plays these sadistic games with his most dedicated worshipper to see if he can make him lose his faith?' So MacLeish changes the ending. Instead of God rewarding Job, Job forgives God. Job forgives God for not creating a perfect world, for not structuring the world so that only good things will happen to people who deserve them. Job forgives God for creating a world in which evil and death and unfairness are possible and sometimes happen to people who don't deserve them."

Ultimately, however, the message of hope which Harold Kushner found in J.B. had less to do with Job's relationship with God, with Job's spirituality, than it had to do with Job's relationship with himself, with his family, with his humanity. In the last moments of the play's final scene, Job returns to his wife and it is she who illuminates what, for Rabbi Kushner, was to become the way forward.

"It is their love for each other," he explains, "not God's generosity, which will bring the new children into the world. Life has hurt them so badly, life has taken away from them everything they held precious and their response is to say, 'Yes and we want more of it. We have learned how unreliable, how painful life can be and we want to go on living.' We don't explain our suffering, we survive it, we respond to it, we choose to go on.

"Job's wife has the beautiful last lines of the play. She says to her husband, 'You looked for justice, didn't you? Well, there is no justice. There is only love.' Then she says, 'The candles in churches are out, the stars have gone out in the sky. Blow on the coal of the heart and we'll see by and by.'

"What she is saying is, don't look for answers to why our children have to suffer and die. Don't look for answers in theology — 'the candles in churches are out' — nor in science — 'the stars have gone out in the sky'. The only place you will find an answer — and it won't be an answer: 'why', it will be an answer:

'how do we go on' — will be in your own heart. 'Blow on the coal of the heart.' What a beautiful image that is. If you have been hurt by life, take the pain, the white hot anger of your grief, and send it out into the world to make the world a slightly brighter and warmer place. On those lines, the play concludes."

In other words, the pain, the suffering, the tragedy we experience has no hidden meaning. It is not directed towards us by a vengeful God, nor is it, most often, the consequence of our own evil doing. The suffering we endure has no meaning until we impose one upon it and then, we are free to choose the nature of that meaning.

"If we choose to give up on God, on faith and on the world because it has been unfair to us," Rabbi Kushner believes, "we give our suffering a negative meaning. If we choose to become more sensitive, compassionate people — to blow on the coal of the heart — then we impose a positive meaning."

The meaning which Harold Kushner has imposed upon his suffering is, against the odds, one of faith. He emerges with a God who has compromised its own power but who is nonetheless a vital presence in the rabbi's life and who is experienced tangibly, in ways which, although not miracles in the biblical sense, are nonetheless miraculous.

"You can't dial up a miracle," he smiles. "You can't order one from God because you deserve it and sometimes we don't realize that we've been given a miracle because it isn't the miracle we asked for. In our case, we asked that our son be able to live a normal life. We didn't get that miracle. The miracle we got was that, when this fourteen year old boy found out he was dying, he was able to handle the news. The miracle was that, when he died, my wife and I were able to survive his death without it destroying our marriage. The miracle was that, out of that experience, I was able to put into words my resolution of God's place in it and turn it into a book which has helped literally millions. I think those are miracles. Miracles don't have to be like the Red Sea."

Harold Kushner does not have a literalist approach to scripture. He neither knows, nor is particularly bothered by, the precise events that led to tales of miraculous events in ancient times. He suspects the biblical accounts of divine intervention were recorded by authors who were "carried away" by some fortuitous occurrence and wrote their stories "more as testaments of faith than accurate reports of what had gone on". This does not mean, however, that Harold Kushner lives in an unerringly rational, pragmatic world.

"People do receive God's help," he insists, "and when that happens, it's a miracle.

I tell people who are terminally ill to pray. First, I tell them to pray for a miracle. Why not? It is never right to leave people totally without hope. Any doctor who says to a very sick patient, 'There is nothing more to do, you're going to die,' ought to have his licence revoked. I believe in telling people what's going on but I think that information should always be phrased with an ingredient of hope. So I say, 'Pray for a miracle and, at the same time, pray that if things don't turn out the way you want, you'll be strong enough and brave enough to handle it.'

"You see, Jews don't actually pray for, Jews pray to. Prayer does not mean asking God to do something. Prayer, in Judaism, means asking God to be with you. The prayer of a terminally ill person need not be, 'Please God, make me healthy.' The prayer of a terminally ill person can be, 'God, be with me because I'm frightened. Be with me so I don't feel alone. Be with me so I don't feel rejected.'"

In much the same way that he believes his family's survival of their tragedy was a miracle, he is certain that God does answer prayers with blessings of courage, hope, strength and love which the recipient had not believed possible.

"I want to share with you," he adds as an afterthought, towards the end of our interview, "one of the most unforgettable experiences of my life. Some years ago, I was invited to speak at John Hopkins Medical Center in Baltimore, Maryland. I was asked to give two talks — to talk to the professional staff at noon and to give a public lecture in the evening. When I finished my talk to the staff, the Chief of Chaplains approached me and said, 'Rabbi Kushner, we have a patient who would love to meet you. He heard you were coming to town, he's read all your books, he would like you to come in and spend a few minutes with him. If you'd rather not do this, I understand, and I'll tell him you were busy and tired. He's a thirty-two year old Episcopal minister and he's dying of AIDS.' I said, 'Sure, I'll talk to him.'

"I followed the chaplain down the corridor, feeling very noble and virtuous — the Jewish Mother Teresa. I went into this hospital room. I saw this emaciated figure hooked up to tubes. I said to him, 'How are you doing?' He said, 'Not too good but I'm getting used to it.' We chatted for a while and he told me how much he'd appreciated my books.

"Then I said to him, 'Do you ever worry that you're going to die without God, that God is punishing you?' He answered, 'No, just the opposite. The only good thing that has come out of this experience is that something I always wanted to believe turns out to be true — that, no matter what you've done with your life, you have not alienated yourself from God's love.'

"He said to me, 'When I was a child, I thought I had to be perfect for people to love me. I thought that, if I ever fell short of perfection, people would reject me and God would reject me. I tried so hard to be perfect. I probably went into the clergy so people would think I was perfect and would love me for it. Every time I did something wrong and every time I told a lie to cover up for what I'd done, I was sure God was as contemptuous of me as I was of myself. Now, lying here with an illness that nobody can cure, the one thing I've learnt is that I have not lost God's love. I have felt his presence in this hospital room.'

"Then he said, 'I'm going to be getting out of this hospital soon, not because I'm getting better but because there's nothing more they can do for me and they need the bed for somebody else. I don't know if my congregation will take me back — now that they've found out I'm gay and I have AIDS and I'm dying — but I hope they will because I have one more sermon to preach. I have to share with them the lesson that this illness has taught me — that no matter how bad you've been in your own eyes, you still have not lost the love of God.'"

"This," Harold Kushner adds, "is a message I would give to the terminally ill and to those on the verge of despair. Pray. Pray for a miracle, pray for a cure, pray for whatever is in your heart but more than anything else, pray that the presence of God will come into your hospital room, so that, whatever the future holds for you, it will not be nearly as frightening and will not be nearly as painful because you won't have to face it alone."

To this point, the rabbi's conversation, again and again, returns. He returns to a God who values goodness above perfection, who could have created a perfect world but elected, instead, a less constrained creation, in which goodness, freely chosen, would be at liberty to flourish.

"Ultimately," says Harold Kushner, "the question is not, 'Why do good people suffer?' Ultimately, the question is not, 'Why does God permit this?' Ultimately, the real question is the one the psalmist asked: 'I lift my eyes unto the hills. From where does my help come?' He doesn't say, 'From where does my malignant tumor come?' He doesn't say, 'From where does my alzheimer's disease come?' He doesn't say, 'From where does my heart condition come?' It doesn't matter where they come from. They're there and he's got to deal with that. The real question is, 'From where does my help come? How will I manage to get through this?' The psalmist's answer, it seems to me, must be our answer as well: 'My help comes from the Lord, maker of heaven and earth.'"

Dr. Barbara Thiering

9

THE REVOLUTION WILL
BE TELEVISED

An interview with Barbara Thiering is frighteningly reminiscent of being called before the school principal. I bring pastries but there's to be no ice breaking, no small talk, no afternoon tea — not just yet. To begin with, she would like to know whether I have any idea what it is that I'm writing. A barrage of questions elicits painful evidence that I lack all but the most rudimentary knowledge of the early history of Christianity. A potted theology course ensues, after which Barbara explains what she believes should be my central themes. Reassured that I have somehow stumbled upon a number of these unaided, she breathes an audible sigh, settles into a comfortable chair and an animated discussion of her work begins.

It does not surprise me that this woman insists upon putting me through my paces. A circus of journalists and scholars has put Barbara through hers, unremittingly, since the 1990 screening of a documentary called *The Riddle of the Dead Sea Scrolls*. Two years later came the publication of her first popular book, *Jesus the Man*. Both created a storm of controversy around the world. Fundamentalists prayed for her soul. Ministers of religion accused her of killing Jesus (again) and putting them out of a job. Theologians and historians boxed themselves into corners which said more about their prejudices than the work they sought to appraise.

Why all the fuss? Quite simply, Barbara Thiering refuted the divinity of Jesus. Moreover, her academic record demands that she be taken seriously.

For more than twenty years, Barbara has been engaged in research centered around the Dead Sea Scrolls, a collection of documents, found in caves at Qumran, in Israel, in 1947. With an understanding of Hebrew, Aramaic and Greek and a background in theology, she secured the respect of a number of international scrolls scholars. In the late 1970s and early 1980s, she published three academic books on the subject — *Redating the Teacher of Righteousness* (1979), *The Gospels and Qumran: a New Hypothesis* (1981) and *The Qumran Origins of the Christian Church* (1983) — which created not a whisper of controversy. It was not until ten years later, when the media got wind of the implications of her work, that a storm of public opinion erupted around her.

Central to the dispute is her re-dating of the scrolls. Much of the scholarly literature produced immediately after the scrolls were discovered saw parallels between the events described in the material and the early development of Christianity.

"The first great articles were written in the 1950s," she recalls. "In 1955, Edmund Wilson, who was a very good journalist, wrote an article for *The New Yorker* in which he claimed that the Dead Sea Scrolls proved that Christianity was simply an episode in human history and should no longer be regarded as divine revelation and dogma. He reached that conclusion by talking to scholars who believed evidence for that position was contained in the scrolls."

Shortly afterwards, however, academic opinion shifted. The scrolls were now thought to have been written at least a century before the rise of Christianity and the Christian connection in the vast majority of published research died down. This earlier date (around 100 B.C.), Barbara believes, was arrived at by a series of errors and miscalculations. If the scrolls are approached consistently, she is certain, they provide their own date for one of their key subjects, the Teacher of Righteousness, and that date is 26 A.D. This, of course, places the Teacher of Righteousness at the center of the crucial years during which

Christianity was evolving in Palestine and Judea, but Barbara goes further. She identifies the Teacher of Righteousness as John the Baptist and another recurring character in the scrolls, the Wicked Priest or Man of a Lie, as the historical figure we know today as Jesus.

This is no hocus-pocus conspiracy theory. Barbara garners her information from the original documents, applying to the New Testament a method of interpretation learnt from the scrolls, called the *pesher* technique. It would be a simple, if time-consuming, matter for other scholars to replicate her studies, testing the validity of the technique and her conclusions but none have yet done so.

Two types of scrolls were found at Qumran — the first, copies of books of the Old Testament, and the second, sectarian writings of the Qumran community, which provide detailed information about the religious practices of the predominantly Essene Jewish sects which lived in the area at the time.

The sectarian writings include tracts, known as *pesharim*, which interpret Old Testament books as prophecies relating to the era in which the Qumran writers lived.

For example, the Qumran scholars took this passage from the Book of Habakkuk: "Woe to him who causes his neighbors to drink; who pours out his venom to make them drunk that he may gaze on their feasts!" They interpreted it as concerning "the Wicked Priest who pursued the Teacher of Righteousness to the house of his exile that he might confuse him with his venomous fury."

The pesharim, Barbara maintains, reveal that the Qumran Jews believed Scripture could be interpreted on two separate levels. On an immediate level, it provided general moral direction and a simple cosmology. Concealed behind that, however, and comprehensible only to those armed with the appropriate method of interpretation, lay a hidden historical meaning.

Barbara applies the same technique to a number of books of the New Testament. She is convinced that the authors of the gospels, Revelation and Acts were familiar with the use of pesharim to interpret the Old Testament and, if this was the method they employed to read Scripture, might they not have written their own sacred works in a similar style? Such an approach to Scripture was very common in the Hellenistic world in which Christianity arose.

Barbara believes it is possible to prove that there is, in these books, a hitherto concealed history of the early Christian church.

Her conclusions are as plausible as they are challenging: Jesus was not born to a virgin, did not die on the cross or walk on water. He did marry (possibly twice) and live to a ripe old age. Jesus was no Son of God but a courageous, liberal reformer of the Jewish faith. The scrolls, she says, were written by Jesus' enemies, the reactionary leaders of traditionalist Jewish sects. Her theories appeal to the rationalist in all of us and dovetail uncannily with what we know of early Christian and Jewish history.

"In the first century A.D.," Barbara explains, "something quite extraordinary happened. The Jewish people were already religious and had already contributed one of the highest theological insights to human culture, namely monotheism and the idea that you shouldn't make statues depicting God. Around them, everybody was believing in multiple gods and making their little statues and worshipping them. So, this was the Jews' special insight. For two thousand years, they'd been saying, 'Moses told us not to make statues and we won't even name God because to name God is to objectify God.' They understood this well before the advent of Christianity.

"Then, around the time of Christianity, the whole world was in turmoil because Hellenism, a new culture, was spreading across the world. There was a great upsurge of the human spirit. It was a wonderful period in which to be alive. Knowledge was no longer the prerogative of a few people up there but of every-body. It was a time such as the one in which we're living now.

"In the pagan world, people were reassessing the gods they had been worship-ping — Isis and Osiris and Diana and so on. They were being educated out of their belief in these old gods and badly needed a new religion to take their place. Into this situation came the Jews and, with good reason, Judaism became the trendy new religion throughout the Pagan world. It became fashionable, I think, largely because of the women at the top of the Roman court, who said, 'Here is something worth doing, a better religion.' They had very good judgement.

"Judaism had many wonderful insights but it also had a great deal of ritual baggage. The Jews were saying, 'If you want this knowledge, you must become a Jew.' They were proselytizing. They wanted power. You had to become a Jew, you had to be circumcised and you had to obey the ritual laws. It was a total change of cultural identity."

The Romans were intrigued by this new religion which appeared so much more sophisticated than their own but were reluctant to adopt its demanding prerequisites. What they required was a form of Judaism stripped of its ritual and cultural appendages and fortuitously, just then, a new Jewish sect arose offering them exactly that.

Jesus, Barbara concludes, was born into this proselytizing movement. He grew up amongst Jews whose mission was to spread their religion abroad but his mission was different. Jesus realized that Judaism's rigid laws were a barrier to its cross-cultural acceptance. He also believed many of its laws were archaic, irrelevant and unjust.

"Jesus said, 'We're going to give the Pagan world what it needs in terms of a new religion but we'll drop the exclusively Jewish aspect,'" Barbara continues. "He was an heroic figure. He was feared and derided for committing heresies, defiling the temple and breaking the law. The law meant, of course, that no blind man was allowed into the presence of God for the whole of his life, no leper, no menstruating woman. These people were obsessed with cleanliness, purity and they believed gentiles were filthy. Jesus dropped those laws and, out of those changes, came Christianity. It was an historical process."

Christianity, however, became much more than a cultural reformation of Judaism. Intrinsic to the religion which the early Christians finally presented to the Pagans was the notion of its founder as a divine human being. This, according to Barbara, also came about as a result of historical process and cultural necessity.

"The Hellenistic world," she says, "badly needed the idea of a human being who was an incarnation of God. That was the great value of their old religions. Half the people were walking around being incarnations of gods. Every great emperor's mother had somehow managed to achieve intercourse with a god. This was the popular myth. This was a way of glorifying humanity, which was what the Greek world wanted because it was in the midst of an era of great humanism. So Jesus was set up for such a treatment. If his version of the Jewish religion was going to work, it needed to incorporate that element. It wasn't sudden. There was an historical process that led to Jesus being deified."

This historical process is what Barbara has uncovered in her work and it provides, she believes, conclusive proof that Jesus' divinity was consciously constructed by those around him. Concealed beneath the stories of miracles and magic in the gospels lies a record of the events which led up to an attempt on his life by reactionary Jewish leaders. Jesus was indeed crucified but he was saved from death by his supporters and his survival was subsequently concealed. Much of the rest of his life was lived in seclusion or under an assumed identity.

IF WHAT BARBARA THIERING POSTULATES IS CORRECT, THE IMPLICATIONS FOR THE future of the Christian definition of God are enormous. There is some doubt, particularly amongst her detractors, whether anything that could be called a Christian church would survive. Barbara, on the other hand, plainly believes her findings are accurate, yet considers herself a Christian and feels that the separation of the historical Jesus from the theological God would be a positive development for Christianity.

"We're now in another great creative period," she begins. "Things are changing very rapidly. New knowledge is everywhere. I think it's just as exciting as it was in the first century and something new will emerge from it.

"Change is coming from so many different directions. The feminists, for instance, are bringing about massive change in the understanding of God. Only two or three times in human history have we changed our image of God. There was polytheism, where there were a whole lot of gods, and there was monotheism, where there was only one God. Then there was the God who was so far off that you couldn't talk about it and the God who was way down here and reincarnated in a human being, but that human being was male. Now, a couple of thousand years later, women are saying that we can no longer speak of God as a superhuman male.

"Then, the big question is, how do we talk about God? Either it will be the ungendered god, not a person at all, or, as some feminists are saying, it will be a goddess. I am very much opposed to the latter option but there are two distinct threads, and that's just one of the things that's happening.

"The other big issue of our time is this question of the separation of Jesus and God. Is Christianity the same thing as the cult of Jesus? That must be the current theological issue that's taken on. There it is. It's a pressing question. The deification of Jesus has proved to be an effective educational tool for the Christian church. When talking to children or less sophisticated people, both the Catholic and Protestant churches have fastened on Jesus because they've felt that an abstract God is something people can't understand — Jesus is something they can.

"There are still people who, for that reason, would say that the question of Jesus and the question of God are inseparable but any theologian will be aware that there can be an enormous gap between the study of the historical Jesus and the question of God. I react strongly to those who say, 'You are destroying religion.' They assume that, by proving that Jesus was not a supernatural figure, this destroys the whole of Christianity. No theologian would agree that was the case. The question of God always has been separate from the question of Jesus.

"In Christian teaching, we say to children, 'Jesus did this, that and the other and he was a good person and this is what God wants you to do.' In that way, it's tied up. Christianity has then gone on to say, 'Jesus was a person who lived two thousand years ago,' and therefore there's history in it. At the same time, the question of God can be a matter which has no relation whatever to history, particularly in the case of a God who is permanent and unchangeable and so on. Christianity has linked the two for educational reasons but it also knows that they're capable of being separated. This has been the case for two thousand years."

Barbara, now in her sixties, has been a Christian for all of her adult life, yet she feels not a moment's remorse about the spanner which she so energetically throws into her religion's works. Each time the conversation veers towards theological revolution, her eyes light up with delight.

"I think I'll state this as a fact," she resumes hurriedly. "As a result of all the books on the historical Jesus which have been written over the past twenty years, the idea of the supernatural Jesus really is finished.

"It was a crude idea, appropriate to a less advanced society. You see, I'm not the only one who's written about the historical Jesus. I'm the one who's saying, 'There is new evidence, look at it.' I'm unique in that respect but, for some years now, people who have usually had a church background, have come to the point of saying, 'It's ridiculous to talk about the Son of God and to worship a human being.' It was one of the heresies, to worship a human being. We had reverted to that. So, recovering the historical Jesus and bringing him right down to earth is a trend that's been going on for twenty years or more. People have been saying, 'Let's stop equating Christianity with the cult of Jesus,' and then they've been digging up whatever evidence was available to point out that he was a perfectly normal human being.

"I came into this scene and said, 'Fine, just do a bit more work. I agree with your motives but you're getting it out of your head or out of the New Testament, which does not lend itself to the kind of treatment you have used, and sort out your prejudices.'

"Often people develop these theories out of their own personal experiences, which they project onto others. I'm saying, 'Good on you for doing it but let's listen to this new evidence.' Fortuitously, there have been two great discoveries of new documents in our century — the Dead Sea Scrolls and the Gnostic literature. The implications of what we find in them must be faced up to."

According to Barbara, the "hard line" of the Catholic church has reacted by ignoring the evidence in the hope that it will go away. Ironically, Barbara believes, this is the branch of Christianity which has least to lose from the debate.

"The Catholics, above all, will survive," she says, "because they have a strong tradition of understanding that Jesus and God are separate. Just look at the classical theology of the eleventh and twelfth centuries, look at Aquinas. He went back to the sixth century B.C. and said that the language we need to talk about God is available to us from Greek philosophy. He was condemned as an heretic by the Bishop of Paris but, since then, has been the foundation of all Catholic theology and they've had this long tradition which talks in completely timeless terms about God.

"Protestants arose out of a reaction to Catholic priestliness. Catholic priests alone had knowledge about God, they were the authorities, they were the scientists, you had to obey what they said and they became totally corrupt. After this came Protestantism, which says that we can find out for ourselves what it's all about and we'll do that by going to the book.

"The Bible had scarcely been read for fifteen hundred years until the Protestants went to the book and made it their priest. They understood it no better than the Catholics but it was a powerful political tool against the priests and that's been the case for the past five hundred years.

"So, Protestants are particularly badly affected by this new collapse because they have a lot invested in the Bible and in history and in Jesus. They've never really gone for this abstract doctrine of God and, as a result, Protestants are disappearing. We're living in the time of the collapse of the great ideologies. It's one a year. There's communism, the British monarchy and, although the collapse of Christianity is less catastrophic, it is in fact happening."

BARBARA THIERING'S HISTORY INFORMS HER WORK. WHETHER LECTURING AT Sydney University or rifling through dusty archives in search of the key that would unlock the meaning of the gospels, she has been driven by a single motivation.

"My religious education was never tied to a belief in magic or superstition," she says. "I could never cope with the notion that my internal salvation and my morality depended on Jesus walking on water. To me, that is magical thinking and very unhealthy thinking. I remain, as I have been all my life, wanting a religious language and actively seeking it but, at the same time, respecting reason."

Barbara's childhood was spent in Sydney's far northern suburbs. The tree-lined streets are a bastion of the middle class, hardly a hotbed of radicalism. Her father, an accountant and liberal thinker, was a pivotal influence on her early years.

"He was a very sensitive, quiet, thoughtful person," she recalls. "He had a love of learning, a love of reason, a love of literature. We never went to church and I was never taught religion at home. Growing up, I was morally serious and a bit studious. I inherited my father's love of reading and studying and, of course, that made me unpopular at school."

In her teens, Barbara side-stepped momentarily into the irrational, rebelling against her upbringing by entering into a brief flirtation with fundamentalism. It did not last long.

"At about that time, a lot of well-meaning people were going around to schools, taking idealistic young teenagers and asking them to give their hearts to Jesus," she recalls. "I went to these camps, of which my mother approved, and saw that people were totally brainwashed. I liked the idea of giving my heart to Jesus — it was a good religious theme and it aroused something in me — but, for the most part, the fundamentalist message was too extreme and the people who stood for it didn't have my respect."

By nineteen, Barbara had shaken off what she saw as the hypocrisy of fundamentalism and had begun a lifelong search for a religious expression that could fire her heart without insulting her intelligence.

"I took myself to our local Presbyterian church," she remembers, "where we had a minister who had broken out of fundamentalism and was deeply influenced by the nineteenth century liberal tradition. He was a very saintly man. He didn't teach resurrection, certainly not the virgin birth — Protestants haven't believed in the virgin birth since the sixteenth century — and we didn't go strongly on Easter. It was primarily a moral teaching."

Entering into an academic career, Barbara studied theology and lectured at Sydney University.

"Sydney's top theologians were all my very good friends and, in fact, they don't agree with all they preach," she laughs. "They are well aware that you say one thing to the people and another amongst yourselves."

Professional and social circumstances led Barbara to spend much of her early adulthood among people who were deeply committed to one or another Christian church, even at times when she was seriously questioning the central tenets of their faith. The result is that today she does not align herself with any denomination and retains a lingering distrust of institutions.

"I was an observer," she says. "I found myself watching how people behaved religiously, seeing how claims that they made were not backed up, seeing that their faith did not make them moral people, seeing some of the truly nasty things that go on under the banner of institutional religion. I came to feel that religion was being used for immoral purposes and this, I thought, was sad because I still believed that, in essence, religion was a good thing."

Looking back, of course, it was all grist for the mill. She can now cheerfully list the redeeming qualities of each of the faiths with which she's had contact and conflict, except perhaps Christian fundamentalism. It is with a certain glee that she announces its death.

"This is another of the major contemporary issues on which I have an opinion," she smiles. "Fundamentalism has collapsed and its collapse is in keeping with the current trend in the collapse of ideologies but, for the most part of this century, it has been a powerful force. It has taken an extreme position and that position was designed to oppose something which no longer exists."

Fundamentalism was the result of cultural pressure and historical process and Barbara is eager to elucidate the finer points of its development. She was doubtless a magnificent lecturer. Her mind leaps across cultures and centuries at breakneck speed, weaving threads of meaning with a rampantly contagious enthusiasm for her subject.

"In the nineteenth century," she explains, "with the first discovery of documents that questioned the creation story, liberalism set in. There was a huge surge of biblical scholarship which established liberalism and which was actually the first blow to Protestantism on the question of the Bible, although it was also a blow to Catholicism. The new liberal thought was that all that was left to Christianity was its moral role. It really was the first stage of what's happening now. At the same time, into that arena came science, with a theory of evolution. The two schools came together — biblical liberalism and Darwinian evolution — and refuted the creation story, which had profound theological effects.

"The first reaction to that was the doctrine of papal infallibility. That was an entirely new nineteenth century doctrine. Probably they had been acting on it before but they'd had no need to assert it. So, the Catholics came out with this doctrine of papal infallibility, asserting that they had the truth and whatever the Pope said was right.

"Then, there was an extreme Protestant reaction, fundamentalism, which had an historical beginning in 1909 in Chicago, Illinios, where a group of American Protestant businessmen put an enormous amount of money into the publication of a series of tracts which aimed to outline 'the fundamentals of the faith'. If you did not believe these fundamentals, they said, you were not a Christian.

"These tracts were distributed to every clergyman and religious teacher in the world. The fundamentals, of course, included the idea that Jesus was the Son of God, the doctrine of the Trinity, the virgin birth, the second coming. So, from 1909 up to recent times, fundamentalism became an established doctrine in the United States. Just as Italy was Catholic and England was Anglican, America's established faith became fundamentalism.

"It was immensely powerful. You subscribed to this and you automatically became a good person. The tele-evangelists set themselves up and made money out of it because anyone who gave money to their church was proving they were all right with God. It moved into its debasement, exactly paralleling the way the Catholic church behaved in the Middle Ages, when it was selling indulgences. The fundamentalist preachers had that same power.

"Psychologically and socially, it was exactly the same thing. The Catholics said: 'We have the power to save you from hellfire. First, we'll tell you there is hellfire and damnation for those who sin. Next, you're obviously going to sin anyway, so we'll tell you that, if you pay us a lot of money, you'll be fine.' It really is exactly parallel and the fundamentalists had the technology to spread it.

"Now, of course, this has been exposed. Just as Protestantism was produced out of the actions of the Catholic church in the Middle Ages, so fundamentalism has been discredited and we are now in this very interesting phase where something new is starting to emerge.

"In the Middle Ages, the issues were defined and the classic doctrines grew out of them. So, now, we too are defining the questions and producing the classic doctrines. The question of Jesus and God is an essential one — whether you can dispense altogether with the cult of Jesus and have a healthier and better Christian religion. This will go down in the history books. Many of the feminist theologians are calling this new direction post-Christian.

"Something as big as Protestantism, at least, is going to emerge or maybe something as big as Christianity itself, when it came out of Judaism in a time of turmoil like this."

The other critical question of our time is, of course, whether anything that can be recognized as religion will survive. Here, Barbara uncharacteristically straddles both camps, planting one foot with the traditionalists and the other with the radical fringe.

Religion, she feels, is so essential to our species that it cannot disappear altogether. The form it evolves into, however, may be quite different from the culturally based institutions which we have identified as religions in the past.

"At times like this," she says, "the real process is the breaking down of some of the things from the past which have become spiritually crippling. That's the process we're in. Usually something emerges. Whether we will call it religion or not is another question.

"Are we beyond religion? We're reassessing the contrast between secularism and sacredness. We're finding that secularism can be far more religious than what is sacred. We're, in a sense, going through another anti-priestly revolt. Previously, Catholicism was opposed by Protestantism and that was the new religion because we had to have religion, just a different set of priests. Now, the big issue could well be, is anything that you can call religion still viable?

"Personally, I don't think there is ever anything totally different. Religion comes out of the questions we all ask ourselves. The starting point, I suppose, is every human being's sense of the presence of God, that need we all have which comes to the surface from time to time. We believe that there must be something greater, something beyond us, beyond this world. We ask questions about creation, we make assumptions based on our own lives. You know, 'I have a big daddy so there must be a Big Daddy.'

"These are psychological questions that human beings have always asked in every different culture and religious institutions have grown up around those questions. People are in desperate need of some sense of direction, some meaning in their lives. 'Why am I here at all? Why should I try to be good?' A religious institution has always grown up to take the form of conscience and to give people a language with which to talk about their sense of God. For thousands of years before Christianity, religions did that. Other religions in other parts of the world do it. You might use the name God for it or you might use another name.

It's something that's within us and we will always ask these questions, so there will always be religion.

"What's at issue here is the conceptual language we use for it and that is very much affected by culture. Whether it's English or Arabic, whether you say God or Allah, that's language. As culture is changing, which it is now, that's going to lead to the most enormous changes in language and no one person or institution will any longer be able determine what must be said. It's not as if anyone has the right or the ability to decide. People will simply observe what we have to say, what the culture throws up."

For the past two thousand years, the world has been shrinking and gradually, year by year, human culture has grown more homogeneous. Christianity spread from east to west with European culture, beginning with the Romans.

"There are some things," says Barbara, "that are just so big that local events are not going to stop them. The future was going to be in the West. The Romans provided a political structure and this very good new religion. For two thousand years, it held the power." Escalating technology, however, recently evened the stakes (if marginally) and in the last century Asian religions have gradually made their way west.

"Now," Barbara explains, "your religion is not so clearly defined by where you live on the planet. The media tycoon, Rupert Murdoch, says we are in the midst of a communications revolution. There have only been three or four great changes in human beings' way of living. There was the agricultural revolution, when we stopped wandering around as nomads and settled down and had farms and grew crops, which meant we developed villages and cities. That was a major change of lifestyle and, really, the only other big one was the industrial revolution, where villages were split from cities. The men generally went off into the cities to work and the women stayed at home. That was just a couple of centuries ago and a total change of lifestyle again.

"Now, we have the communications revolution. Why go to the office when you can sit at home, as I do every day, in nice surroundings with your computer, your fax and your phone, which put you in immediate contact with anybody anywhere in the world? We're just at the beginning of it but, even now, with this Internet system, I can sit in front of my screen and communicate, in great scientific detail, with someone in another part of the world. Why go to the crumbling buildings that need renovation? Why say I'm a great scholar because I go to this university or I'm not such a great scholar because I go to another one? All that's on the way out. Cities will go — the very same cities that were built up through the industrial revolution. Why go into a smoky city? People are staying at home.

"That means a total change of lifestyle — one world, one culture. I'm not going to think a certain thing because I happen to live on the Arabian Peninsula or in the United States. Religions have often been a way of saying, 'My culture's better than your culture, I live on the Arabian Peninsula so I'm Muslim, I live on the edge of Europe so I'm Catholic.' Global communication means we're not going to have religions determined by local cultures and we'll all be equally in touch with Islam and with Christianity. That's unstoppable, unless someone bans electronic communication completely, which is unlikely."

This, according to Barbara, is sounding another death knell for institutional Christian churches and, while Catholicism was holding its own in the God versus Jesus debate, it doesn't fare nearly so well when the communications revolution comes into play. The Catholic church is reacting to change by narrowing its vision and reverting to the rigid dogma of its pre-Vatican Two stance — a direction totally out of keeping with contemporary thought.

"It insists that certain parts of the population are desperate for a strong line," she says, "not so much on the nature of God and what will happen when they die but on what they should do while they're alive, on morality. The church says they need a voice of authority: 'This is what you must do, don't spend ten years trying to figure it out for yourselves.'

"Perhaps there are people in the world who have less time and space for thinking, who are more passive and want to be told. However, we are in midst of this tremendous social change. All of us — potentially everyone in the world — are capable of sitting in front of that little box and the little box will tell us what to do.

"What comes over the box is not likely to come from the .Catholic church because their language is no longer universal. The Catholic idea is that it's so because the Pope says it's so but that's not going to come across through television. Catholicism relies on one person and the nature of television demands variety.

"Because of the universal availability of knowledge, the same level of education will soon be available to everybody. We've only had television for fifty years or less. Give it another hundred years and it will be a worldwide medium of education. There will still be people who are passive but I think they will not be asking the questions the church has dictated."

Change, says Barbara, is inevitable "because none of us can help it. When new knowledge comes, we must go along with it to survive. We're bound together by our questions and by the answers to them. This is what being human is about." What is not so certain is how each of us will react to change. The Vatican has taken one approach. Barbara has chosen the polar opposite.

"The moral issue," she believes, "is whether you go with these changes out of honesty and out of religious sensitivity. Where will morality and religious sensitivity and honesty lead you? Will they lead you to dig your heels in and say, 'The old way is the right way' and, 'These wicked, evil people are destroying God'? Will you go back to the Latin mass? At the same time, some of the wicked, evil people going the new way are saying they're doing it out of honesty and out of religious sensitivity too. Change will come and I don't think we need to deplore the fact that, out there, are all these people we're hurting because we're giving them different answers to their questions."

DISPENSING WITH FORMALITY AND WITH SOME OF HER HEADMISTRESSLY ZEAL, Barbara now decides it's time for tea. While she clatters about in the kitchen, I am offered the run of the house. She lives high above Sydney harbor. A stone path winds its way up a steep incline from the road. Her desk affords a spectacular view across forested hills and water dotted with bobbing white boats. One of her sons is currently staying in the guest room downstairs. Barbara has three children (a daughter who is a teacher, and two sons — a lawyer and a psychiatrist) and four grandchildren.

Returning to the kitchen, I find the kettle bubbling and Barbara setting out biscuits and pastries on a floral china plate. We discuss the north shore, comparing notes on our childhoods here. We talk about Sunday school. Barbara went once — her mother thought it was the right thing to do — and was bitterly disappointed.

I went twice. We made raffia octopi and colored in drawings of Jesus feeding the five thousand. Later, my mother asked, 'How was Sunday school?' I said, 'We made raffia octopi and I'm never going back.' "Yes," Barbara sympathizes. "You would know what I'm talking about. There must be a lot of us with those stories."

Settled back down in the lounge room, juggling plates of biscuits and cups of tea, I finally ask the question that's been troubling me since we began. Through all her research, Barbara has somehow maintained a belief that God exists. Does she ever feel tempted to simply join ranks with the atheists and be done with it?

Barbara audibly draws in breath.

"Now, stop me if you want to because this is a whole theological course coming up." Before I can respond, she's away.

"It's very often the case that the questions you ask define the answers. You've taken for granted that we should be saying, 'There is something.' To assume the existence of God is to make a statue, to make an image. We exist. I exist. Here I am, alive, and one day I won't exist any more, I'll be dead. There was a time when I didn't exist, before I was born. Existence is a property of human beings. Yet, we say, 'God exists, there is a God.' That means, as with human beings, that there is a time when God exists and a time when God ceases to exist. We suppose a thing like ourselves, an existing object like ourselves, because we cannot conceive that there could be anything that does not have the property of existence. However, through our instinctive religious sense, we know that God is more than that. God is not a human being, so we shouldn't say there is a God.

"If an atheist, in saying there is not a God, really means, 'I refuse to postulate the existence of God and God is, in Buddhist terms, the beyond or the ultimate,' if the atheist really means that, then I go along with the atheist, as do all theologians, because the whole job of theology is to stop the objectification, to stop the making of God in one's own image. Another atheist might say that there is nothing greater at all. Then, of course, I would disagree."

Be that as it may, I am inquisitive about the concept of God with which Barbara has been left after years of questioning and rationalizing. She has stripped away much of the myth and magic from her religion, which suits her temperament, though, I must say, it's anathema to mine.

Surely there was a point at which she found herself staring into an abyss, watching the pieces of her faith fall away beneath her. I ask her to describe what comes to mind when she thinks of God.

"You can't," she retorts good naturedly. "As soon as you think of God, you need to put brackets around it because you're only thinking in your own terms and your own language. I'm thinking in English. My thinking is inadequate for something better expressed in Hindi.

"You cannot think about God, you cannot have any knowledge of God but, at the same time, you have to, in order to cope with your personal religious needs.

"In fact, you cannot know God in any way because there is nothing you can say about God that is true. All you are saying is that your human language, which is extremely limited, finds this a suitable way of talking at the moment and it helps. It's a bit of a long sentence to put after each thing you say but that's what you really mean. Language helps to some extent but you can get beyond language. To attain that physical state, where you're no longer striving to go outwards or to find words or to do anything at all — that perfect poise — that's what you're striving for."

So the conversation circumambulates, around and around, in an attempt to define what, if not myth and magic, is at least a mystery. We finally agree to describe it as an absence of form.

"I think about God because I want to," Barbara concedes, "and as soon as I think, I cancel it out, but the spiritual and physical effects are very important. I have to eat and I have to think about God."

Yet, when she thinks, is it of an objective absence? After all our fine intentions — to avoid gender and image, graven statues and name and form — have we nonetheless created God out of history and culture and wishful thinking? When Barbara prays, is it to our collective imagination or to nothing at all?

"That you put it that way shows you understand," she laughs, "so, full marks."

I think this means I've just passed Theology One.

"I have to say I don't know. The satisfying thing is to break down the existing answer, the one that was there before, and to do that is the process of growth. I admire the scientists who are trying to reconcile theological and scientific language. Paul Davies says you must think in terms of the order in the universe. It could have evolved differently. Why did it go this way? In entirely modern scientific language, he is trying to accommodate theological language and that's wonderful. Just reading his books imparts that sense of the greatness of everything. It imparts a religious sense, a sense of awe.

"So, I can think about science and I can think about God," she says finally, "and I can say this is better than the previous thing, but that's all I can say. What I say now, if it survived, would be quite ridiculous in a hundred years. At the moment, it works. That's all."

Floyd Red Crow Westerman

10

FOR ALL
MY RELATIONS

THE YEAR WAS 1946. THE SCENE MIGHT HAVE BEEN ANY MISSION SCHOOL IN South Dakota. A dozen timid, frightened Native American boys — all new recruits, having been removed forcibly, that very day, from their families — marched from dormitory to amenities block, where their long hair was cropped close before they were stripped naked, doused with pesticide, handed a scrubbing brush and marched into the showers. For many, this was their first taste of white America.

Among them was Floyd Westerman, a proud, ten year old Dakota Indian, tugged that morning from his family on the Sisseton-Wahpeton reservation, which means "by the shining waters" or "where the waters come out of the earth". Young Floyd, like most of his peers, was handy around horses. Sisseton-Wahpeton is sixty miles wide by about seventy miles long and back in 1946, no one on it owned a car. Each family's lifeline was its horse and wagon.

Today, Floyd Westerman has made a name for himself as a folksinger, a political activist and a Hollywood actor, best known as Chief Ten Bears, the sagacious head of tribe in Kevin Costner's blockbuster film, *Dances With Wolves*. Today, he refers to reservations like the one on which he was raised as "nothing more than concentration camps."

"From 1890 until 1930," he says, "you couldn't leave them. If you wanted to go from one reservation to another, you needed to have a white person with you. Only in 'America the free' could this have happened. We couldn't own a horse or a mule or a cow or a shovel without the government knowing about it. The only Indians to whom they gave anything were the ones who became Christian. If you became Christian, they'd give you a shovel or a horse or a head of cattle to feed your family. It was coercion by starvation and many families did become Christian as a result."

Floyd's family, however, had a long tradition of resistance. His grandfather, Red Crow, was part of an Indian delegation to Washington DC, back in 1858.

"He was one of the few who didn't want Christianity. He wanted the right to practice the Indian religion and he wanted to keep several wives and he was pretty adamant about it. They killed him. It was an assassination. The delegates were all in one room of this huge building in Washington and each Indian had just a blanket and a place on the floor for his possessions. Some white men came in and asked my grandfather to get his possessions and follow them and that was the last anyone saw of him, until he was found dead, hanging from a tree in Washington DC. In those days, they didn't transfer the bodies back to the homelands, so he's there, in the Arlington military cemetery."

Later in life, Floyd would adopt his grandfather's name. He would be known as Floyd Red Crow Westerman. Like his grandfather, he would grow in courage and learn to speak his mind. On that winter afternoon in 1946, however, he stood shivering, scrubbed raw, in the mission school amenities block, waiting for a supervisor to check that every inch of his small body was perfectly clean.

TEN YEARS PASSED. THE YEAR WAS 1956. FLOYD WESTERMAN WAS A YOUNG MAN. After college, he spent some time back on Sisseton-Wahpeton, where, following a long hiatus, he began to rebuild relationships with his family. Little had changed since his childhood. The reservation land was the least arable in the state, incapable of supporting its population. His family and their neighbors lived, much of the time, on what he calls a "poverty diet" of sugar and starch, rationed out free by the government. Diabetes afflicted his people as a plague. Residents were finally free to come and go from the reservations as they pleased. Often they'd travel to Rosebud or Pine Ridge to visit friends and relatives but racism in neighboring towns was virulent. A shopping expedition was rarely accomplished without incident.

Floyd found himself stranded between two worlds, unwelcome in the one for which he was educated and a stranger to the one in which he was born. At school, he'd been forbidden to speak his language, practice his religion or sing traditional songs. Even on the reservation, only the older folk — fifty-five years of age and above — had been permitted to participate in Indian ceremonies for such a long while that traditional culture had been forced underground.

Floyd divided his time between the reservation and traveling with friends to big cities, like Minneapolis and Denver, where he worked at odd jobs and played guitar in nightclubs and bars. Then, just as life began to paint itself in Floyd's favor, just as he began to find work as a musician and to rebuild tenuous links back home, he received word that his father and mother, one after the other, had died.

From that moment, Floyd Westerman's life dipped towards its lowest ebb. Looking back, some forty years later, he remembers a shiftless young man, roaming from one city to the next, drinking too much, trailed always by a dark cloud of grief.

"I didn't feel like I cared to live," he says. "Everything was meaningless. After all that time I had been separated from my family, I was finally making my connections back and they left this earth for the spirit world, my mother in a very tragic way and my father with cancer. Things seemed pointless. So I fought my way through the city streets of America and had my bouts with alcoholism, jail and prison.

"I was lost for eight or ten years but then survival started to happen all over again. It was a phase and, out of it, I started looking around and trying to find reasons to go on. Usually, those reasons are within yourself. When you're in a situation like that, if you go to be by yourself and if you come out of there without doing harm to yourself, then you come out much stronger. A lot of people go through that when they experience loss.

"I don't think alcoholism was as damaging to me as it was to other members of my family — my brothers and sisters — because through it all, there was this thread of survival. Through it all, I felt the gift of being able to play music and produce music and that became the next thing I started to do. That was my way of striking back — to write songs and put out a record."

IT WAS EARLY IN THE EVENING OF FEBRUARY 29TH, 1973. FLOYD WESTERMAN WAS sitting, with a small group of American Indian Movement (AIM) faithful in a dusty meeting room in Minneapolis. Floyd had been involved with AIM since its inception in 1968.

"That was my new family, my new reason for living. It was survival for all of us," he remembers. "The American Indian Movement was a defiant act in the middle of an America that didn't care and couldn't learn to care."

Floyd had released his first album, *Custer Died For Your Sins*, in 1970. "My songs were born at the time when AIM was born and they went hand in hand." His songwriting spoke directly to an awakening Native American political consciousness and wherever AIM gathered, for a ceremony, a celebration, a meeting or demonstration, Floyd was there to play guitar and sing his songs.

On this particular evening, a meeting had been called to discuss the events which were unfolding on Pine Ridge reservation. On the previous afternoon, more than three hundred Indians had driven in convoy to the tiny hamlet of Wounded Knee. Most of those traveling were local Oglalas. Many were women and children. A few were AIM supporters who had been invited along to lend a hand.

The sun had been setting behind the Black Hills as the convoy pulled into Wounded Knee. A meeting was convened. AIM luminaries, Dennis Banks and Russell Means, addressed the crowd, as did a spokesperson for the traditional Oglalas, Pedro Bissonnette.

The meeting had issued a public statement, demanding official hearings on Oglala treaty rights and an investigation into alleged misconduct by the Bureau of Indian Affairs (BIA). The statement was endorsed by the area's eight leading chiefs and medicine people and was considered an official document of the Oglala nation, demanding its right to sovereignty and self-determination and an end to government manipulation through the BIA. The gathering had then sat through the night, awaiting a response.

When the government response arrived, however, it was not the one which the meeting had anticipated. The following day, Wounded Knee had been surrounded by the combined forces of the FBI, the US Marshall Service and the BIA police. This tiny gathering had challenged the United States Government, nation to nation, and Washington had met the challenge with an outrageous show of force. There were helicopters, armored personnel carriers, infrared lights, automatic weapons and great stockpiles of ammunition. The demonstrators had no option but to sit tight.

As word filtered back to Minneapolis, the movement mobilised its resources. It was evident, within hours of the establishment of the blockade, that neither side would surrender its position easily. Those on the outside would need to raise both funds and public sympathy quickly if the encampment at Wounded Knee was not to end in desolation, starvation and bloodshed. Plans were formulated, media releases written and Floyd, known fondly as the *eyapaha*, or town crier, was dispatched on a national tour, explaining the Native American position to the American public through his songs and posting back donations and tour profits to finance legal, publicity and survival costs.

What followed was a seventy-three day siege, during which arms and supplies were carried into Wounded Knee by sympathizers, under the cover of dark, and days were spent waiting for some guarantee that the federal government would address the besieged demonstrators' demands.

Twenty-two years later, an older, wiser Floyd Westerman looks back on this time from his family home in suburban Los Angeles. He is still bemused by the government's overreaction, he is still horrified by the loss of life but he sees, with hindsight, the bureaucratic insanity of the era and he does not for a minute regret spending months on the road in solidarity with his cousins and sisters and brothers who remained defiantly in their bunker.

"The fact that they were sitting there, making these demands," he says, "labelled the government and the American people as occupiers of another people's land." He alludes to shady deals with gas corporations and uranium miners for rights to reservation land, he talks about BIA puppet governments and their "goon squads" which ruled reservation life by force and he explains that "Nixon was running for President and wanted to keep all this quiet.

"There was a lot of confusion. A lot of people were dying on the reservations. It was very tense. Adding fuel to the fire, the government had developed an FBI program called COINTELPRO, Counter Intelligence Program, which was created to debilitate and dissect minority movements like the Black Panthers, the Chicano Brown Berets and the American Indian Movement. All the minorities had efforts going at this time and the FBI tried to disrupt them by infiltrating them with agents. So this was the background to the confrontation at Wounded Knee."

On March 9th, amidst rumor of an unbridled attack by government forces, a heavy exchange of fire broke out and a young Oglala was wounded. On March 11th, following a meeting of elders, the demonstrators announced the re-formation of the Independent Oglala Nation and insisted on treaty negotiations with the US Government on equal terms. On March 26th, the last remaining telephone line to Wounded Knee was cut and media crews were ordered to leave. Within hours, the village was showered by gunfire and a US marshall was seriously wounded.

All this, Floyd heard on the Indian grapevine and the evening news as he zig-zagged his way across America, from campus to coffeehouse to town hall. Each new bulletin from Pine Ridge cemented his conviction that he must defend the rights of the besieged reservation folk with the only weapons at his disposal — his guitar, his voice, his songs.

Towards the end of March, the government began negotiations with the local Oglalas who, once again, demanded a committee to review the Treaty of 1868. On April 5th, a delegation was sent from Wounded Knee to Washington, where they learnt that the government would not begin negotiations until the Wounded Knee camp had disarmed. On April 17th, a Cherokee demonstrator was killed. On April 26th, the sound of gunfire rang out through most of the day and the first Oglala at the camp was shot dead. On May 4th, the government promised a meeting to examine the treaty if the tiny township would disarm. On May 5th, the Wounded Knee activists agreed to do so.

"After that," Floyd recalls, "they promptly arrested all our leaders. Nothing came of discussions about the treaty and the BIA was never seriously investi-gated. Fifteen years passed before our leaders were vindicated and freed but even so, it was never publicised that it was the government's wrongdoing that was the cause of all this."

WHEN ASKED, MANY YEARS LATER, TO RECOUNT THE MOST SIGNIFICANT MOMENT OF his spiritual life, Floyd replies, without hesitation, that it was "my experience of all that happened when the American Indian Movement formed."

The American Indian Movement was born in the 1960s, as a coming together of concerned young Native Americans, most of whom had grown up in mission schools, had moved to the cities and had, like Floyd, done their time in jail or prison, on the bottle and wandering aimlessly from one underpaid job to the next.

It began as an effort to battle the relocation programs which, at the time, were moving large numbers of Native Americans from their reservations to the cities. They would arrive, with little education or training, to face the worst possible racism from employers, landlords, government departments and the police. AIM's initial goals were in the areas of employment, housing and education, as well as mounting active opposition to police brutality.

Primarily, AIM was a political organization, yet, early in its history, it recognized the necessity of uniting the hearts, as well as the minds, of Native Americans. Just as the colonial power had stripped Indian nations of their land and their sovereignty, it had also tried to rob them of their cultures, outlawing religious ceremonies and restricting the use of native languages. Products of mission schools, almost exclusively, the early AIM organizers were amongst this policy's primary victims. Thus, they made pilgrimages back to the reservations, in search of the remnants of a culture which they might reclaim.

"We found out," Floyd smiles, "after going back and talking to the older people, that something of our culture was still alive and that straightened us all out. We knew we had to fight for that. We began to just outright hold our ceremonies and to do it in an outspoken way, as a challenge, so the government would have to see it. We came together, as an organisation, for our generations and for our culture and for our lives and for our land and for our spirituality.

"We found that, in spite of the systematic genocide which took place; in spite of the fact that, before 1930, Indians could not practice their religion at all; in spite of the fact that we had been living in a kind of limbo on these concentration camp reservations; in spite of all that, much of it had survived. In many places, it went underground and nobody knew that our parents and grandparents were practicing these ceremonies. It was kept alive that way."

By 1970, AIM had set up its first Survival School, in an attempt to help young Indians adjust to white society without losing sight of their historical and cultural roots. Around this time, AIM also became involved in local battles for treaty rights and land claims and became a defender of Native American cultural and religious, as well as political, freedom.

"One of our priorities," Floyd explains, "is still to have our spirituality recognized by the government. It's an institutional process. First of all, the churches don't want to recognize our religion because they still have their missionaries on our land. Then, the government doesn't want to recognise our religion because they would have to cede a lot of our land back to us. Our spirituality, you see, is related to thousands-of-years-old sacred sites and many of these are on lands which have been taken away. Most of the huge national parks are sacred land areas, where other Indian nations, as well as ours, are in litigation. These cases are still not decided. So there is a hesitancy in the government to acknowledge our religion because it's related to the land, just as Aboriginal religion in Australia and other indigenous religions are related to the land."

Despite these hurdles, the formal recognition of Native American religion remains on the movement's agenda and the recovery of Native American culture remains an ongoing task.

"We hung onto a lot of it," Floyd admits, "but we're still relearning much of what was lost. Our culture is essentially intact and it's a matter of filling in the empty spots. I think it's the same way with all the Indian nations here. The filling in of those empty spots is a transition we're going through now."

For Floyd, that process of recovery began in the very early days of the American Indian Movement. The first time, he says, that he knew the Great Spirit was a reality and felt its presence close by was around 1969, when AIM invited a group of Lakota elders to hold, for its members, a pipe ceremony.

"That was the first time I had seen the pipe ceremony," says Floyd. "There was a group of maybe sixty people — kids and everything — but when the pipe came out, there was complete silence. I had never known anything like it and I realized then that this is what makes a people adhere without any commands, makes people understand without words and makes the people go on without struggle. Those kind of things, when they continue to happen, resolve everything."

The Lakota elders explained that the sacred pipe was a gift from White Buffalo Calf Woman, who taught the people that its spiraling smoke was their link with the Great Spirit. According to legend, it was at a mid-summer festival, long ago, that White Buffalo Calf Woman appeared. There was little game to be caught that year and the people were starving. Two hunters, walking over the hills, spied what they thought was a buffalo coming towards them but as she drew near, they realized that it was a woman, so beautiful and ethereal that she could only have come from the spirit world. She told the young hunters to return to their tribe and have their leaders prepare for her visit the next morning.

At daybreak, the people gathered and as promised, White Buffalo Calf Woman appeared. In her hand, she carried the sacred pipe. She stepped into the tipi which had been prepared for her, the elders followed and her first gift to the Lakota people was to teach them the pipe ceremony. She also passed on instruction for other sacred Native American rituals, including the sweat lodge and the sundance.

When she left, four days later, she asked the people to follow her to the top of a nearby hill. On reaching the summit, she transformed again into the guise of a buffalo, before gradually vanishing. When the people turned their gaze beyond the hill, they saw a herd of terrestrial buffalo and realized that their time of famine was over.

"The White Buffalo Calf Woman," Floyd explains, "was an envoy from the Great Spirit. Most people understand the term God. That's what the Great Spirit is. Some people call him God, some people call him Buddha, some people call him Allah, we call him the Great Spirit. It's the same being. It's just that we have a more defined belief about him, even without writing any of it down."

When Floyd travels, as he does often, both as musician and activist, he likes to introduce his hosts to a little Native American spirituality. He has conducted sweat lodges in Australia and Europe, as well as in the United States and when he's at home in California, he often runs sweats for friends and neighbors.

First, a small shelter is built, traditionally of willow branches and buckskin. A pit is dug in the center, into which red-hot rocks are placed. Water and sacred herbs are sprinkled onto the rocks, filling the lodge with clouds of steam.

"Then we sit," says Floyd, "and pray to God in the darkness and we heal. Whenever I run into someone who's having troubles and I can do that, I hold a sweat lodge for them. I regularly run the sweat lodge ceremony for a lot of people around. In there, I find myself being a part of the whole, with all my people, and I find an ongoing regeneration and rebirth.

"I don't have those overwhelmed feelings that many Indian people get when they don't know their own spirituality. A lot of people have heard my records and have written to me saying that they feel society is so overwhelming but when they hear my songs, all my songs together, they come away feeling that they can handle it. I think that's the way spirituality is too, when you go back and find that rebirth."

The greatest rebirth, for Floyd, comes each year when he returns to South Dakota for the summer festivals, to the sound of voices raised in song, the cry of eagle-bone whistles and the rhythmic heartbeat of the drum.

"In the old days," he says, "many people would just quit their jobs and go back and be part of the ceremonies all summer and white people couldn't understand that.

"The main ceremony we go back for is the sundance. You prepare for it for a week. You go to the sweat lodge twice a day and you make ready and you build your psyche up to go without food and water in the sun for four days, while you pray to God through the tree. The tree is a relative. The tree is the center of life. There's a collective power that we get when we all do this together and dance around the tree for four days.

"In that ceremony, an interesting thing happens. A clown comes by with some food and iced water, while we're all very thirsty, and he tempts us. Then, symbolically, we take the water and give it back to the tree. That's a very difficult thing to do but it gives everyone strength to know that we're all doing it."

That collective strength might also allow participants to pierce their flesh with traditional skewers and perhaps to attach those skewers, with a long piece of thong, to the sacred tree, around which they dance, until the skewers have pulled themselves free. All the while, the dancers pray for their people, their families and for the renewal of all life on earth.

"It's not easy," Floyd admits, "but there is that collective strength. This is our most sacred ceremony. It is the old connection of humanity to the earth. The tree is a relative. We pray to God through the tree. The sundance ceremony is thousands of years old."

There has been an enormous revival of interest in traditional Native American spirituality in recent years. Many Indians are now questioning the doctrines and the policies of the churches and, with good reason, Floyd says, they are turning away.

"The churches sit on our reservations. They say, 'Thou shalt not steal', yet every one of them has been able to, very discreetly, obtain land which is not theirs. They have been violating the Ten Commandments. We have a fifty thousand year history with our spirituality, whereas Christianity is only two thousand years old and already isn't fulfilling what it was created for. It's a power grab."

Native American religion has survived, against enormous odds, he claims, because it is a living spiritual system. Books can be burned and used to beat reluctant converts into submission. An oral tradition lives from generation to generation in the deeds and hearts and minds of its adherents.

"An oral spirituality is something that is learned through values and a way of life. In our case, it is about living on and with the earth," he explains. "I think something that is written down becomes a tool for power and tries to conform people to these things that are black and white. If you have an understanding of the way to live, you don't need to write anything down."

When Floyd speaks of European society and culture, he gives the impression that a number of its central tenets puzzle him as deeply today as they did when, as a small boy, he was thrown in the deep end at mission school and instructed to sink or swim.

"As Indians," he announces, with a glint of mischief in his eyes, "we're always getting together. In our own way, we're anthropologists, studying white culture constantly and commenting on it. That's how we vent our anger. If I went around angry all the time, I'd probably have died of cancer long ago. I think that helps us to survive, along with the values of our spirituality and our culture, without getting too chewed up in the society that's chewing everybody else up. We have values that keep us out of that.

"One of the values of Indian life that's helped us to survive, often on as little as $2,000 per family per year, is that you live with fewer possessions and you live with a more spiritual sense. When you have fewer possessions, you don't get caught up in this society as a consumer. You don't get caught up in that mentality of success or 'me, me, me.' Everyone in society is driven by a kind of blindness or passion. Whether it's called success or money, that's what they're driven by and it just eats everybody up. Indians aren't really into that. When you have a spiritual way of life, like our old ways or other old ways, the spiritual teachings give you an understanding about life that doesn't cause you to be a driven person. It puts your ego in a humble place. That, to me, is one explanation of how we've been able to survive."

White society in America, as far as Floyd can see, operates on a bewilderingly counter-productive set of principles, valuing independence above community, personal freedom above family and success above happiness.

"White people have a real difficult problem," he asserts. "They're very lonely people and that's because the families break up so early. There's no longstanding connection to families. Everybody moves away from each other as soon as they can. They put their parents in the old folks' homes. What kind of longstanding connection is that? I've got all my cousins and uncles and aunts, all elders to me and all telling me things, and there are all my nephews and nieces, hundreds of them all around, and you're right in the centre of it and that's where the happiness is."

In part, he suspects, the reason for this longstanding connection is that respect for the young and for the elders is enshrined in every facet of Native American life and all life, to Native Americans, is viewed in continuity.

"Our elders remain with us, to offer advice while they're alive, and they don't go to some other place when they die," he says. "They remain here, around where they have always lived and continue to help the ones who are here. When we're in ceremonies and prayer, we're always talking to our relatives on the other side. They're right there. Many times, in and around ceremonies, we see certain things. We might see one of our relatives in one of our other relatives, a coyote or a bear, when the spirit happens at the right time. All the signs have spiritual meaning. While you're in your most secret moment, you know, your relatives are right there watching you."

So, in Native American culture, connection to family and community never ends. It evolves from one form to another but there is a constant concern and caring.

"I feel for people who don't have that sort of connection with their heritage," Floyd says, "and I always take a real concern if I run into someone I know who is that way. I think people, trying to survive in society, are very lonely because they're not connected to anyone else. It can be a lonely world, I can see. It's that loneliness that creates a big emptiness. That's why they always have to go out at night. They don't know how to live their lives in a spiritual sense, so they go out and try to fill their lives with things to do. They've got to have their toys. I think, most people, when they lose their central values in life, end up running around pointlessly.

"Of all the minority people in the United States, the Indians have the highest number, per capita, in prison. We're one half of one percent of the total population but we have the highest number in prison, the highest number of homeless in the cities. In the cities, there's a lot of homelessness but when you get back to the reservations, that's not a problem. There's a whole cultural existence that carries through in the values of life that we express. Instead of being caught up with success, we get caught up with our families and with survival. A real humanity exists in living that way.

"When I go back home, every summer, and we hold our dances and our ceremonies, that's one of the best feelings I have — when we're dancing back home, with the sound of the drum and the singing and many people dancing and the sound of children playing. When you're right in there, going around in that circle and you're standing in the midst of all your people, dancing, that's true happiness."

The New Age movement, which has grown exponentially over the last two decades, has appropriated aspects of Native American culture as part of its search for a new spirituality. It's a process which Floyd has watched sympathetically but can't condone. He believes that the impulse is right — a return to pre-Christian spiritual values — but the approach is all wrong. Plundering another people's cultural heritage, he believes, is no substitute for recovering one's own.

"Unfortunately, we run into this a lot in America," he says with a wry smile. "There are people who are not Indian but they say they're Indian. We call them the Wannabe Tribe. They wanna be Indian. They put out a book and they probably live in a commune somewhere and they come down out of the mountains with this book and two years later, they're Indian. We have a problem with that. There are people going around the country, setting up symposiums and teaching people these concepts which are Indian and they say they're theirs.

"We are very guarded about our ways but somehow, in the early nineteen hundreds, some of the inner sanctums of our religion were written down and they've been there for people who have given up on their own religions to pick up on. Christians, who have come over to a New Age vision of life, use concepts of Indian belief to create what I call a generic religion. These people are not from here. They're foreigners who try to take up a religion which really isn't theirs. Often they're people who have given up on the Christian religion and are searching. They used to have a guru in India and go there but that's too far away and too expensive, so they've found out they're right next door to the Native American spirituality.

"A lot of people are doing the sweat lodge and our fear is that it will be ten years down the road and they'll be doing sweat lodges very differently from how we do them. It would be like a cult. These people could misuse the Native American traditions and learn them in the wrong way because they don't live them. It becomes a colonial impulse. It's just another phase that colonists will go through when they find out that their ways are no good."

This is not to say that Floyd objects to Europeans sitting in on a genuine Native American sweat lodge, from time to time, in the interest of mutual

understanding. He simply believes that it would be more spiritually and culturally productive, for all concerned, if white people directed their spiritual gaze,
not towards his heritage, but back to their early European roots. If they are looking for a pre-Christian religion, he advises them to explore one of their own.

"All people had an old religion," he insists. "They should go back to their own
Celtic religion. It was very similar to ours. It revolved around the solstice moon.
It's still there and there's a growing interest in that now in America, along with
this New Age. The Celtic and Gaelic ways are coming back and that's what we
want them to do — not come to ours but go back to their own ways.

"I was speaking earlier about the fact that the tree is a relative. Well, that's
your old religion too. That's the oldest religion on earth. That's how the
Christmas tree gets in the house. Christianity wanted you to stop your old festivals but they never could get your ancestors to stop bringing the tree into the
house, so they got them to disconnect from the tree. What the Christians did
was they moved Christ's birthday. Christ was born in June but they moved his
birthday six months forward and called it Christ's mass, so it would seem more
important than the tree which your relatives were bringing into the house. It
was to sever their connection to that tree.

"It's just blatantly chopped down now, and put in the house and decorated,
but there was a time when you brought the tree into the house and danced
around it and gave water to the tree — in a sense, giving back. That was the
winter ceremony. That was December 23rd, on the solstice moon. The tree was
decorated with sacred colors. That was the early Christmas tree. You brought
offerings to the tree, not to each other. They turned it into a real capitalistic
thing, this tree thing."

WITH AGE HAS COME WISDOM. THE POLITICS OF AIM, THE CULTURAL PRACTICES
of his people and his career as an artist, as well as his roles as husband and father,
all have a common purpose for Floyd. They are the links that help to bind him
to a chain of tradition, which evolves with the experiences of the present and is
mindful of centuries of history.

On a superficial level, this perspective has helped him to conquer his personal demons, but the personal is political. Certainly, it is always so for Floyd and,
in recent years, his political work has grown to encompass, not only indigenous
issues, but the environmental cause as well. Indeed, this is how our paths first

cross: at a media function, in 1989, in the bowels of an opulent Sydney hotel, where, once again, Floyd has been called upon to explain to an audience of white folk about the importance of renewing their cultural ties with nature, with the earth, with that sacred tree.

Floyd sits on a podium with the musician Sting, the documentary filmmaker Jean-Paul Dutilleux and a Native American named Raoni from deep in the Amazon forest of Brazil. This is the final leg of the Rainforest Foundation world tour. For months now, this unlikely crew has been traveling the world, raising funds and consciousness about the plight of Raoni's people, whose traditional way of life and land are under siege from corporate and government interests. Floyd has been invited along to speak for a people who, long ago, saw Europeans invade and strip their land. He speaks slowly, measuring every word, and softly, in the deep whisper of wind through his native Black Hills.

"It was one hundred and fifty years ago," he begins, "that the gold miners came to our land and with them came the diseases — smallpox and others. Then, along came the farmers and ranchers, who took the best land and left us with the worst. Then the dam projects came in on the rivers. So everything we've faced is parallel with what Raoni is facing. In those days, there was no hope for us but in this day and age, there can be help for Raoni because we live in a society where, if that rainforest goes, so do we, and there is something we can do."

Long salt-and-pepper braids hang across his ribboned shirt. A landscape of lines is deeply etched around his lively brown eyes. He is the last to speak and, in comparatively few words, explains why he has temporarily put his AIM work aside to travel the world with this caravan of born-again greenies.

"Some people say we have to save the Indian way of life and other people say we have to save the forests," he offers. "I say, we must save the forests. While we fight for our land rights and human rights in the United States, I would put that aside because humanity is just one living species within the forest. I think the right to clean air, clean water and unpolluted land is a human right, so the understanding of all these issues is coming to one place. Every one of these issues broadens people's minds and brings us all around to the same way of thinking — that we've got to start doing something for our children and their children. I think human rights are vitally important but we've got to save the planet first. Without a planet, there is no sense in fighting for human rights."

At question time, he is asked whether he feels optimistic about the planet's future.

"I wouldn't say that," he laughs, "but I think there's a direction in which to go. There's a way to live and there's a way to die and you don't have to die this way. We're at a point where the fork in the road is right there. If we go one way, we'll destroy ourselves quickly. If we go another way, things can possibly be saved. We're right at that point. I'm optimistic that human consensus can decide on a pretty good direction and we can get together and put pressure on the corporations. I believe that human consensus works and it brings pressure on the culprits, the corporations, who mass-produce and create a waste they can't deal with. However, I'm not so sure about the corporate mentality. I'm not so sure that they'll be willing to follow up.

"The corporations just want more. They destroy one area and move on to the next. We've been on the road for months and, while eating in restaurants, at the next table there are often these big businessmen sitting around. They travel all over the world, planning the next step of destruction and they couldn't care less about what we're doing. In fact, they'd probably criticize us.

"The last strands of pure life, pure water, pure air are being attacked and if that goes, there are probably just twenty years left for society as we know it. It's going to be the end of living and the beginning of survival. When the world's out of balance and cannot support you in the right way, it's the beginning of survival. Who will survive? It's hard to say. I know Raoni and his people will have a better chance than anyone else. Perhaps the first world now will later be the last."

A tough audience of cynical media types has been lured to this event by the presence of an international celebrity and the promise of a colorful photo opportunity. As the conference closes, a rabble of reporters descends and Sting and Raoni are engulfed in a sea of flashing lights. From my perch on a table at the back of the room, I glimpse Floyd, having plainly invoked some shield of invisibility, making his way quietly through the commotion to an exit on the right. As he closes the door behind him, he turns to flash a conspiratorial smile.

The following morning, I return to the hotel. Its long, carpeted corridors are once again silent. Were it not for the occasional appearance in the dining room of a South American Indian — dressed traditionally and sporting the great protruding lip plate for which Raoni's people, the Kayapo, are known — the management might even convince itself that the Rainforest Foundation and its attendant media circus has skipped town.

I wait in the lobby for the illusive Mr Westerman who, I am told, will be just a few minutes, having recently emerged from the sauna. To tell the truth, the publicist confides, he's been approximating a sweat lodge in the sauna, with a team of inquisitive Australians, for much of the morning. Tomorrow, he will construct a more traditional sweat lodge and share the ceremony with a gathering of local Aboriginal people.

Floyd Westerman is a tall man. He greets me at the door to his room with a firm handshake, lowers himself into a comfortable chair and sits, with shoulders rounded, his elbows firmly planted on his knees.

"I have been thinking," he begins, with a furrowed brow, "about the things I've learned on this tour. It has really brought home to me the fact that we're on the doorstep of a great tragedy. I don't worry so much about myself — I feel I've lived some — but traveling throughout the world and realizing how bad the situation is, I start worrying about my children. I worry about the younger generations. What is going to happen to them? Not that I can save them from anything but how are they going to survive? It's going to be a desperate situation in ten years. It's going to be very bad and my youngest one will only be twenty-two. How are they going to survive if there's a greenhouse effect?

"These are the things I've become sensitive to. If there's so much pollution all over, what's the future going to hold? So, when I get back home, I'm going to be thinking, 'Well, I tried. I made some effort.' There's no one person who can save this earth, no one corporation, no one government, no one technology. We're all in this boat together. It's just that the river of life that we're riding down is very polluted. We're all riding that same river and what we leave behind will be difficult for generations, if there are any, to come."

This is hardly the voice of optimism, albeit guarded, from yesterday's media event. This is the voice of a man whose own message has recently begun to affect him deeply.

"I think there is a nightmare up ahead," he continues, "and we Indian people knew this more than two hundred years ago, when the USA was just starting out and the white man was wasting one piece of land and moving on to another and polluting the most sacred thing on earth — the water. It's in a critical condition right now. When children start getting cancers in such great numbers, that means something's very wrong. There's a big concern in America now about people developing strange illnesses from polluted water. That's America's demise and we're all stuck in it. America consumes 60% of the gross world product, while the rest of the world lives on the rest. America is destroying so much of the earth and so many corporations are looking the other way. All they're concerned about is profit."

If there is to be a way forward, he suggests, it will involve learning from the values of cultures like his own and Raoni's and the pre-Christian religions of Europe. He has come to believe that the contemporary search for a gratifying spirituality is far more than a personal quest. It is a vital step in laying the foundations for a sustainable society to come.

"Many of the old religions have much to do with living with the earth," he explains. "They're about having a non-profit economy, which harms the earth less, which doesn't use up the energies of the earth, which encourages us to live from energies that don't pollute. Enshrined in these religions is a set of values which address issues of living on the earth without chewing it up and destroying it. Within those values, I think, lie the answers to every one of America's problems. If we were allowed to live our way and anybody who came to our land lived our way, we would all be in a very different situation.

"It starts with a basic understanding about respect for all life. Everything stems from that. When we pray in ceremonies, we include one phrase, which is actually a prayer in itself: we say, 'for all my relations' and that means all living things. That is the basic approach to living on the earth — for all your relatives — and who you should pray for — all your relatives — and that's why we say it at the beginning and end of each ceremony.

"I think spirituality is different from religion. There are people who are following organized religion and people who live by a spirituality that goes far beyond that. My spirituality is based around the land and to desecrate the land is to heap contempt upon the creator. When people live a lifestyle that desecrates the land, they'll eventually start disappearing themselves."

WHEN NEXT I SEE FLOYD, IT IS IN THE CINEMA. I AM IN THE CINEMA, HE IS ON the screen. The role of Chief Ten Bears, I think, fits him well. He has acquired the broad perspective that only comes from a fully lived life. He has developed that rare combination of an over-arching idealism, shot through with a strong pragmatic streak. When I speak to him again, some time later, he is proud of all that *Dances With Wolves* has achieved.

"When young people saw that movie," he smiles, "a lot of them started growing their hair long. They always knew they were Indian but they didn't know what it was like back then. They saw Dances With Wolves and it instilled something in them. Each one's experience of the film might have been different but all the same, they started turning around. When you see young people growing their hair long again and going to these ceremonies and learning the language, it gives you hope and it's a generational thing. I think *Dances With Wolves* turned that generation around."

Even growing up in the comparatively enlightened 1990s, Floyd believes it is a battle for the next generation to understand the heritage into which it was born. It is a battle which his own children, ranging in age from twenty-eight right down to twenty, need not tackle alone.

"I make sure my kids have experienced the ceremonies," he says, with some pride. "They might not understand all the answers yet but they have a better understanding than I did of the whys and the whens of all this. Most of our children are learning the old language right now. We have our own schools on the reservation and we're making that a priority, so you can practice the religion with the language. They go hand in hand. That's how the language has stayed alive, through the religion."

All Native American families are not, however, as concerned with reclaiming their cultural heritage as Floyd's and he still sees young people on the streets, treading the same path that he walked back in the 1950s and early 1960s.

"It's difficult if they don't know the spiritual way of the Indian," he admits. "If they do know, there's no problem. That's why there's so much alcoholism. These young people are on the streets, drinking alcohol, because they were brought up in the city with very shallow Christian values. They look in a mirror and see an Indian but they do everything like a white man and they're treated as third-class citizens, which makes it even more confusing. There are a lot of young people who are living in San Francisco. They know they're Indian but they say they're from Oakland, California.

"As soon as they find out more about themselves and their people, their true identity comes out. Once they make the trip back to their old ways, it's like completing a circle of life for them. They know, when they start learning their own language and doing their own Indian ceremonies, that the circle is complete and everything is understandable. I think Indians are still learning. "

Floyd Westerman's struggle continues also, now often in the international arena.

He has traveled to Europe fifty-seven times to lobby heads of state and appear before United Nations committees investigating Native American treaty rights.

"I continue to travel with the human rights efforts," he explains. "After the government did not negotiate with our demands when we came out of Wounded Knee, we went to a world podium at the United Nations in Geneva, Switzerland. We took with us the solidarity of Indians from Bolivia, Guatemala, Canada and South America. We went to the Human Rights Commission and continued our efforts in a worldwide forum. So we do have recognition in the United Nations and we go there every year.

"It's a matter of being part of the struggle, seeking our sovereignty and seeking our human rights and religious rights and land rights and they all come together under our spiritual rights. So, my political work continues, even though I also do concert tours and record albums and make these movies."

After a lifetime as a singer and songwriter, Floyd has fallen into acting only recently and, he insists, quite accidentally.

"It happened this way," he says. "There was an Indian actor who was very famous. His name was Will Samson. He was the tall Indian in *One Flew Over the Cuckoo's Nest* and, at the time, he was the actor of the day. This was just before he died and he couldn't make it to a reading so he asked me to do it instead. He set up everything and it started then. So, it's just been the last ten years I've been doing that."

His other current project is the development of a television series which will document the atrocities committed against each Native American nation, one by one, since the arrival of the first Europeans.

"It will be an holocaust series," he explains. "It will show, historically, that America was involved in an holocaust in obtaining land. I want to outline how each state played an active role in the holocaust. The Jewish people, here in America, have created an holocaust museum to show the world holocaust on them. Well, in a way, it's been a world holocaust on us too. The First World War didn't begin in 1914 because, as Indians, we were fighting all of Europe. We were fighting Germans, English, Irish, Dutch, French. They were all coming here and we had to fight them all.

"At that time, the Indians were portrayed as the savages, attacking the poor settlers in covered wagons but, actually, we were being invaded and we were defending our land and our children and our way of life. That point of view is never illustrated by Hollywood. It still shows the Indians attacking in a John Wayne movie. They continue to screen those. The holocaust series would be historically accurate and would be in America's face for all time.

"It's the same story all over the world. I think an holocaust series would be good for Australia too. Nobody says anything when it comes to the taking of Aboriginal or Indian or Hawaiian lands. Even today, in Central and South America, our Indian relatives have no voice and no one to represent them. They are governed by a Spanish ruling class. In Canada, there are four and a half million Indians. They make up about a quarter of the population. There is an indigenous point of view in this world that needs to be asserted. It's part of our regaining control of our destiny."

Floyd Westerman is a man with an abundant agenda. He is a man who has lived hard but well. He maintains an extensive schedule and finds time to enjoy both his own culture and the melting pot of American life. He has accomplished more than enough, in sixty short years, for two or more people, yet the external achievements of this world are not, for him, the yard posts by which to measure a life.

"We Indians know that we're all on this earth, in this life, in this reality, for just a few winters," he adds, towards the end of our final interview. "We know that, for all time, we will be in the other reality. So, every day is getting ready for that other reality, not just living in this one. This is only temporary. If you live eighty years, that's just a few winters. I've lived sixty and I'll be lucky if I live another ten and what a short life that is. Another ten winters is short. Life is short. We tell our children, 'Don't cry, be happy, life is short.' In your youth, it's all fantasy. Then, you start surviving and it's only a short time between when you start surviving and when you go to the spirit world. We acknowledge the spirit world because that's where we go for all time and it's just a few winters off. It might be tomorrow for you or me."

Bernadette Cozart

11

IN THE GARDEN
OF THE ONE MOST HIGH

"I'M A PORTLY BLACK WOMAN WITH A PURPLE HAT," BERNADETTE EXPLAINS. "I'LL be in a white van, on 57th at Park, in ten minutes."

A diminutive blonde woman in black shorts, shirt and boots, I am arranging, on my first visit to New York, to meet a complete stranger on a street corner for an excursion into Harlem.

Bernadette is unmistakably the woman she described, limping boldly through traffic, nursing a gardening injury. She ushers me to the van where the driver has the engine running. We take the scenic route to Harlem, via New Jersey, to pick up a hibiscus and half a dozen indoor plants. On the way, she explains a little about the Greening of Harlem Coalition.

Bernadette and a troupe of volunteers make guerilla raids on asphalt playgrounds and vacant lots. Over weeks and months, as local residents become involved, rubble is carted off, paving is chipped away and gardens teeming with flowers, herbs and vegetables emerge in their place. Interestingly, when the gardeners leave, the fruits of their labor remain. The gardens continue to be tended by neighbors and explored by children but never vandalized, even in the roughest parts of town.

The van screeches to a halt at a busy intersection on 135th Street. Bernadette and I tumble out, clutching a bundle of gardening books and the hibiscus. We stop at a vendor to buy nectarines and peaches and ford a dusty river of buses, blue smoke spewing vans and long black cabs (the yellow ones don't venture this far uptown), before arriving safely at the gate of the primary school opposite. Outside the tall grey fence, concrete stretches as far as the eye can see. Behind the wire, a tiny patch of Eden is blooming.

Bernadette worked with the youngsters here to design and plant a garden playground. Their concept is a mini-Harlem, complete with a jungle gym in the center that represents the Apollo Theatre. Harlem, however, never looked this cheery. Tiny blue and pink and yellow flower faces wave in the hot summer breeze. Sturdy wooden play equipment rises out of a sea of green.

"I meet a lot of kids, working on these gardens," Bernadette begins as we peer through the fence. "This is New York City and no one has a front or back yard so nature opens up a whole new world for these kids. It's like, 'Wow, we didn't know this existed.' They might as well be on Mars."

Bernadette, beaming, points out a dozen varieties of wildflower, before turning on her good heel and bustling me, through an exodus of small dark faces, around the corner to the high school in an adjacent street.

"Interacting with nature is spiritually nurturing," she explains as we walk. "It's empowering, which is one of the reasons why, I've always felt, the patriarchy is so interested in removing so much of it from the planet. I don't think the Great Spirit — whether you want to refer to it as male or female doesn't really matter to me — made so much green for no reason. It's not natural for people to live outside of nature."

We wind our way through a maze of long, drab, dark corridors which look like those in learning institutions everywhere. They all lead, however, towards a central courtyard which appears suddenly ahead, a dazzling patch of green. This garden was sponsored by the Japanese government as a gesture of multicultural goodwill. Just twelve months ago, it was a rectangle of cement. Today, a bamboo water fountain trickles against a far wall. Ivy threatens to obscure bricks.

We sit in a wooden pagoda and listen for a while to sirens, horns, airplanes and the rustling of leaves.

"If I take away from you the knowledge of the seasons and you live on a planet that goes through them, I am disempowering you because you no longer know how to live," Bernadette continues. "If you don't know how to live, then you have to live within my constrictions and confines. It's a method of controlling people. We're all on the grid, we turn on the faucet and we get water, we flip the switch and we get light. We don't know how to live any other way. We can't get off our credit cards. We have a whole system set upon us that is based on exploitation and the subjugation of other people. It's not a necessary system. The system was set up to benefit a very few and to keep control.

"I think you set up a psychosis in personalities that way, keeping people under the thumb and divorced from nature. All the man-made asphalt, concrete, glass and steel is a real terror. It's cold, hard, unnatural, unfeeling. It makes people cold, hard, unnatural, unfeeling — it does. What effect do you get from people sitting in a garden? Quite different."

Bernadette's itinerant work on vacant lots has, over the years, led to grudging official acceptance, to the point where she is now furnished with a council wage. She has helped create gardens with young women at the School for Pregnant and Parenting Teens, with prisoners on work release, with drug addicts in rehab, with AIDS patients, senior citizens and the mentally and emotionally ill. A good deal of her work, these days, involves helping students transform the asphalt deserts in neighborhood schools. She couldn't be happier.

"I see such changes in the kids, from itty-bitty ones to teenagers," she smiles broadly, rummaging through her bag for a peach. "It brings out their more nurturing, more calming, more healing side. The biggest deal, for them, is to find out that they are part of nature. There's this wonderful, beautiful universe which they discover. You should see them when they find out that they're affiliated with something so grand. It cannot help but make them feel better about themselves. It's a gift to watch them interact with nature and to teach them basic gardening in an area, like Harlem, where everything is beat up and run down and generally not beautiful. Taking over a vacant lot and watching it change gives them hope. It's the power of transformation and that power of transformation also raises their self-esteem. The greatest thing you can give a child is self-esteem: 'If I can take this awful, trash-ridden lot and change it into this lovely little oasis, what in my life can I not change?' That's the important part.

"Another thing about working with kids, in this urban setting, is that I see daily what gardening does for them, in terms of respect for life. They certainly aren't going to get that from the mass media culture of ours, nor, unfortunately, from many other aspects of their lives. By working with nature, following nature, even worshipping nature, you automatically develop a respect for life because what is nature but life?

"Putting them in this situation and giving them the 'R' word — responsibility — makes an enormous difference, particularly to young males. This plant is a living, breathing thing. It hurts just like you hurt, it can get sick just like you can get sick. This is not your basketball. You can't throw it in the corner when you get tired of it. You, now, are in the responsible position of doing for it everything your mother has done for you. You're going to have to feed it, protect it, take care of it.

"Of course, at first, because the machismo is there, they don't want me to see them doing this, but some of these guys do things like showing up an hour early to work and staying an hour late, just to make sure their personal little plot is the best. Then they go 'dis' the other guy. I'm always very careful not to laugh."

Bernadette is a true believer in nature as a political tool and a spiritual elixir. Hers is as much a liberation theology as Desmond Tutu's, though it springs from pagan wells.

"It's something very simple, yet the power of it is profound," she says. "It even makes a difference to how the kids interacted with each other. They're more respectful to each other, kinder, more caring. So, I get a chance, every day, to understand how powerful the effects of the environment are, in terms of the psyche and human development.

"Here's a group of kids growing up in a neighborhood that is just shot to hell. What's the message being sent out here? This is psychological warfare. You can't say it's not. We're talking about conditions which replicate themselves from one coast to the other in every major urban area across this country. If you've ever been to Harlem — you know what? — you've been to Watts, you've been to Woodward Avenue in Detroit, you've been to the south side of Chicago, you've been to Brixton in London and probably some place in Sydney too. You don't have to do all that traveling. It's global. All over the world, it's the same thing."

A young guy careers by with a basketball and stops to say hi.

"The most important thing I tell my kids is that you should be the best you that you can be," Bernadette grins. "Don't be somebody else or someone else's idea of who you are. Be the best 'you' that you can be. The essential thing, I always tell them, is to save yourself. What's the first law of nature? Self-preservation. The best thing any of us can do is to honestly and openly — without any shenanigans — seek out our one true path. That is one of the strongest things you can do, not just for yourself but for the planet as a whole, and many people are blocked from that."

Bernadette's kids are less blocked than many around here. She watches for the changes in the way they hold themselves, the way they speak, the way they band together when one of her gardens is under threat. She wants them to follow their dreams in much the same way she followed hers against the odds and came out trumps.

IF EVER THERE WAS A VOCATION, GARDENING WAS BERNADETTE'S. GROWING UP in a small town in the Mid-West, she was never encouraged to take up the rake and shovel but she was unstoppable. Inspired by an aunt — the only independent woman she knew — who was a florist, she was never happier than when a seed she'd planted showed the first signs of growth. Flowers and trees and earth and insects were her life and she struggled to make them her career. She studied, worked in private gardens and, most recently, in New York's sprawling Central Park, before founding the Greening of Harlem Coalition in 1989.

It began when she was commissioned to create a garden for Harlem Hospital and, instead of doing all the work herself, she decided to enlist the support of the community. The first park the Coalition tackled was Colonel Charles Young Park, on the corner of 143rd Street and Lennox Avenue. Onlookers thought they were crazy. "People felt like you needed an Uzi [gun] just to walk in there," Bernadette laughs. Vacant buildings in the neighborhood had become crack houses and brothels and the park was littered with syringes, vials and broken glass. The Coalition was, however, undaunted. They marched in and started carting off trash. It wasn't long before inquisitive neighbors joined the effort and now, the park's African Garden is ablaze with five and a half thousand tulips.

"Every time we reclaim a space," Bernadette explains, "the negative elements just pack up and leave." That's partly the power of cooperation but it's also a sign that Mother Nature is at work. Gardening is Bernadette's profession and her recreation. It is also her spiritual path. When a bunch of people come together to honor nature, she believes, little miracles start happening around them.

"Much of what I know, or think I know, comes from interacting with nature. Mostly it's listening to that voice," she confides, having asked that we refrain from discussing spiritual matters until we're well out of earshot because "a lot of people think this side of my work is nuts".

"Nature is the greatest teacher there is. My spiritual nourishment comes from observing her in all her glory, from watching waves wash upon a shore to working in the garden to discovering the wonders of the animal kingdom to beholding a storm. My favorite things are thunderstorms.

"I'm not saying that's for everybody. I don't think it is. The old saying, 'There are many roads that lead to the center,' is true. Everyone's path is not the same, everyone's teachers are not the same and everyone does not need, necessarily, to be taught the same lessons.

"Nonetheless, a spirituality centered in nature is a spirituality that says everybody is valuable. Your neighbor is valuable, as well as yourself. Everything is glorious, no matter who or what it is. Everybody is a star. Is there not a place for everything in nature? We have arid lands, we have lush and green tropical lands, we have lands with temperate climates such as this, we have frozen waste to the north and all of it is valuable. We have more species of plants, animals and micro-organisms than we will ever have life breath to count. It's all necessary and it's all connected and it's all valuable to the whole. This is the type of society I'm talking about and this is the type of spirituality I'm talking about.

"The pre-Christian Mother religions knew all this. They were based on nature. Nature is plentiful. She is abundance. She's all inclusive. The stratified, classified system of the patriarchy doesn't exist in nature. Only the people under the patriarchy are running around thinking this group is better than that group. If you ask the Mother, the chrysanthemum's not mightier than a rose. They're equal."

Which brings us to one of Bernadette's favorite topics.

"I've noticed, over the years," she says, "that nature is often referred to as something wild and feral and needing to be controlled and conquered, which is the same label that's always slapped on women. Women and the earth are the same to me, particularly in terms of the things that have been stolen from us."

Bernadette spent her childhood in a poor, God-fearing community, confronted by symbols of inequity at every turn. There, she began to identify the culprits in this robbery and their victims. Not yet in her teens, she remembers deciding that a life like her mother's and the neighborhood women's was not for her.

"I saw marriage and childbearing as a way of controlling a lot of your energy, resources and time," she says, "because these weren't necessarily being offered as paths of choice. They were more like control.

"I made up my mind that I was not going to be defined by outside forces. There would be no traditional women's roles. I wasn't going to do what women do — forget it. I would seek and find that voice that, in so many women, is stomped out by the time they're seven. I would hold onto it and I would hear my own voice and I would follow it."

This voice of Bernadette's encouraged an interest in spirituality. She was raised in a church-going family and never doubted that a sense of spirit was vital to a full and purposeful life. The challenge, however, was to find a religious framework against which her moral fiber would not rile.

"Growing up in an oppressed community," Bernadette recalls, "and looking at the role of the church there, what I saw, again and again, was men in positions of authority and power and control and women doing all the work, really all the necessary work, to keep the churches going. To this day, nothing has changed. The women get very little, if anything, in return for their work and all the positions of power and prestige go to males.

"Too many times, particularly in poor areas, I would see the controlling factors of these churches — ministers with fancy cars, dressed to the nines — and where was the money coming from? The money was coming from the sweat and labor of women, who were making their fifty-four cents to the dollar that a man made, if they were indeed working at all. I thought about the positive impact that many of the churches should have had on the community and it wasn't happening. It was cosmetic and I think it's even worse now than it was twenty or thirty years ago. It's almost all show."

With the advent of the women's movement in the late 1960s, Bernadette began to think more deeply about the nature of oppression in the church. She read voraciously, she listened to the stories of other women and her worst suspicions were confirmed.

"I started to think about the effect it must have on a young girl to be told that she's a second-class citizen. We're looking at psychological warfare again because, if you're in church and you're a little kid, the person who's standing there in the pulpit, as far as you're concerned, is God. If he tells you you're a second-class citizen by virtue of being a female, just think about the impact that's going to have.

"In most of the world's religions, I notice, women fall into two categories. The first claims we are in a natural state of grace and, because Scripture says that in order to be in that state, one must become as a child, women are therefore child-like and need to be looked after. The second says that women are the cause of all the problems — you know, Eve, the apple, the serpent — and are inherently wicked and therefore need to be, particularly sexually, watched out for. Take your pick, either way you're in jail. It does not matter whether one is in *purdah*, concealed behind a thousand veils, or whether one is simply restricted in what and whom one can be in life. Where is the difference and what is the damage of hearing this from the highest authority you know?"

The damage, she quickly realized, was inestimable and, while her friends laugh at her ability to see conspiracies at every turn, Bernadette does not feel it in the least far fetched to assert that organized religion has been used, consciously and effectively, to oppress the laity.

"What you're up against," she insists, "is what the old left meant when they said, 'religion is an opiate of the masses' and it's used to control. That's the difference between religion and spirituality. It's a big difference because one is about empowerment and the other is about enslavement. Religion, as it is taught in this country, is pure dogma and it's about controlling people, controlling people's thoughts. It has nothing to do with empowering people.

"The church makes mental zombies of people. How? Through guilt and fear. Think about it. 'You were born in sin, you are unworthy of salvation, you will be damned, you will be burned, let me destroy your entire self-esteem here.' Of course, you will carry guilt and fear. On a spiritual plane, what does this do? Let's get down to the meat and bones of it. First of all, you have to understand those two emotions. Guilt is the slayer of the heart and fear is the slayer of the mind. If you get someone in both those places, you have created a living zombie. It's no wonder so many of us are members of the walking wounded.

"The best protection is always to look at what they vilify. If they tell you to look left, you'd better turn your head right. It's that simple. You'll be surprised at what you'll find and a lot of it, you have to make a conscious effort not to see."

BERNADETTE TOOK HER OWN ADVICE. AS FEMINISM MARCHED INTO THE 1970S, ITS focus expanded from contemporary issues to include a reassessment of history. Landmark feminist works on pre-history, and archeology were published. Merlin

Stone's *When God Was a Woman* (1976) and Marija Gimbutas' *The Goddesses and Gods of Old Europe* (1974) appeared in book stores, along with a range of investigations into the witch hunts of the sixteenth century. Plainly, this was a direction in which the church had not intended she go looking, so Bernadette devoured each new book with glee.

Her reading on the witch hunts led her to conclude that such carnage could only be the result of a deliberate attempt to oppress something which had resisted less violent means. Her reading on excavations of sites dating back to the Neolithic and even Upper Paleolithic periods began to hint at what that something might have been.

Bernadette became interested in Minoan civilisation, so named for the spectacular Palace of Minos at Knossos (1600-1400 BC) on the island of Crete. Historians had written extensively about Minoan culture for thousands of years but it was not until the latter part of this century that anyone noticed one startling and crucial point: in Minoan civilisation, there appears to have been absolute equality between women and men.

The Minoans developed what we would consider an advanced society with a high standard of living. They created the first paved roads in Europe, extensive viaducts, unheard of feats of indoor plumbing and civic amenities the likes of which would not be seen anywhere else in the world for many hundreds of years. Minoan society also placed unique emphasis on public welfare. Artwork of the time shows women in high public positions and the Minoans' religious faith centered around a female deity, representing the creative force of nature.

Ironically, this pinnacle of Bronze Age civilisation was probably destroyed by earthquakes and tidal waves but it is now commonly believed to have been the last bastion of pre-patriarchal societies which were widespread on earth from as far back as 25,000 BC

These societies — signs of which have been found from Malta to Mesopotamia, from Russia to the British Isles and in pockets throughout Asia — have been identified by a number of common factors. Archeologists, noticing little difference in status between dwellings and graves, believe they had egalitarian social structures, with little discrimination on the basis of class or sex. An absence of battle motifs in art and architecture and a lack of any hard archeological evidence (weapons, armor, fortifications and so on) to the contrary has led many scholars to conclude that these societies were also predominantly peaceful. Finally, there is a prevalence of female imagery in sculptures, paintings and architectural remains, and many of these appear to be dedicated to a goddess of nature.

These societies are thought to have been matrifocal, rather than matriarchal. There is no evidence to suggest that men were oppressed in these cultures in the same way that women have been oppressed by a patriarchal world view and an exclusively male vision of the divine. The old religion of the Goddess appears to have been inclusive, rather than exclusive. As Bernadette would say, "The chrysanthemum was not mightier than the rose." The old religion appears to have honored the processes of life and nature, including fertility, sexuality, birth, health, frailty and death. Remnants of it can still be found in the Wiccan faith which has survived in European civilisation up to the present day.

Here, at last, Bernadette found hints of a spirituality she could call her own — a spirituality which was life-honouring, rather than life-denying and which, as far as she could tell, had seen the world through many thousands of years of comparative social justice and peace. It was also a spirituality which fitted in nicely with her work in the garden.

"I frankly believe that it was a woman who discovered farming," she asserts. "You see, some of the characteristics for which women are noted are patience and endurance. Nature does not give up her secrets readily. You must earn them. It's about watching. Being a gardener, I guess I have an insight into that. A friend of mine once said that gardening is eighty percent observation, and he's right. There's no such thing as a good gardener who is not observant. It takes patience. You're talking about going through the seasons and it takes a good ten years before you know what the hell you're doing.

"I would say most women have a good deal of patience. I always figure that some woman, watching a spider spin a web, figured out how to weave. It's that darn simple. Watching a bird build a nest, another woman figured out how to make a basket. Carpentry is similar to a beaver building a dam. There are limitless lessons that can be taught to the human race by nature. Nature is the first and foremost teacher. The secret to living an abundant and well life is to get into the flow. The universe is a river. It's a wonderful cosmic river and, when one is in that flow, things go well. When one is not, that's when you have problems. In many cases, I feel, people have been pushed out of that flow from birth, they've been taught wrong. That's the cause of much misery and unhappiness on the planet and it's perpetrated by those who would like to control everything, including nature."

The pre-patriarchal societies about which Bernadette read were overrun by invaders who came from the far north of Europe and the far south, beyond Mesopotamia. They brought with them an early patriarchal warrior culture and their predominantly male gods. These tribes, Bernadette now believes, began the slow march towards the exploitation of women and nature which was to become the dominant cultural pattern throughout the world. The small pockets of woman-centered, earth-honoring spirituality which remained were ruthlessly wiped out. With the advent of Christianity, despite hopeful beginnings, the persecution accelerated, culminating in the witch hunts of the sixteenth century and, Bernadette believes, the similarly motivated African slave trade.

"I had looked everywhere," Bernadette resumes. "I had looked into all the branches of Christianity I could think of. Then I began to turn my gaze farther afield. I started with the big four — Buddhism, Islam, Hinduism, Judaism — but always that face was missing. Wherever I turned, I felt that void. Then, I began to learn about the old religions of the Goddess and, for the first time, I looked into the face of the One Most High and saw my own face reflected there.

"I can look in a mirror and see the face of Yemaja looking back at me. I can see Kwan Yin. I can see all these faces and it makes a difference. I feel like I am one with something far greater than myself and I am one with many and I feel that, quite frankly, I am being led. I do. I think she does look down at me and she takes very good care of me — far better than I'd do on my own. I don't believe in luck and I don't believe in coincidences. I have had some phenomenal things happen in my life that are just like, 'I can't believe this is happening.' Opportunities have been orchestrated, obstacles moved out of my way and blessings given to me."

The energy, the sense of freedom, power and support that overwhelmed her when she saw that reflection gave Bernadette her first sure understanding of why the old religions had been crushed, why witches had been burned at the stake and why relatively egalitarian societies, like some of those in Africa and Native America, had been driven into slavery and starvation.

"In recent years," Bernadette explains, "we've discovered a great deal about women's true history. Now we've taken another step. We're examining women's hidden role in spirituality and that's going to be the big one.

"Our cultures have been taken away from us. Patriarchy co-opted the old religions to a grand extent. The whole Judeo-Christian thing is primarily other people's ideas, turned around to suit these guys' particular prejudices and needs. Our power has been taken from us, our culture has been taken from us, even our space has been taken from us. Remember that famous essay by Virginia Woolf, *A Room of One's Own*. Many sites around the world, sacred to women, were co-opted by the church. That's no accident. Women combining together has always been looked upon as a grand threat to the patriarchy. There's much done to keep women apart, to keep women from banding together. Why is this? It's because of the power and the strength of women when they are banded together. Women naturally bond. We can't help ourselves, can't stop ourselves from doing it. The only way to stop this patriarchal nonsense from perpetuating itself is for women to come together, reclaim that space and get to know who we are spiritually."

LET'S TRACK BACK A FEW YEARS TO A WARM NEW YORK MORNING IN MAY, 1991. Spring is a frantic time in Bernadette's gardens. Children bustle from plot to plot, in preparation for the summer holidays and Bernadette has her hands full supervising and planting in dozens of lots which all demand her attention at once. On this particular morning, however, she had left her gardening gloves behind and was making her way downtown to the swanky Waldorf Astoria for breakfast. A friend of hers, Helen Hunt, a wealthy Texan business woman, had asked her to address a women's conference about her work. With the workload in the gardens, she was tempted to decline but Helen had helped her out from time to time and besides, says Bernadette, "she was one of the very first people I talked to who didn't think I was totally nuts and I was impressed by that."

"There was no way I was going to tell her no but I was also on roller skates. I didn't prepare what I was going to say and I found myself standing up, looking at sixteen hundred women who were dedicated to the betterment of women all over the world. It was a wonderful sight and a great audience to find yourself talking to but, without a speech, a little nerve-racking."

Undeterred, Bernadette launched into an impromptu address which had such an impact that many of those women remember it to this day.

"I said, 'My subject is going to be the Great Goddess,' and my opening statement to them was that, if they could not look in the mirror and see the face of the One Most High in their own reflection, they would never know power. That was the opening statement. Needless to say, it got very quiet but I went on to tell them that, if they looked in a mirror and could not see Yemaja, if they could not see Bridget, if they could not see Kwan Yin, if they could not see the One Most High, the most powerful aspect of the universe in themselves, they could never truly value themselves. How could they? Then, if they looked in that mirror and saw Lilith or any other goddess who has been maligned, I told them that they shouldn't be upset because we strong women get a bad rap."

This was the first time Bernadette had gone public with her beliefs and she is still, as I mentioned, wary of who she speaks to about them and when. Perhaps that's because language is not her preferred medium of expression. Like nature, Bernadette speaks most profoundly through her gardens and, through her plans for a Goddess Garden in the middle of Harlem, she speaks most powerfully and intimately of all.

"At the present time, I have three possible sites," she begins, "and I want the garden to be constructed by women as much as possible. The garden is going to be divided into four parts, which represent the four seasons and the four directions. In the center, another garden will represent the three faces of the Mother and there will also be a nine-by-nine, round reflecting pool, with the twenty-eight faces of the moon moving around it. The garden is designed to be viewed at night, with the moon and all white flowers.

"In the southern quadrant, there will be a very large cauldron. The south, of course, is the warrior face of the Mother, which deals with the will. In the north, we want to put a cave. We want to actually construct a cave and embed it with crystals. The northern face of the Mother deals with productivity and the Mother's ability to manifest. The western face of the Mother deals with, amongst other things, adolescence and insanity, with emotions and the heart, and it's the face of the Mother from which she can tell you the secrets of your heart and the secrets of others' hearts as well. In the west, we're going to create a waterfall. Then, in the east, I am going to hang huge chimes. The east is illumination and wisdom and intelligence. There will be plants to correspond with each quadrant.

"Other works we've been talking about include a wall of heroines and statuettes representing female deities. There will also be spaces for different cultures from around the world. It's important that something like this is done for women by women and, personally, I hope it takes off and that there'll be goddess gardens all over."

When Bernadette mentions the Goddess, she is not merely transposing female imagery onto a male notion of God, nor is she speaking purely in terms of psychological archetypes. Just as the old matrifocal societies were fundamentally different from the world we know today, so Bernadette's Goddess is sufficiently different from our male gods to recreate civilisation anew.

"I'm thinking about something that is a living, breathing force throughout the cosmos," she explains. "I'm talking about something very real and tangible that is female in nature and she is real. She's waiting for us — her daughters and her sons because she has sons as well as daughters.

"When I talk about the Mother and I talk about the patriarchy, I want to be real clear because I know there are a lot of women who don't think the way I do. I am not talking about recreating the hamburger machine. I don't want a new machine that says that women are everything and men are nothing.

"I liken the patriarchy to a runaway, hell-bound train, with a lunatic as a conductor. The conductor, if you were to take a global poll, would probably be an American, straight, white, male millionaire. My idea of stopping this hell-bound train is not just to change the conductor. I don't think you've done anything if you decide, 'Well, we're progressive because now the conductor is a woman or the conductor is Black or Latin or Asian or Native.' My objective is to wreck the train. It's totally different. Look at this hell-bound train and all the misery that it brings and has brought around the globe. This train has killed countless millions of people through the witch hunts and the holocaust and so forth. I'm not about recreating this train. I'm about destroying it."

Guys, breathe a sigh of relief. Bernadette's brand of spiritual feminism will take no prisoners. After the revolution, as in her vision of pre-patriarchal Europe, life will be a whole lot sweeter for all of us.

"There's a big difference," says Bernadette, "between a man who is comfortable with his mother side and one who is not in touch with it at all, who's in fear of it or suppresses it. We all run into the patriarchal one but, if you ever run into the other one, it's immediately obvious. Even if a woman is not woman-centered enough to be able to name it, she can feel it nonetheless. A lot of men are sincerely, actively seeking this aspect of themselves because the patriarchy destroys quality of life for everybody.

"When I talk about the Goddess, I'm thinking of a balanced, whole force and I believe there's an aspect of the Mother that is male. I really do.

"How maleness is defined by the Mother and how maleness is defined by the patriarchy are, however, two different things. People are both male and female.

I don't mean that in terms of sexual orientation. I mean it in terms of spiritual and mental orientation. We're both and it's just as important for a man to be able to raise his nurturing side as it is for a woman to be able to raise her warrior, because you're out of bounds if you can't. The old teachings recognized this. In human beings, it's important for female and male to be in harmony with each other, not striving for dominance over one another. That's like the left hand trying to fight with the right hand.

"A man is just as much hamburger as a woman. Look at all the wars that have been fought, the arms and legs and eyesight that have been lost. Look at all the forms of human degradation and misery inflicted upon men. They also are not allowed to express all the sides of themselves. We're human beings first, not just male or female, black or white. You're never, under the patriarchy, going to be allowed to express yourself as a human being. That's what I'm saying."

Men are not the problem. Maleness is not even the problem, according to Bernadette. "The world is out of balance," she says. That is the problem. "The yin and the yang are just not there."

The Maiden, Mother and the Crone spoke of birth, the fullness of life, death and transformation. Their rituals celebrated the sacredness of nature and of a full, corporeal, creative, human life. The female form, which brings forth new life, was an obvious symbol and an obvious image for the divine.

Then, the needle spun from pole to pole. The Father, Son and Holy Spirit spoke of birth, the suffering of life, death and transformation. In Asia, this world was *maya* [illusion]. In Europe, it was wrought with temptation, debasement and sin. The aim was no longer to immerse oneself in life's currents but to resist them. The female form, which brings forth new life, became an obvious symbol of evil.

"The more nurturing, loving face of the One Most High," says Bernadette, "is no longer with us." As half of the world has been disenfranchised, so half of the face of the divine has been cast aside. In thirty thousand years, if some future civilisation stumbles upon our relics, they will find the remains of graves and dwellings which indicate a society in which there was an enormous gulf between female and male, rich and poor, black and white, Native, Latin and Asian. What else will they find? Plutonium, amassed weaponry, one hell of a lot of plastic, phallic towers reaching hundreds of feet into the sky and temples and shrines containing predominantly male figures, many of them suffering, perhaps representing a god who lived in the sky.

"If you look at people around the world," says Bernadette, "their needs, their wants, their desires really do not change. I don't care what language they're speaking, what religion they practise, the color of their skin, the continent they're living on, the food they eat. It really doesn't change when you get down to that bottom line.

"So what are all these little false divisions that have been put upon the world for the last six thousand years? What's this about? Why do we have nation against nation and, in fact, war in the middle of the home at this point? A friend of mine used to say, 'Always follow the money trail.' Well, it's true. Who benefits? Most people on the planet really want to live a useful, productive, happy existence.

"Most people are not greedy. They want to be comfortable. They don't need forty-two cars, six Olympic-size swimming pools and a Lear jet. They want to live in peace. They don't want to live in fear of their neighbors or have their neighbors living in fear of them. They want their children to be well and healthy and have decent opportunities. You start listening and you realize that everybody actually thinks this way, no matter who they are or where they're at. So, why can't this be and what are the forces that are getting in between everybody's happiness here?"

The money trail, according to Bernadette, mostly leads to the conductors on the train — the ideological descendants of those ruffian invaders from the north.

"However, they're on the way out," Bernadette adds. "I hope, I believe, change is in the air and we will recover a sense of balance."

I too am given a hint, just three weeks later, that goddess gardens might well "spring up all over" and that Bernadette's grand historical saga could play its way to a happy ending.

IT IS LESS THAN A MONTH SINCE I SHARED A PEACH WITH BERNADETTE IN A PAGODA in the middle of Harlem. It is natural that I should think of her as I stand in a circle of a dozen eccentrically dressed women, holding onto a velvet ribbon and humming.

Ruth had decided on a goddess party and, in the absence of a goddess garden in Sydney, had gathered her favorite female friends in her apartment. Each dressed as a goddess (from screen stars to the denizens of Olympus), each brought a plate of goddess food (from ambrosia to liquorice candy) and each arrived with a poem, a painting or a ritual to share.

216

A more secular lot you couldn't hope to find, yet we now hum our way through the seventh chakra, giddy with energy and red wine, while Amy-Jane reads from an ancient Celtic chant. Tonight we have painted a giant tree of life on a wall in Ruth's study, we have read tarot, gazed into crystal balls and played "goddess pass the parcel". We have also learned that all of us, in our quietest moments and since we were very small, have created an cherished and image that is both female and divine.

Tenzin Gyatso, the fourteenth Dalai Lama

12

TO LIGHT THE MIDDLE WAY

For as long as space endures
And for as long as living beings remain,
Until then may I, too,
Abide to dispel the misery in this world.
"THE BODHISATTVA'S WAY OF LIFE," SHANTIDEVA

EACH DAY DAWNS MUCH LIKE ANOTHER IN TAKTSER, A TINY RURAL VILLAGE IN Amdo, on the north-eastern frontier of Tibet. The sun creeps above the horizon, turning the snowy peak of Mount Ami-chiri to gold. Clumps of junipers, poplars, fruit, and nut trees cast long shadows and deer venture above the treeline, onto alpine pastures, to graze.

In a nearby monastery, beneath a broad green and gold roof, monks sit in quiet meditation. In the valley, butter lamps have already been lit in family shrines, smoke spirals skywards from cooking fires, children laugh and squeal, bounding into cold morning air and men feed and water livestock, before returning indoors for a breakfast of barley meal and hot butter tea.

On this particular morning, Lhamo Thondup picks up his wooden bowl and, hugging it tight in the folds of his jacket, runs on his tiny, two year old legs to the stable, where his mother is milking the *dzomos* — gentle, doe-eyed creatures, part cow, part yak. Lhamo Thondup lifts his bowl, with a mischievous grin, and his mother fills it with warm milk, which he gulps down before running outside to play.

The sun has risen higher now, catching the turquoise tiles on the roof and filtering softly into the courtyard. The little boy wanders inside, where he begins his favourite game of wrapping up parcels then marching purposefully to the front gate, as if setting out on a long adventure. Already, he dreams of traveling to the great Tibetan capital of Lhasa. He imagines the Potala, winter palace of the Dalai Lamas and seat of government, with its white walls towering above the city and its roofs all shiny gold. He imagines rippling seas of burgundy and yellow, when monks gather to chant in its vast halls. He imagines the bustling life of the marketplace below.

Lhamo Thondup gathers up his parcels and perches himself on the side of a hill, from where he can see the men and women of the village working in the fields. He has not been watching them long when he notices a band of traders making its way along the winding path that leads to his home.

By the time Lhamo Thondup arrives breathless at the door, the travelers have been welcomed by his parents and are preparing their tea in the kitchen. He spies the travelers' servant, on his way to join his masters, and the little boy follows close behind. When the servant takes a seat, Lhamo Thondup climbs onto his knee and immediately begins to play with a string of beads hanging from the stranger's neck.

"You can have the beads if you tell me who I am," the stranger smiles.

"You are a lama from Sera," the boy replies, quite confident, despite the fact that this man is not dressed as a monk. To clinch the deal, Lhamo Thondup goes on to name two more members of the party.

The travelers spend the night with the boy's family and when they rise before daybreak to continue their journey, Lhamo Thondup is already waiting for them, begging to be taken to Lhasa. Only the promise that they will soon return can quiet him.

When they do return, as promised, several months later, the party of travelers has grown and the servant, to whom the boy had shown such affection, is dressed in the robes of a lama from the renowned Sera monastery near Lhasa. The beads he had worn around his neck, it soon transpires, had once belonged to the thirteenth Dalai Lama, whose reincarnation this team of monks and high officials is seeking.

They are following a trail of clues which have led them unerringly to this peasant family in Taktser. Soon after the thirteenth Dalai Lama's death, a series of unusual cloud formations, shot through with rainbows, began to hover north-east of Lhasa. The Dalai Lama's body was seated ceremonially, facing south, in his chamber. One day, a group of monks arrived to find that his head had mysteriously turned to the north-east. At the same time, a giant star-shaped fungus grew on the north-east wall, towards which the Dalai Lama's corpse now appeared to be gazing. Following that gaze further, over vast plateaus and mountain ranges, the monks finally arrived at Taktser.

There had been further clues: a vision, seen in the sacred lake, Lhamo Latso, of a tiny village in a secluded valley; a vision of a farm house with a roof fringed by turquoise tiles; a vision of a monastery with gold and green about its eaves. There were those who remembered also that the thirteenth Dalai Lama had once stopped, on a pilgrimage, in a field near Lhamo Thondup's family home and had left a pair of his old boots there — a sure sign, in local superstition, that the ruler would one day return.

So the monks spend another day with Lhamo Thondup. They have brought with them two identical black rosaries. The boy chooses the one which belonged to the thirteenth Dalai Lama and quickly strings it about his neck. The same test is repeated with two yellow sets of beads. They offer him two drums — one large and ornate, one small and plain. The boy chooses the smaller one, which also belonged to the Dalai Lama, and begins to beat it in the traditional Buddhist manner. He is offered two walking sticks. At this, he hesitates, before finally selecting the correct one. Only much later do the monks discover that both sticks, at one time, belonged to the thirteenth Dalai Lama. One he had given away and the other he had kept with him until the day he died. Finally, a physical examination of the boy uncovers the eight distinctive signs which mark all Dalai Lamas as incarnations of Chenrezig, Buddha of compassion.

By now, of course, Lhamo Thondup's initially baffled parents realise that their son has been selected as the next embodiment of one of the great Tibetan lamas but not for a moment do they imagine they might be living alongside the Dalai Lama himself.

After months of wrangling with local Chinese officials, the emissaries are eventually granted permission to take their young charge, his parents and two of his brothers with them to Lhasa.

In the autumn of 1939, three years after the search party set out, it returns in a grand procession, with the four year old child on a gilded palanquin. At a ceremony the following February, Lhamo Thondup is enthroned as the four-teenth Dalai Lama and receives a new name, Tenzin Gyatso, Ocean of Wisdom.

I READ THIS STORY WHEN I WAS TEN YEARS OLD. MY MOTHER HAD HIS HOLINESS' memoirs in paperback. It was one of those well-thumbed books, with musty smelling pages that fell out and scattered on the floor if you didn't hold it just the right way. My mother also had Heinrich Harrer's *Seven Years in Tibet* — she'd read it in her late teens — so Tibetophilia was hereditary in our household.

While other young girls dreamed of traveling to London or New York, I lay in bed at night and imagined crossing the high passes of the Himalayas. The story of Tibet was part fairy tale, part tragedy. I marveled at the mysterious feats of ancient hermits and great monks. I rode in archery contests, in the summer, on the banks of the Kyichu river. I strolled with the young ruler through the exotic gardens of the Norbulingka, his summer palace. Yet, always, I was aware that the Tibet of which I read existed now only in memories and books.

THE SUN RISES OVER THE POTALA, CATCHING THE ORNAMENTS ON ITS GREAT ROOF and streaming into the Barkor marketplace below. One of the few great Buddhist monuments that remains intact in Tibet today, the winter palace still stands high above the city of Lhasa, a constant reminder of days of greater freedom, when Tibetan sovereignty seemed almost unassailable.

Those days were more than forty-five years ago but the older people remember them clearly and the younger ones cherish myths and stories, passed on by parents and grandparents. Some among the crowd, now filling the marketplace in the early morning light, look up at the Potala and offer silent prayers for the long life of the Dalai Lama, still hoping, after forty-five years of Chinese occupation, that their one-time ruler — spiritual and temporal — will some day secure their freedom and return.

At just sixteen, Tenzin Gyatso had the full responsibilities of a head of government thrust upon him, when the parliament in Lhasa found it could no longer keep the peace between the Chinese invading forces and the Tibetan people.

Both the Dalai Lama and the local government saw that it was futile for their tiny population to meet the might of the Chinese military with force. The young ruler appealed to the international community for assistance. None came. He embarked on a course of negotiation but as successive treaties were broken and the Tibetan people grew more resentful of the occupying army, the threat of guerilla warfare and bloody Chinese reprisals loomed large.

In these days of pro-active international relations, it is difficult to believe that, in 1950, when the People's Liberation Army began its invasion of Tibet, there was barely a whimper of protest from the world beyond. In 1959, the Tibetan people rose up against the occupying Chinese forces. The rebellion was extinguished violently and the Dalai Lama fled to India. Many of his people followed close behind him.

The Indian government permitted him to set up a government in exile at the northern hill station of Dharamsala, in Himachal Pradesh. Since then, more than one hundred thousand Tibetans have crossed icy Himalayan passes to join His Holiness' battle for freedom in his homeland and to help him reestablish Tibetan culture in the outside world.

The uprising and its immediate aftermath saw eighty-seven thousand Tibetans die in the defence of their nation's freedom but still there was hardly a word of protest from the world beyond. Since that time, an estimated 1.2 million Tibetans (one-sixth of the total population) have died at the hands of the Chinese military or as a result of imprisonment or starvation. The Russian author, Aleksandr Solzhenitsyn, has described the Chinese administration of Tibet as "more brutal and inhumane than any other communist regime in the world".

Tibet has seen the sacking and destruction of more than six thousand of its once magnificent monasteries and temples, its children have been sent to China for corrective education, there has been compulsory sterilisation and abortion, and restrictions on teaching the Tibetan language in schools have been imposed. Tibetan history has been rewritten, its borders have been redrawn and more than seven million Chinese have been settled in the region, so that Tibetans now form a minority in their own land.

The Tibetan people have been subjected to one of the most violent instances of genocide this century has seen. Even the Dalai Lama, who is characteristically slow to pass judgment, admits that there is no other term to adequately describe the systematic oppression of his people.

"The Chinese say that Tibet lacks human resources," he offers, quizzically. "This is how they justify the enormous population transfer of Chinese. Yet, at the same time, they carry out very strict birth control, forced abortion and sterilisation amongst the Tibetan community. What else can this be but a deliberate measure?

Some of my friends have described it as a 'final solution' by the Chinese.

"It is not like Nazi Germany, where the government admitted that the Jewish community should be eliminated. The Chinese use very beautiful words like liberation, development and progress. Nonetheless, these things are happening. If you look closely, the only explanation can be that some kind of systematic program of genocide has been embarked upon in Tibet."

His Holiness goes on to tell the story of a Chinese doctor who was working in a hospital in Lhasa and confessed to a local Tibetan that the government sets quotas for abortions.

"The doctors," the Dalai Lama explains, "are compelled to fill these quotas, which means there are times when they administer injections to kill an unborn child without the parents' consent. Later, when the child has died, they remove it, telling the parents its death resulted from some other cause.

"I have also heard, from a Tibetan refugee who traveled to India from a remote region of Amdo, that sterilisation has been carried out on girls as young as fourteen and fifteen years old. So this is not a matter of encouraging limited children but of ensuring that these girls have no children at all. Clearly that is the case."

In conversations with the Dalai Lama, this is a recurring theme. He travels the globe, covering as many as 250,000 miles in a year, delivering Buddhist teachings, bringing the plight of his people to the attention of the world and discussing his concern for human rights among all people.

"We are all brothers and sisters," he often says. "Despite differences of culture and history and background, we are all, deep down, the same human beings. We all have the desire for happiness and joy and we all wish to overcome human suffering. On this basis, we can meet and have understanding. On this basis, we can develop gentleness, compassion and a sense of universal responsibility."

His concern for human rights springs from many years of Buddhist study and practice, as does his interest in the environment. When the Dalai Lama received the Nobel Prize for Peace in 1989, special mention was made of his commitment to the environment. Respect for the natural world is, he says, inherent in his faith.

Traditionally, Tibet was a Buddhist state. To the Tibetan people, all life was sacred and was only to be sacrificed for the most essential human needs. Tibetans managed to live sustainably for centuries in a precariously balanced environment because Buddhism pervaded every aspect of their lives and they believed unshakingly that life was to be lived in harmony with nature, not in a battle against it.

The Chinese invasion, however, brought in its wake widescale environmental devastation. The Chinese know Tibet as Xizang, which means 'Western Treasure House' and, for the People's Republic, that is precisely what it has been.

Prior to 1950, the Tibetan population was small and the land was ecologically stable. Visitors to Tibet in the 1930s and 1940s reported spectacular wilderness populated by birds, antelopes, musk deer, leopards, gazelles, wolves and bears. It was described as "one great zoological garden" in a 1930 issue of National Geographic magazine.

Recent accounts have painted a very different picture. The American nature photographer and writer, Galen Rowell, reported that he found much of the Tibetan landscape devastated. "For three weeks we walked, over one hundred miles in all. We saw virtually nothing. The wildlife had disappeared." As had the forests. Today, sixty-eight percent of Tibet's forests have been destroyed and the roads that first brought the military to the roof of the world now carry timber back to China. This, the Dalai Lama says, saddens him as much as the oppression of his people.

"An attitude of carelessness towards the environment," he explains, "is equivalent to an attitude of carelessness towards your home or your family. We need to show a far greater sense of responsibility towards the earth, our mother.

"I say this, particularly as a Buddhist, who is concerned for the welfare of all sentient beings. A central tenet of Buddhism is the philosophy of interdependence. If something happens over here, then something somewhere else will be affected. Everything is linked. Life is built on chain reactions. Therefore, it is important to recognize, not only the oneness of all human beings, but also our responsibility to other species on the planet."

The environmental destruction of Tibet is, he says, the result of both a vastly increased population and inappropriate land use. Chinese agricultural policies have led to land degradation and famine. Overcultivation and conversion of high-altitude grazing land to more intensive farmland has resulted in crop failure, wind erosion and the starvation of herds. Soon after the Chinese invasion, farmers were moved into collectives and directed to grow winter wheat instead of the traditional barley. China took much of that wheat home to feed its own population until soil became depleted and Tibet experienced its first recorded famine.

All this, the Tibetan people bore relatively peacefully. Each year, on March 10, independence demonstrations, marking the anniversary of the 1959 uprising, would rock Lhasa but these went largely unnoticed in the outside world. Then in 1987, the largest protests for many years were witnessed in the capital. Western travelers, who had recently been permitted to visit Tibet, documented the events thoroughly and images of the riots were splashed across the pages of newspapers around the globe. Further demonstrations were reported in March 1988. In March 1989, the situation became so difficult for the Chinese government that it evicted all foreigners from the capital and imposed martial law. There followed a month of almost ceaseless independence demonstrations, during which many Tibetans (a number of them monks and nuns) were injured, imprisoned and killed.

The aftermath of the demonstrations was not dissimilar from what followed the massacre in Tiananmen Square. House-to-house searches were conducted for those who were involved in the unrest. Any Tibetans found with wounds indicating possible involvement in riots were automatically arrested. Some reports suggested that whole families were shot dead without trial. Observers estimate a total of several hundred demonstrators were killed and thousands of Tibetans imprisoned in what even the Tibetan Region Party Secretary, Hu Jintao, described as "merciless reprisals".

There is general agreement that, prior to Chinese occupation, the Tibetan government was far from perfect. It was feudal, monarchic and in many ways repressive but it did not subdue its people with anything like the ferocity of the current Chinese rule. Before occupation made the nation ungovernable, the Dalai Lama had already begun to institute substantial democratic reforms and, during their time in India, he and the Tibetan government in exile have worked to develop a representative parliament for their people.

"Right from the beginning," His Holiness insists, "we have worked towards a genuinely democratic system. Already, in 1961, we were discussing a democratic constitution. Then, in 1963, we adopted a draft constitution for a future Tibet."

He makes reference to Mahatma Gandhi, from whom he has drawn much inspiration, and points out that Gandhi's direct involvement in Indian politics came to an end as soon as his people achieved liberation from British rule.

"In recent years," he continues, "the democratisation process has intensified and, since 1969, I have made it clear that, whether the institution of the Dalai Lama may or may not continue, entirely depends on the wishes of the Tibetan people. In either case, in a future Tibet, I do not wish to participate in government leadership."

This is a matter of hot debate amongst the Tibetan refugee community, to whom the institution of the Dalai Lama means a great deal more than it does to His

Holiness himself. Most Tibetans, if pressed, will confess they find it inconceivable that there could come a time when a Dalai Lama was not both their religious and political guide. The current incarnation, however, prefers to leave the question open.

"It is a human institution," he has often said, "and these things change with circumstances."

He goes on to explain that, long before the institution of the Dalai Lamas, the Lord of Infinite Compassion incarnated in human form and, for as long as there are sentient beings who suffer, *bodhisattvas* — the incarnation of Chenrezig among them — will return. They will remain the embodiments of compassion, whether they bear the title, Dalai Lama, or not.

A *bodhisattva*, in the Mahayana Buddhist tradition as it is practised in Tibet, is a highly-realized being who has renounced the final step to enlightenment, in which all ties are severed with this material world, and has chosen, instead, to reincarnate again and again until all sentient beings attain enlightenment and mortal suffering is finally conquered. The Dalai Lama is such a being. His pledge is to work to alleviate the suffering of humanity in each successive life until, when he finally achieves the ultimate peace of *nirvana*, he will carry all earthbound beings with him.

I AM NOT A BUDDHIST. I MEDITATE TOO LITTLE AND MY PRACTICE IS DERIVED FROM NO particular school. I don't take a position on *bodhisattvas* but I hope they exist and, if they do exist, I don't know of anyone more likely to be one than Tenzin Gyatso.

When finally we meet, some twenty-two years after I first heard his name, the Dalai Lama's effect on me is unlike that of anyone else whose path I've crossed in putting together this book. He is charming, witty, humble, wise, honest. His laugh dances around him. His tranquillity fills an entire room, seeps out the door, along staircases, through air conditioning ducts. People confess that they're unusually cheerful ten floors below his suite. He meets hard-nosed politicians and they go about their business, with absurd smiles on their faces, for days. Everyone he meets — which is perhaps why Chinese heads of state do not go out of their way to meet him — falls under his spell.

By supernatural means or not, he has come to embody compassion. His attitude to the invaders of his homeland is a case in point. Not for a moment does he forget the suffering of his people. Not a day goes by when he is not actively engaged in securing their freedom. Certainly, in the conversation we have, high up in a harborside hotel in Sydney, this is foremost in his mind. He returns to it again and again. Yet he makes a point of reminding me that his argument is with the policies of the government in Beijing, not with the people of China.

"As a Buddhist monk," he smiles impishly (the Dalai Lama smiles much of the time), "I pray that all sentient beings, and particularly all human beings, should be happy and should overcome suffering. There is no point in excluding the more than one billion human beings who live in China. As a Buddhist practitioner, I am equally concerned with the rights of the Chinese people and I have a very strong feeling that, when liberty, democracy and freedom prevail in China, we Tibetans will be able to contribute to their peace of mind."

He is certain that day will come. "It is only a matter of time," he says. China cannot forever remain immune to the forces of freedom and democracy whose influence is being felt in other parts of the world.

To hurry that process along with armed struggle is, however, unthinkable. His Holiness confesses to an admiration for the courage of the Khampa soldiers who escorted him out of Tibet in 1959 and waged a long guerilla battle with the Chinese military from their bases in the hill country of Kham.

"Nonetheless," he says, "violence is the wrong approach, both morally and practically. Practically, it is almost suicidal. Morally, we are Buddhists. Our first objective is to help others. If we cannot do that, we must, at least, try not to harm them. That is why, in the Tibetan struggle, non-violence is the only way."

There is no end, he says, to the situations in which this philosophy of non-violence can be applied and, with that, he tilts his head back and the air rings again with his staccato laugh.

"Sometimes," he admits, still chuckling, "I think I'm a little bit of an idealist. I think our world should be run on the basic principles of democracy, freedom and liberty. I think that, if those principles are our foundation, then our ultimate goal should be a demilitarized world. I know this goal appears a long way off and there are many obstacles but I believe that, if we are constant in our determination and effort, then we may some day achieve it."

Consistent with his optimism is the Dalai Lama's attitude to the repercussions of his escape into exile.

"In one way," he says, "the occupation of Tibet and all that has come from it are very sad. In another way, however, that negative event provides us with new opportunities. It is now possible for us to have closer contact with the wider world and with people from other religious backgrounds and cultural heritages.

Through these personal contacts, we have learnt many things.

"In the past, the Tibetan attitude was one of isolation. That created a very great mystique but, politically, it contributed to our problems. Now, whenever the opportunity arises, we try to have contact with our human brothers and sisters. We have learnt much from them and I think we have also contributed something to the world. In many places, Buddhist centers have been established. Perhaps seven hundred new Buddhist centers have sprung up in various countries."

Life in exile has been a time of constantly expanding horizons for the Dalai Lama. Even as a child, he was fascinated by science and technology. He spent hours, in the Potala, gazing into an old telescope and he was renowned for his passion for pulling old machinery apart and putting it back together in perfect working order. If he was not the Dalai Lama, Tenzin Gyatso confesses, he might have become an engineer or a technician.

Watch repairs are, perhaps, his best known pastime. "I've repaired a number of what appeared to be hopeless cases for my family and friends," he notes. He also surprised Potala staff when, in his teens, with a young driver accomplice, he dismantled three of his predecessor's no longer functioning automobiles and soon had two of them ready to hit the rudimentary roads of Lhasa.

Since moving to India, his interest in Western science has developed to encompass areas as diverse as psychology and quantum physics. Wherever possible, his religious and political tours are punctuated by visits to laboratories and scientific conferences.

Modern science, he says, has refined concepts which have existed for thousands of years in Buddhism. The Buddhist notion of the impermanence of all material phenomena has been confirmed, quite literally, by physicists.

"Matter," he adds with apparent delight, "is energy, constantly changing, disintegrating, reforming from one moment to the next. Nor are the concepts of atoms and particles new to Buddhism."

The Dalai Lama is a firm believer in the religion/science interface. A greater understanding of the humanities, philosophy and spirituality, he says, can help to fill the moral vacuum in which many scientists are forced to operate. For those who practice religion, he believes, science offers sometimes to confirm, and at other times to challenge, long-held beliefs. In either case, this is useful because spiritual knowledge must always be tested in the laboratories of logic and personal experience.

Meetings with scientists have largely served to confirm his personal cosmology but he believes it is a two-way street. The task at hand is to achieve a balance between scientific progress and spiritual development.

"We live in a world which is very much dependent upon technology and science," he explains, "and science has contributed much to the alleviation of human suffering. However, if we pay attention only to our material progress, without equally developing our inner nature, it can only lead to dissatisfaction and perhaps even greater suffering than was there to begin with."

His Holiness has also made a conscious effort to meet with leaders of a number of world religions and, here too, he has learned as much as he has been able to impart.

"When I was in Tibet," he confides, "we felt that our religion was the best and other religions were only so-so. Then, you see, I came to the outside world and had the opportunity to meet many people from very different traditions. Through personal contact, I have developed a genuine, deep realization that all the different religions are equally effective, in that they all have the potential to produce truly good and selfless human beings."

Of course, he acknowledges, there are vast differences between cosmologies and theologies.

"There are fundamental differences," he asserts. "Buddhism, Jainism and some other ancient Indian traditions, for example, do not accept the theory of God. Other religions have God, the creator, as the basic tenet of their faith. These are big differences. Even between the godless religions, there are differences. Buddhists do not accept the theory of soul or permanent self. Self, we say, is momentarily changing. It is not something which exists independently."

Consciousness, the Dalai Lama believes, is produced by consciousness. "There is no way to posit consciousness except as a continuation of former moments of consciousness." Thus, in Tibetan Buddhism, consciousness has no beginning, the universe has no beginning, the cycle of rebirth has no beginning and there is no creator God who set all this in motion. Our state of consciousness now is dependent on our state of consciousness a moment ago. This is the fundamental principle of the law of karma, in which our thoughts and actions in the present will dictate the nature of our life and lives in the future.

"As you can see," His Holiness continues, "these are big differences — quite big enough to fight each other over — but what would be the use? There is no use. In the past, in the name of religion, there has been a great deal of suffering. This is very sad and it is also unnecessary. If you look closely at the different religions — not necessarily on an intellectual level but through genuine communication, dialogue and personal experience — then you will see that all the different religions have the same potential to make better shape of the whole human race."

The Dalai Lama also meets a constant stream of Western seekers, who come to Dharamsala and to his lectures around the world, in search of spiritual direction and sustenance. In the 1960s and 1970s, he says, it was very fashionable, in the West, to study Eastern philosophy. Today, however, "the excitement has died down a little" and those who come to him are fewer in number but "generally more serious".

His Holiness suspects that this earlier fascination with the East was largely a result of young people's dissatisfaction with the lack of readily accessible experiential teachings in their own faiths. Certainly, he says, Buddhism possesses many very effective techniques for meditation and the training of the mind but he does not unreservedly recommend it for all Western seekers. He is a firm believer in the study of comparative religion and in shopping around.

"Choosing amongst the different philosophies is a personal matter," he explains. "We should not allow the philosophical differences to cloud the common aim and the common result. I always look at the result, not the method, and all the different religions have produced selfless, compassionate human beings. There are many different paths because religion has been designed to suit the diverse needs and dispositions of human beings. So, a greater variety of religions can suit a greater variety of human beings.

"Sometimes people ask me whether it would be best to have just one world religion. My answer is, no. A diversity of religions is far better. Each religion has its own specialty. I have learnt a great deal from my Christian brothers and sisters and there are certain Buddhist techniques — particularly for the training of the mind — which some of my Christian brothers and sisters have adopted without altering, in any way, their central beliefs."

His Holiness makes a point of actively encouraging cross-pollination between Buddhism and other world religions because, he says, it helps to build tolerance.

"In these days of fast communication, we should increase our efforts to learn about each other's systems and develop a sense of mutual respect. I think close contact between religions is both essential and possible, particularly if we maintain our focus, not on the differences but on the common goal."

This is a lesson which, the Dalai Lama believes, applies equally in international religious and political spheres.

"Our minor differences," he insists, "can be transcended by a global perspective, a bigger goal. On a practical level, when you look at a problem from very close, it appears very big. It appears insurmountable. If you look at the same problem from a distance, from a wider perspective, then it becomes smaller. It is the same problem, yet it appears smaller. It is also very useful to examine a problem from different angles. This, too, is a very good method for overcoming differences."

For prior generations, he says, this sense of global understanding was an admirable goal. Today, however, it is a necessity. We live in an "entirely different world situation" but we still approach our problems as if nothing has changed.

"The world is becoming smaller and smaller," he continues. "The interdependent nature of all things is now much clearer. Today, every crisis in a different part of the world is, I think, a global crisis. This is true of the economic situation, the political situation and also of the ecological problem. One or two nations cannot solve these problems. All of humanity must work together. We need to develop, in concert, a long-term agenda and work accordingly.

"So, the world situation is showing us that humanity needs to take a wider perspective, a holistic view. A sense of universal responsibility is the key. We must combine that motivation with a realisation of the oneness of all humanity."

Speaking with His Holiness on almost any subject, the conversation will eventually return to the common essence of all. This, I think, is the source of much of his optimism. He believes an utopia is ultimately possible because he is certain that human nature is fundamentally good.

"How to develop that sense of universal responsibility?" The Dalai Lama pauses, furrows his brow for a moment in thought. "I have always felt that compassion and wisdom are the keys."

This might appear a tall order but the Dalai Lama goes on quickly to explain his conviction that compassion, kindness and gentleness are essential to the inner nature of all human beings.

"This I believe: our basic human nature is gentleness," he smiles. "From birth to death, one of the most important factors for sustaining healthy human life is affection. This would not be possible if we did not possess a core of gentleness, kindness and compassion.

"There are people who believe that human nature is essentially aggressive and yes, in human history, there have been many wars and many negative feelings. However, if we look closely, I truly believe that the dominant force of the human mind is a positive one. The hatred, the anger, the jealousy, all constantly come and go but they are not the dominant force. There is much human affection. If human nature was essentially aggressive and merciless, I don't think we would face the overpopulation problem that we see today. The majority of humanity is very much, I think, under the influence of compassion and love."

This, says the Dalai Lama, is the gift of all the great world religions. We are born with this basic human nature and religious training, in every faith, is designed to keep negative emotions in check and to encourage that essence — which Christians might call a spark of divinity — to grow.

In Buddhism, each individual is personally responsible for their present state and future growth, which can only be achieved by cultivating their essential nature. Those faiths which emphasize a supreme creator God appear, on the surface, to be very different. Not so, the Dalai Lama asserts. "They have as their purpose the fulfilment of God's intentions, they see us all as creations of one God and they teach us that we should cherish, respect, love and be of service to our fellow human brothers and sisters."

In this respect, His Holiness believes, "religion is a positive force" but we must not lose sight of the fact that the salutary qualities it encourages are more important than its philosophical trappings. In other words, while an intricate religious practise can surely encourage the development of our inner nature, it is not the only route to that end.

"I think, today, the human population numbers more than five billion but the genuine believers, the people who are really implementing religious teaching in their daily lives, probably number less than one billion," the Dalai Lama explains. "The remaining four billion are, in reality, non-believers. Therefore, they are the majority and we must be concerned about them. They too are our brothers and sisters. They also need daily happiness, satisfaction and a brighter future.

"When we are born, we are free from any ideology or religion but we are not free from affection, gentleness or any of these good human qualities. Later, as intelligence develops, we use all sorts of methods to extend these basic qualities but we can make a distinction between religious traditions and human goodness. It is possible to be a very affectionate person, a good person, a warm-hearted person, without religion. Religion is a luxury, whereas compassion, kindness and forgiveness are necessities for survival."

These necessities, he believes, are not the sole property of any church. They ought to be nurtured in schools, in universities, in families. They ought to be the fundamental area of study from which our intellectual disciplines spring. Whether we are scientists or lawyers or economists or politicians, he insists, our work will be more fruitful — for ourselves and others — if we have been given the opportunity to pay equal attention to our development as complete human beings.

In these days of widespread dissatisfaction with many institutional religions, this means that, at times, even the Dalai Lama finds he must disassociate his teachings on compassion from the spiritual tradition out of which they spring. This does not particularly bother him.

"When I speak about compassion, love and forgiveness," he explains, "some people have the impression that this is an exclusively religious subject and, if they do not subscribe to any religious belief, they are sometimes inclined to reject these basic human qualities also. I think that is a misunderstanding.

"You see, there are two kinds of spirituality and one is founded primarily on these basic good qualities. This I call the universal religion. There is no need for a sophisticated teaching or philosophy. This is a spirituality which we can all hold in common, whether we are Buddhists, Hindus, Christians, Muslims, Jews or have no religion at all. So long as we are human beings, these qualities, from birth, are already there. Our task is to nurture these good qualities and that is a task that we all can share."

So, while he would not be comfortable with a situation in which the diversity of world faiths was subsumed into one amorphous belief, the Dalai Lama feels certain that there is a single thread running through all world religions and through the best of our political ideologies also. When we acknowledge that thread, we acknowledge our common essence, our common birthright, and we take the first tentative steps towards the development of that universal responsibility of which His Holiness so often speaks.

"Genuine compassion," he adds, placing his hands firmly on his knees and meeting my gaze to be sure I'm paying attention, "comes from seeing the other person as just like myself — someone who wants happiness, who does not want suffering and who has every right to achieve happiness, to overcome suffering. Genuine compassion means that, irrespective of the other person's attitude to me, I recognize them as my brother or sister. Genuine compassion means I feel a closeness and a sense of responsibility towards them as another sentient being."

234

HIGH ABOVE THE KANGRA VALLEY, DHARAMSALA NESTLES INTO THE SIDE OF THE Himalayan foothills. From there a road winds higher still, through forests dotted with rhododendrons, to McLeod Ganj. Rounding the last bend, suddenly white houses appear among trees and prayer flags fly from roofs, from poles, from anything that stands upright. In a clearing, three monks sit under umbrellas in meditation. A woman, bent beneath a load of firewood, trudges up a steep incline.

Follow the road from the town to its end and you will come upon the home of the fourteenth Dalai Lama. Already, at five in the morning, lights are burning in his study. His Holiness has been awake since four, chanting and meditating. He also likes to exercise in the early hours and keeps exercise machines for this purpose. In half an hour he will eat a breakfast of bread and honey, with some tea. After breakfast, he will study the Buddhist scriptures until he breaks for lunch. His afternoons are composed mostly of political and social work, meeting with a steady stream of visitors from East and West and delivering teachings. At six, he stops for a cup of tea — Tibetan monks consume no solid food after midday — and around nine or ten, he sleeps.

In the evenings, when he has time to himself, he often listens to the radio — he particularly enjoys the BBC World Service — or watches documentaries on television. Wildlife documentaries are his favorites. Dramas are of no particular interest and besides, he laughs, they're often programmed too late for a lama who must rise at four. Gardening is another hobby and he still likes to stroll about his garden and the nearby hills, losing his troubles and his attendants, as he did in Lhasa as a small boy.

McLeod Ganj is not like other parts of India. Up here, the dust and rabble of the plains are quelled by a persistent atmosphere of peace. Twenty years after I first read about Tibet, I am standing at a crossroad here and I have come with a question. Again and again, Tenzin Gyatso refers to himself as "just a simple Buddhist monk". How then to explain the spell he casts over this town, over five-star hotels, over auditoriums, over everyone he meets?

In essence, the wisdom that he imparts is simple. The attraction is that he believes it so wholeheartedly and that he lives it so completely. The Dalai Lama has come to embody, not only for six million Tibetans but for countless others around the world, those very qualities which he so often mentions. He is a beacon at the end of a road, calling out to us that, while the journey is long and sometimes arduous, the prize is within our reach.

Professor Matthew Fox

13

THE MYSTIC IN
THE MACHINE

This I am. This I am.
I am what you love.
I am what you enjoy.
I am what you serve.
I am what you long for.
I am what you desire.
I am what you intend.
I am all that is.

MEDITATIONS WITH JULIAN OF NORWICH.

MY TWO CHIEF VISIONS OF MATTHEW FOX LIE UNCOMFORTABLY SIDE-BY-SIDE. IN the first, he sits on the stump of a great, old Californian redwood tree. His hands are folded in his lap. His damp gaze is turned beseechingly skywards. His shock of grey hair is tousled. He looks, to me, like a tiny boy awaiting rescue in a dark and alien forest. He looks a little like the kids you see waiting to be claimed at information desks in shopping malls.

In my second memory, Matthew Fox bounds gleefully about a playing field, leading two hundred or so seminar-goers in a spiral dance, urging them to revel in their dizziness, laughing and insisting that wobbly knees, spinning heads and mysticism go hand in hand.

The first image is from a photograph I saw in *Rolling Stone* magazine back in 1991. The second is the scene of our initial meeting.

It is the summer of 1992 and Matthew Fox is still a Dominican priest. He has recently emerged from a year's silence imposed by the Vatican. During this "enforced sabbatical" as he calls it, he has complied with the letter, if not the spirit, of the Vatican's law. For twelve months, he has not addressed a workshop, he has not published a book, nor has he publicly uttered one controversial word. He has spent time with those other pariahs of the Catholic church, the liberation theologians of South America, and has been guided through a Native American vision quest by his friend and colleague, Buck Ghosthorse.

Time for reflection has, however, not elicited the change of heart for which his superiors had hoped. He remains critical of the inflexible hierarchy of his church, critical of its patriarchy and its incomplete theology. He remains determined to reinvigorate Christian life with a return to a deep ecumenical mysticism, which he calls Creation Spirituality. In short, he is taking up his work, with renewed energy, precisely where he left it twelve months ago.

Thus, he reaches out for a woman's hand and she grabs hold of another, who grabs another and another until a chain of hundreds is formed, encircling the oval, and Matthew leads us all in a wild spiral towards the center, where we meet and spiral out again, singing and weaving and laughing. By games like these, apparently, the Catholic church is threatened.

Matthew Fox is no stranger to controversy. He has spent ten years of his life engaged in intermittent skirmishes with the church of Rome. He was first silenced in 1988, after it deemed his book, *Original Blessing*, "dangerous and deviant." When this achieved nothing but a quantum leap in his renown, he was ordered to return from his Institute for Culture and Creation Spirituality (ICCS) at Holy Names College in Oakland, just outside San Francisco, to a priory in Chicago where he might be kept on a shorter leash.

Among the church's problems with ICCS was Matthew's choice of a faculty, which, at the time the complaints reached their peak, included "physicists, artists and social changers," along with a Yoruba priestess, a Nigerian drummer, a Zen Buddhist, a Lakota medicine man, a Sufi and one of the luminaries of the women's spirituality movement, a Wiccan practitioner named Starhawk.

None raised the ire of the Vatican as completely as Starhawk. Her employment, according to Rome, amounted to an "espousal of witchcraft." Matthew's superiors demanded that Starhawk's position be terminated. Characteristically, he refused, explaining that he found this "rancor towards witches unbelievable.

As if Christians, in killing anywhere from three hundred thousand to three million through the centuries, have not had enough of witch-hunts."

Nor did he shift camp to Chicago. In the spring of 1993, twenty-six years after he entered the priesthood, Matthew Fox was finally expelled from the Dominican order.

Eighteen months later, we meet again, this time in the supremely traditional Clift Hotel in San Francisco. Outside, mist billows up from the bay and mingles with the smell of brewing coffee from a dozen nearby diners. Indoors, Mozart plays and bellboys tread noiselessly on plush carpet.

Matthew Fox is standing beneath a heavy chandelier, bidding farewell to new friends made last night at a lecture he gave with the British biologist, Rupert Sheldrake. His speaking schedule has not diminished even slightly since this most recent upheaval.

"I suppose," he begins, as we sink into enormous armchairs, "I've become an un-priest. They haven't taken away my priesthood but they've forbidden me to work as a priest."

He had seen it coming for years but it was the way it came that hurt because it was not the Vatican but his own order, buckling beneath pressure from Rome, that expelled him.

"Some of those people had known me for thirty-five years," he adds, "and they were ready to drop me for political reasons. They wanted the Vatican off their backs. I understand the pressure but this was not solely about me. It was a political decision. I'm a theologian and I happen to be a public one at this time. So, for them to serve me up means that any other theologian is also grist for their mill. There's an issue at stake."

Behind this fiery talk of politics, disappointment is the prevailing emotion. The works of Matthew Fox reflect a man whose life is committed to joy. In person, however, he leaves an impression that heaven, tauntingly, is having him trailed by a cloud of gentle, gray sadness. Despite a bright wit, an earthy sensuality and a hunger for knowledge, the air around him is infused with a sense of solitary longing.

To the Dutch Dominicans, he expresses gratitude.

"They supported me very strongly," he smiles. "They offered me 'religious asylum,' as they called it, in Holland. They were wonderful and they fought for me in all this. I was very moved. They showed strength, they showed courage, they stood up."

They were, however, a tiny minority.

Albert Nolan, a South African Dominican, was another supporter. He said to Matthew: "You North Americans are so into individualism that you don't understand solidarity at all. This is why the Dominicans have thrown you overboard. It's because they have no sense of solidarity."

"That," Matthew confesses, "is the disappointment. The virtue I've always admired most is courage and I've seen so little courage in the Catholic church and the Dominican order today. That's what most disappoints me. I believe that, without courage, there is no spirituality. Courage is two French words for a large heart and without a large heart you're not a spiritual person. You might be a religious person — you might be shuffling clerics or ideologies around — but I look for large hearts and I've been disappointed, frankly, by the rarity of courage in our religious institutions."

A rarity of courage and a rarity of vision. Indeed, the church in Rome has grown so blind that it appears no longer to recognize its own religion. In spite of the eclectic faculty at ICCS, Matthew Fox draws the majority of his inspiration from the Bible and the works of a reputable collection of Christian mystics and saints.

Meister Eckhart, Thomas Aquinas, Teresa of Avila, Francis of Assisi, Julian of Norwich and Hildegard of Bingen are frequently recurring sources, as are The Song of Solomon, Genesis, Exodus, Jeremiah, Paul's letters, the gospels and large tracts of the Old and New Testaments. Are these authors too, in the eyes of Rome, "dangerous and deviant"?

"Anyone can look at my books," Matthew explains. "I don't write about popes and bishops. They've always bored me. They came after me, I didn't go after them. I've been writing about the mystics. I've been writing about spirituality, which is the heart of Christianity, the heart of any religion. It's incredible to me that a guy who writes six hundred page books on St Thomas Aquinas and Hildergard of Bingen can be thought to be doing something wrong."

Yet plainly Matthew Fox was. So what was the problem? What was it, in his work, that proved so threatening that, while priests accused of child abuse were shuffled from parish to parish or sent on long sabbaticals, he was deemed unfit to continue practicing his vocation?

"Number one," he says, "they objected to the fact that I called myself a feminist theologian. I didn't know feminism was an heresy. Number two, I referred to God as 'mother'. Well, all the good medieval mystics and Jesus and the Bible referred to God as mother. Number three, I called God 'child'. This tells you much more about the Vatican than it does about God. They're afraid of children and afraid of women."

It seems an incongruous accusation to level at Catholicism, in which the incarnation, the birth and life of Jesus and the Mother Mary, have been celebrated so energetically. Haven't generations of Catholics heard the words, 'Suffer the little children to come unto me'?

"Exactly. You'd think they'd have remembered that story," Matthew laughs. "It just shows that their real problem wasn't theological."

In fact, a commission of three Dominicans was set up to examine his works for heresy and all were given a clean bill of health.

"The real issue is the very reason that they're uncomfortable with the base communities in Latin America," Matthew suggests. "They can't control them. It's a power issue and Creation Spirituality has all these base communities — over two hundred of them — populated by women and gays and lesbians and artists and people they can't control.

"That's what it's all about. It's about control and power and the fact that we have a movement going. It's a pity. They would rather die with their ideology intact and the churches empty than take a move into the next era. This affects all progressive movements in the church today. Wherever there's life, they're trying to stomp it out and replace it with their dictatorship. The Pope comes to the country and there's all this baby-kissing but what's going on behind the scenes in this papacy, with *Opus Dei* and all, is as corrupt as anything since the Borgias. They will die with their patriarchal shoes on if they continue this way."

Die they will, if the public continues to vote with its feet. The blow of exile from his order has been softened by his resounding public acceptance. At a time when cavernous churches are a quarter full at best, Matthew Fox attracts crowds of hundreds all over the world. His vision of a new Christian spirituality, which draws from its ancient traditions — as well as from recent developments in science, the arts, philosophy and the wisdom of other world religions — has struck a chord in the contemporary psyche.

Matthew Fox offers an alternative to the dry liberals and traditionalists on the one hand, and the effusive fundamentalists on the other. In a society starved of a cosmology, his work infuses the Scriptures with a sense of meaning that ignites the imagination without affronting contemporary rationalism.

His work has grown out of a longstanding infatuation with the mystic roots of Catholicism ("I've always said I was a twelfth century French Catholic, not a Roman Catholic," he jokes) and out of a life which has afforded ample time for solitary reflection.

TIMOTHY JAMES FOX, AS HE WAS KNOWN THEN, WAS BORN ON DECEMBER 21, 1940, the middle child of seven (three girls and four boys). He grew up in Madison, Wisconsin, amongst tree-lined streets, rolling fields and great mirrors of lakes where a small boy could fish or swim or dream.

"That whole experience of God in nature was very important to me as a child," he says now. "Also, the Native Americans are strong in Wisconsin and I had Native American dreams from the time I was young. The spirits are still in the land — no question about it."

Madison is a university town and his father, George, who was once on the all-American team, was assistant football coach at the University of Wisconsin. George Fox was a tough, no-nonsense man. He hailed from a working class neighborhood in Chicago, where he'd been rescued from violence and neglect at home and placed in the care of Augustinian priests. As a result, George Fox was a staunch Catholic, who raised his family with equal doses of blind faith and stern discipline.

Timothy's mother, Beatrice, was also a powerful influence. Of British and Jewish descent, she was raised a liberal Episcopalian and later converted to Catholicism in the interests of family unity. Even beside her husband's dominating personality, she retained a sense of her own strength and independence and might well have been responsible for the note of feminism that crept, from time to time, into Fox family life.

"My parents were gender-just," Matthew recalls. "When we were teenagers, my father sat us down and said, 'I don't make enough money to send you all to college, so I'll send the girls to college and you boys will have to find scholarships because they're more available to boys than girls.' For an Irishman in the 1950s, that wasn't bad. My parents were both very assertive so we had great arguments but I never experienced sexual oppression in the family context."

At age twelve, Timothy contracted polio. An eleven year old friend had died in the epidemic earlier that year, so he understood the balance in which his life hung. When the initial ravages of the disease subsided, he was left without the use of his legs and the doctors were uncertain whether he would ever walk on them again.

"It was," says Matthew, "a time of deep letting go."

Foremost among the dreams to be jettisoned was the one in which he saw himself following father and brothers onto the football field. While, even his father conceded he had always been the skinnier, more bookish of his sons, in the Fox family there was no question that the boys would all do their Dad proud on college teams.

"I had imagined that I was going to be this big football player," Matthew explains, "but I couldn't even walk. It was an important moment in my own personal history because it forced me to let go of my father and of that particular image of masculinity."

Physically fragile, immobile and isolated from other children, Timothy spent the best part of a year quarantined in hospital. His parents visited him regularly and so did a young Dominican brother, offering consolation, companionship and food for intellectual and spiritual thought.

"It was a mystical time for me," Matthew smiles. "That Dominican brother became almost a surrogate father. He was a very joyful man, very contemplative. His beauty and joyfulness drew me in."

It was the beginning of a lifelong friendship and a time of inner transformation. Over the course of that year, his family noticed a change in him. Matthew too remembers reaching decisions that would affect the rest of his life. When he regained the use of his legs, he was "overwhelmed with gratitude to the universe" and he promised he would take neither his legs nor his life for granted.

"I think that's a good definition of mysticism," he adds. "A mystic takes nothing for granted."

When his strength returned, he went back to school, where friends and faculty noticed Timothy had become a more intense, introspective young man.

"My friends were Protestant and Jewish and agnostic and we would have long philosophical debates."

He remembers sitting for hours, listening to Beethoven, lost in the music. He discovered Shakespeare and devoured the classics.

"I remember reading Tolstoy when I was in high school. *War and Peace* blew my soul right open. I wanted to explore that."

At the same time, he began attending mass with renewed enthusiasm and would often remain behind, talking to the parish priest.

"He gave me Aquinas and GK Chesterton to read. I loved the idea that faith and thinking could go together. Ideas were important to me."

He visited a Dominican priory in Iowa. The brothers were chanting the office in Latin. The air in the chapel was dark and heavy with incense and burning candle wax. He was moved by both the esthetics and the sense of community. He was also impressed that the Dominicans were an intellectual order, with a strong tradition of academic achievement.

At nineteen, Timothy formally joined the order and was sent to a Dominican farm in Minnesota, beside the Mississippi river. There, he was given a new name and the ties to his old life were ceremonially cut.

"I will always be grateful to the Dominican order," he says quietly, even now. "They gave me a lot in terms of tradition and rites of passage. Very few men of my generation had a rite of passage but I definitely did. They didn't call it that but that's what it was when you took the habit, took a new name and they told you to leave your family. It was a rite of passage and it was powerful. You were stepping into a male bonding thing with an older generation. In fact, you were bonding with a seven hundred year old tradition. These were invaluable gifts."

Matthew thrived in this new environment, waking at five each morning to pray, immersing himself in the ritual and struggling to understand its mysteries. At year's end, he moved to the Aquinas Institute in Illinios and then in Iowa, where he fed his voracious appetite for learning. From there, he pleaded to be sent to Paris to study for a Doctorate in Spirituality at the Institut Catholique. He graduated *summa cum laude*, among the most distinguished students in the Institut's recent history.

It was in Paris that Matthew was set on the path that would finally set him at loggerheads with the Vatican. His mentor there was the French Dominican and historian, Father Chenu.

"When he named the difference between Creation Spirituality and the fall-redemption tradition, immediately I got it," Matthew recalls. "I said, 'Oh, my family was creation-centered and the church is this other thing but it doesn't have to be that way, does it?'"

Matthew devoured the works of the Catholic mystics. "I felt my generation wasn't going to be interested in religion. We were interested in spirituality," he says. He struggled with the relationship between the contemplative experience of divinity and the necessity he felt to work for justice in the wider world.

"It was the late 1960s," he remembers, "and my number one question was: "What is the nature of social justice in relation to mystical experience?" The Civil Rights movement and the Anti-Vietnam war movement were going on in America. These things were important to me. Then, when I came back in 1970, there was the gay and lesbian movement, the women's movement and, of course, now the ecological movement.

"I taught for four years in a women's college in the early 1970s and this confirmed my feminism. Already I was a feminist in the sense that I found Mary Daly and Rosemary Ruther's work more interesting than what the men were writing about. These women were writing about language and symbol and metaphor, which is so close to spirituality. I found that male agenda, about sin and redemption, boring. You could memorize it in an hour and then what?

"Listening to women's stories in this college also woke me up. Some of them were middle-aged and they had to fight their husbands, who had MBAs and were running the city of Chicago, because they wanted to come to college. I was blown away. Then, hearing stories of how many women had been raped, I was horrified. I definitely picked up on the interesting questions that feminists were asking."

Also in the 1970s, he stumbled upon the work of the fourteenth century Dominican mystic and theologian, Meister Eckhart, whose work, like Matthew's, was a source of conflict with his superiors. Eckhart spoke to the peasants in their own dialect, insisting on their equality with the aristocratic classes because all people, he said, were created in the image of the divine. He was the most popular preacher in Europe in his day and has since influenced the likes of Karl Marx, Carl Jung, the Quakers and the Radical Protestants.

"I realized that this was my Dominican brother and that we thought alike," says Matthew. He also realized that Eckhart, himself, had been influenced by a long tradition of mysticism and Creation Spirituality within the Catholic church. Matthew set about uncovering it and, around it, gradually constructed his own cosmology.

"THERE WAS AN AUSTRALIAN METHODIST MINISTER SPEAKING IN AFRICA," MATTHEW likes to recount. "As he gave his lecture, he stopped after each sentence and it was translated into Swahili. He came to the culmination of his lecture, which was this sentence: 'In Sydney, Australia, today, the number one spiritual problem is loneliness.' The translator turned to him a bit puzzled, so he repeated the sentence. The translator went off and huddled with four or five other Africans.

Finally, he came back to the microphone and he said, 'I'm sorry, Sir, but in our language, there is no word for loneliness.'

"There is no word for loneliness among the native peoples of this planet," Matthew continues with mock surprise. "Western civilization, in the last three hundred years, has invented loneliness — cosmic loneliness — and with cosmic loneliness, comes cosmic arrogance. That is why we are, at the same time, both lonely and treating the other species — the rainforests, the soil, the water, the air — with arrogance. The problem is that the West has lost its sense of the universe, its sense of cosmology. We've lost the tradition of the Cosmic Christ."

This Cosmic Christ, of which Matthew often speaks, is, he says, an ancient archetype, found in the Judaic writings, as well as in Christianity, found in Buddhism ("the Cosmic Buddha, the Buddha-nature in every flower") and in indigenous and matrifocal spiritual traditions. The Cosmic Christ is the divine spirit or divine wisdom that is present in every living thing.

"The soil is divine. It's sacred. There is divinity in there," Matthew asserts. "The Cosmic Christ is there. The same is true of the rainforests and of all the species on this planet and of all the galaxies. The reason we can willy-nilly destroy the soil and the water and the air and the forests, as we do, is that we don't believe in the Cosmic Christ. We don't believe in the sacredness of all being.

"We have this theological idea, that Newton gave us, that God is behind the universe with an oil can. That's called theism. God's out there and we're here. In my opinion, theism is radically immoral. It's obsolete. It's religious dualism. God is not out there. Carl Jung says that there are two ways to lose your soul and one is to worship a God out there. We are in divinity and divinity is in us. That is panentheism. It's perfectly orthodox. It's mysticism. Mysticism is the experience of divinity around us and within us."

This is the central tenet of Matthew's work and it is also a recurring theme in the writings of generations of influential Christian thinkers, including Jesus himself.

"Jesus teaches mysticism — panentheism — whenever he preaches that the kingdom and queendom of God is among us," Matthew explains. "He says, 'Don't look there. It's here now.' Where? Wherever we are. Divinity is here. Thomas Aquinas said that God became human in order that human beings might become divine. Clement of Alexandria said the same thing."

The Cosmic Christ is also present in the meditations of the twelfth century

German abbess, Hildegard of Bingen, when she writes:

I, the fiery life of divine wisdom,
I ignite the beauty of the plains,
I sparkle the waters,
I burn in the sun and the moon and the stars.
With wisdom I order all rightly . . .
I adorn all the earth.
I am the breeze that nurtures all things green ...
I am the rain coming from the dew
that causes the grasses to laugh with joy of life.
I call forth tears, the aroma of holy work.
I am the yearning for good.

The Cosmic Christ is present in St Francis of Assisi's *Canticle of Brother Sun*, when he writes:

All praise be yours, my Lord, through all that you have made,
and first my Lord Brother Sun,
Who brings the day; and light you give us through him.
How beautiful he is, how radiant in all his splendor!
Of you, Most High, he bears the likeness ...
All praise be yours, my Lord, through Sister Moon and Stars;
In the heavens you have made them bright
and precious and fair ...
All praise be yours, my Lord, through Sister Earth, our mother;
Who feeds us in her sovereignty and produces
Various fruits and coloured flowers and herbs.

The Cosmic Christ is present in the book of Jeremiah:
Before I formed you in the womb I knew you, before you came to birth I
consecrated you; I have appointed you as prophet to the nations.

Panentheism is a constant stream running through all the world's religions because, Matthew explains, it is a universal human experience.

"Every human being is a mystic. What does it mean to be a mystic? To experience the divine child. To hang upside down on a tree when we were young. To do ring-around-the-rosy dances until we fell down in a trance, knowing it was good for us. To get high on the wind and the silence at the top of a mountain. To experience union with the ocean and the eons of memory that are implied every time a wave washes up to greet us. We were all mystics once. Mysticism is our intuition, in which we experience the oneness of all things. Mysticism is heart knowledge."

Yet the mystical tradition is not taught in our theological colleges and seminaries. Our churches and synagogues, says Matthew, "have been sleeping on their treasures of mysticism for three hundred years. Mysticism has become a dirty word in the West. Our civilization has left us without a cosmology and therefore without ways of learning our mystical capacity."

One reason for this, he believes, is the split which occurred in the seventeenth century between theology and science.

"During the Newtonian era, mysticism was silenced in the West. That's when our souls became cosmically lonely and that's when our civilisation became cosmically arrogant.

"Science, without the mystical traditions, went its way to explore the universe but it lost the grounding in justice and in wisdom that religious traditions bring. Religion, on the other hand, having turned the universe over to the scientists, became more and more introspective. Theologians said, 'We'll take the soul.' They kept looking in until, today, much of religion can talk to you about nothing but your personal savior. They've lost God the Creator entirely and they've lost the Trinity, the sense of God the Spirit that works through all religions and all cultures."

As a result, all that is left to much of mainstream Christianity is a theology of the historical Jesus, which has, in turn, led to the extremism of the fundamentalist Christians.

"To zero in so totally on Jesus that you lose sight of God the Creator and God the Spirit, is, I feel, a heresy," Matthew says. "I'm not putting down the historical Jesus. I am simply pointing out that, during the Enlightenment era, our theological enterprise put all its eggs in the basket of the historical Jesus and we have deposed the Cosmic Christ because it was not respectable to be mystical during the machine era. You don't want mystics in a machine. They'll foul it up, for sure."

This is Matthew's passion and his goal: that Christianity should reclaim its rich tradition of mysticism and offer it as a salve to an ailing Western world. The routes to an experiential Christianity have been tried and tested over thousands of years ("our art is a yoga, our music is a yoga, even our science is a yoga," he says) but the churches withhold, from a starving society, the very nourishment it needs.

"Mysticism is a tradition of experience," he insists. When Matthew becomes passionate, his features grow visibly more angular and his ordinarily gentle gaze fires lightning bolts. "We have to move from believing in God to experiencing God and I think all young people yearn for this. Frankly, I think it's the big appeal of drugs, for example. It has also been the big appeal of Eastern spiritual paths. It's the appeal of transcendent experience and it's such an indictment that Western religion is not offering it."

Yet there is hope and, interestingly, Matthew believes, it is coming from science. It is science, not religion, that is leaving the mechanistic Newtonian worldview behind. Scientists, like Paul Davies and Rupert Sheldrake, describe a universe which is perfectly rational but in which the mystic might also thrive.

"Einstein said that mysticism — he wasn't afraid to use the word — is a cosmic, religious feeling and it is the basis of all science and all art. Indeed, he said that the purpose of science and art was to awaken this cosmic, religious feeling."

That is precisely, Matthew believes, what science is doing today. It is beginning to create, for us, a cosmology.

"Let me give you one story from contemporary science," he offers. "One is enough.

"When the universe began, about fifteen billion years ago, as a seven hundred and fifty thousand year fireball that expanded as the universe expanded, there was a decision made, in the first second, on our behalf. The decision was that the expansion of the fireball would be at such a rate that, if it were one millionth of a millionth of a millionth of a second slower or faster over seven hundred and fifty thousand years, you and I would not be here today. The earth would not have evolved as the hospitable planet it has.

"It's an awesome story. It makes mystics of everyone. It reminds me of Julian of Norwich's words: 'We have been loved since before the beginning.' This is why physicists are coming out of the closet as mystics — this plus a lot of other stories. Ninety percent of all scientists, I would say, are drawn to science because of the mysticism and the beauty of it."

To Matthew, these scientists are beginning to describe the original blessing which is so crucial to his own faith. Creation Spirituality is a tradition which begins with divine blessing. It is a tradition that remembers we were all blessed with divine breath and divine intention and sees that as the pivotal moment in our evolution, rather than the Augustinian notion of original sin. As far as we know, the universe is around fifteen billion years old and, "from the very first second of that fireball," Matthew says, "the universe has been blessing us."

Original blessing, he believes, is more scripturally accurate than original sin, which only gained a place in theological debate with the work of St Augustine in the fourth century AD. It is not mentioned in the scriptures, and the Jews, who share with Christians the same story of creation and fall, do not have a theology of original sin. Original blessing is also less anthropocentric.

"Sin is only as old as the human race," Matthew laughs. "That means it's not much more than four million years old. So, to begin religion with sin is to leave out fifteen billion years of the creative activity of nature and God."

The Western preoccupation with original sin springs, once again, from a theology which places undue emphasis on the historical Jesus as personal savior, at the expense of God the Creator and the Cosmic Christ. In Creation Spirituality, God is understood to have given birth to, and to reside as spirit within, all living things.

"Thus," says Matthew, "we are crucifying the Christ all over again when we oppress God's creation, which is God's garden in which God dwells. It is an expression of the divine one, the Cosmic Christ. God is not out there, appointing us stewards of creation, as if we were here to do the dirty work of an absentee landlord. Rather, divinity is in creation and, when creation flourishes and is radiant, divinity flourishes. When creation is crucified, the Christ dies all over again.

"St Thomas Aquinas says that 'the first and primary meaning of salvation is to preserve things in the good.' I think that is as rich a definition of the agenda in an ecological age as we're going to get. To preserve things in the good, we first have to recognize the good. That's what a blessing theology is. Blessing is a theological word for goodness. We have to find the deep down goodness of things, the deep down goodness of the universe, of this creation story that brought us here, through a lot of travail and suffering, but which has made so beautiful a planet.

"That's why I begin the naming of the spiritual journey in terms of original blessing. We're here to return blessing for blessing. That is basic gratitude. Just as our universe began with compassion, so Jesus and other spiritual avatars teach us to find the compassion again and to return goodness for goodness. Their message has always been about carrying on the work of the universe, which is a work of compassion, and returning blessing for blessing."

In this way, Matthew Fox binds his mystical temperament with the quest for a theology of justice which has propelled him on his spiritual odyssey since the days when he was a young man, exploring Paris and politics in the 1960s. For him, the transcendent experience is never enough. Like Desmond Tutu, he insists that Moses communed with God, then set his people free. Jesus spent time in solitude, then went about his business of healing the sick, feeding the hungry and raising the dead. Mysticism, Matthew believes, inspires tangible, compassionate, sometimes revolutionary action.

"Meister Eckhart says that, if the only prayer you said in your whole life was, 'thank you', that would suffice, but when you say thank you, activity and responsibility are implied. Thank you are not just words but a lifestyle — a lifestyle of reverence and gratitude — and that, I think, is the basic morality for our times.

"Bede Griffith, the monk who lived in India for over fifty years, said that if Christianity cannot recover its mystical tradition and teach it, it should fold up and go out of business. To that I say, 'Amen,' because it is only out of the mystical tradition that our prophetic work to transform society will be authentically radical and rooted. Authentic action comes out of respect for mystery and wonder and the glorious surprise of our being here."

"I DON'T WRITE ABOUT WHAT I HAVEN'T EXPERIENCED," MATTHEW FOX HAS SAID when pressed to elaborate on the recurring celebration of eros in his work.

Today he goes on to quote extensively from The Song of Solomon, much of which he has obviously committed to memory.

"The woman says: 'My lover is radiant and ruddy, he stands out among ten thousand, his head is pure gold, his locks are like thick palm leaves and are as black as the raven, his teeth are bathed in milk, his eyes are like doves beside brooks of water, his cheeks are like beds of spice, his arms are rods of gold.'

"This lady's seen something! She has seen the Cosmic Christ in her lover. That's what falling in love is. It is a mystical experience. It is a transfiguration, theophany experience.

"The man responds: 'How beautiful you are my dearest, how beautiful. Your eyes are like doves behind your veil, you hair is like a flock of goats streaming down Mount Gilead, your teeth are like a flock of ewes ready to be shorn, your lips are like a scarlet thread, the cheeks behind your veil are like a pomegranate spliced in two.'

"This stuff is erotic! This is delicious! These people are seeing something beyond words, something divine in one another."

Matthew pauses for a moment and sits quietly, watching his folded hands. Disappointment washes, once more, across his features, softening them and in an instant, moves on.

"When I look at my life as a sexual human being," he ventures, "and at what the Catholic church has taught me — sub-consciously and consciously, verbally and non-verbally, over the fifty-four years I've been on this planet — I can summarize it in one word: regret. I've always felt that the church, like St Augustine, wishes sexuality would go away. St Augustine has been so influential and, for him, original sin was our sexuality. He had a problem — no question about it.

"There is, however, another tradition, besides that of the neurotic St Augustine, whose dualism and patriarchal fear of women and sexuality has dominated the Western Christian conscience. There's another tradition, far more ancient, in our Bible, and that is the tradition that treats sexuality with praise.

"We Jews and Christians and other Westerners who come out of this heritage have a whole book in our Bible that does nothing but praise the God of sexuality and the experience of the Cosmic Christ between lovers. It portrays lovemaking as Cosmic Christ meeting Cosmic Christ. I am talking about the song of songs — The Song of Solomon — which ninety-eight percent of rabbis, ministers and priests never get to study because it's cosmological and mystical and that's not considered serious theology.

"You see the churches have fallen into moralizing about sex — they have all these lists of rules and sins — but what I'm saying is that sexuality is essentially mystical. Lovemaking is one of the deepest acts of prayer in which adults can engage. It is art as meditation and the song of songs is a celebration of that. It's a celebration of the Cosmic Christ who has been birthed."

The Augustinian theology of sexual repression, Matthew believes, could only have taken hold in a religion which had lost sight of the sanctity of creation. If God was truly perceived as the Divine Creator who had, indeed, made everything 'good' and infused each human being with a spark of its own divinity, then surely sexual union would be hallowed, rather than mistrusted. Surely our sexuality would be celebrated as the fountain of the blessing that is life.

"Lust is a holy time," he insists. "None of us would be here if it weren't for the gift of lust between our parents and origins are always sacred moments. We need to celebrate this and also celebrate the fact that, as we grow up, we inherit this same gift of lust.

"Lust by itself is, of course, not all of our sexuality. Meister Eckhart says, 'If you want to treat your passions well, don't go into asceticism, don't mortify your senses and kill them. Rather, put on your passions a bridle of love.' It's a wonderful image. What's a bridle? A steering instrument for a stallion. There's a stallion of lust inside all of us. There's a stallion of anger inside all of us. Our passions are holy. We can't go any place important without them but we need to bridle them. We need to steer them. If you can't steer them, then they're going to run your life."

Having chosen, in place of the bridle, to bolt the horse in the stable, the Catholic church, particularly, has developed an unhealthy obsession with sexuality which plays itself out in misogyny, homophobia and a preoccupation with celibacy. Meanwhile, the church is rocked by the debate on the ordination of women, steadies itself against allegations of child abuse and continues to advocate the birth of children in situations of abject poverty and emotional and physical danger.

"Another way to approach sexuality," Matthew continues, "is in terms of the seven *chakras* or energy centers that are described in Eastern spiritual traditions. One of the first things that happens to people in our program at ICCS is a sexual awakening because we're bringing together the sexual and the spiritual. We don't go along with this dualistic ideology. They come together through art as meditation because, in play or in dance, you can't separate your sexual energy from any other energy and you don't want to.

"So, some years ago, there was an English woman in her thirties doing the program and, about six weeks into it, in the middle of my class, she said to everyone: 'Oh, I'm feeling so sexual. I want to give everybody the number of my room tonight,' and they're all going, 'God, this woman is really discovering herself!'

"I thought about this and, at the next class, I said: 'A sexual awakening is very important. It's one of our chakras and therefore it's very important. However, it's only one of seven. So, it's silly to build your whole life around it because it's one-seventh of your total energy.'

"I think that's worth noting. It must be included — you want to open it up — but it's not everything. Now, if you look at the Catholic church's preoccupations, sexual morality is not one-seventh. It's about ninety-nine percent, whether you're talking about abortion or birth control or homosexuality. All these issues that they're so keen on just illustrate that they have things way out of proportion."

The same can be said of the church's infatuation with celibacy, the sanctity of which has been stressed to such an extent that any other lifestyle is presumed to be less than ideal. This, in turn, reinforces Augustine's concept of original sin and, before we know it, we're back with Eve in the garden, propagating the dualistic notion that women, sexuality and indeed the physical world are all signposts on the highway of temptation.

"Both lust and chastity are holy," Matthew insists. "Celibacy has a long history, not just in the West but in other religions too. I remember visiting a large monastic ruin in Germany. It was a Medieval monastery and it held over a thousand men in its time. So I was standing in this ruin and saying to myself, 'Why would so many people choose this lifestyle?' Then, it dawned on me — birth control. It was the most effective form of birth control and people institutionalized it and honored it.

"There have been other reasons for celibacy also. Rosemary Ruther has written about one particular fourth century woman who, she says, was typical of many. She was Roman, not a Christian. When she was twelve, she was married to a fifty year old. She'd had something like four children and three miscarriages by the time she was seventeen.

"At eighteen, she discovered Christianity and what did that mean? She took a vow of celibacy, left her husband and her kids and got her dowry back. That's not a bad deal under those circumstances. She sailed for Jerusalem and she set up a hostel or a convent there. It was a place of refuge for other women who had been in awful marriages and they too became Christian and took a vow of celibacy. In the fourth century, a vow of celibacy was a very political act. It meant emancipation for women. You can imagine that it became pretty popular.

"So I think celibacy has played many roles in cultural and religious history but when it gets to be an end in itself, it's perverted. It was never meant to be that. It's meant to be a means for purifying our intentions and therefore being more grateful for love and sexuality. It's exactly like fasting. Go without food or water for three days and there's no question, your sense of appreciation heightens when you take that first sip.

"That's why I write about the art of celibacy, instead of the vow of celibacy.

The vow of celibacy is pretty worn down in the West but I think there's still a need for the art of celibacy. To make celibacy into an art, we have to separate it from the ideology of putting down the body and sexuality. I also think it should be temporary for most people."

Much of Matthew's life has been lived in celibacy and much of it has been lived alone. Perhaps he would have chosen such a life, whether his church had demanded it of him or not. He speaks wistfully and with some detachment of friendships. His betrayal by the Dominicans colors his thoughts.

"You see people of your own generation and younger sell out," he says slowly, quietly. "To be disappointed in human nature is difficult and you realize there are times when you have to look for support to the non-human world, whether it's angels or animals or trees or the soil or the stars. We can't just depend on the human because the human disappoints so often. Human nature is disappointing a good deal of the time. I see people younger than me who are so old and rigid and that's a disappointment. Friends have disappointed me at times in my life and, I guess, I may have disappointed them too, but the human community is important to me, and so are friends who come and go."

His spiritual nourishment, he says, comes from those friends, as well as nature, music, ideas, meditation, his reading of the works of the mystics and the extended community he has drawn around him through his work. However, hints in his conversation of truly deep friendships, friendships founded on trust, are rare.

It's not that we don't speak of people. We speak of his father, who, towards the end of his life, watched the escalation of friction between Matthew and his superiors with despair. George Fox never understood the impulse which propelled his son to battle for theological change and he admitted as much. It would have sat more comfortably with him if Matthew had adopted the pious obedience which George Fox associated with his faith. This was a tension in their relationship of which both were painfully aware.

We speak also of his mother, whom he admires, and of great souls, like Bede Griffith and Father Chenu, whose names are writ large on his life. I suggest that the best evidence he has given of true companionship is a brief description of Tristan, a white spitz who, for seventeen years, was his dog.

"I'm half Celtic," Matthew laughs, as if this explains everything. "I'm half Irish, quarter Jewish, quarter English and it's a deep part of Celtic spirituality, this relationship with animals, the recognition of their spirit. Also, I had a very special dog. If you had met him, he'd have been your spiritual director too."

Animals, he says, are "wise, silent, mysterious" and, most importantly, "they're doing their work". Tristan's work was to sniff around the house, dig holes and lie in the sun. He was "busy being a dog," Matthew continues. "That was his work and that was wonderful. He was not waylaid in the process. He was not deceived by money or fame or reputation. He got on with his work.

"Animals are connected to the great work of the universe, whereas, we humans are often busy making up our work. Rilke had a great line: 'Somewhere there is an ancient enmity between the great work and our daily lives.' We become disconnected from the great work and create our own little worlds.

"There's a purity about animals' connection to their work. It's very Buddhist. Thomas Merton, the Catholic monk, said that every non-two-legged creature is a saint and my dog was a saint. He taught me many things. So, as I say, it's very Celtic, to have animals as spiritual directors and I have a little of that in my blood."

There have been times when he's felt animals have made more loyal friends than human beings but, he concedes, he likes people and he clings to a good deal of hope for *homo sapiens* as a species.

"Perhaps I'm naive," Matthew smiles, "but I'm hopeful. You need it to live day by day. I have a lot of hope for the younger generation. I think the shift from modernism to post-modernism is very hopeful. There are pitfalls all around but I think the ecological crisis, and its potential to wake us up, is hopeful. I think there's a real spirituality emerging. By that I mean a genuine thirst for spiritual experience and I think we can reinvent our forms of religion.

"Without a spiritual awakening, there is no hope. Technology is not going to save us, science isn't going to save us, government isn't going to save us. It has to do with the heart — heart work and heart awakening — which, in turn, will reinvent other forms of human endeavor, from education to politics to economics to business to religion. That's where my hope lies. I think that's where the spirit works and the spirit, fortunately, has a much bigger imagination than we or our institutions."

Eckhart speaks of the *via negativa*, the dark night of the soul, a time of wholehearted letting go. For our society and our spirituality, Matthew believes, this is such a time.

"Whenever people grow up spiritually, we go through processes of letting go of previous images of God," he explains and again quotes Eckhart:

"'I pray God to rid me of God,' he said. It's a wonderful prayer. It's very radical. It's very Zen. It means to quit projecting onto God, quit making God over in our image, let God be God and show her face in whatever new ways it shows.

"There are so many images of God. Aquinas, in *Sheer Joy*, lists the images of God to be found in the Bible. There are about fifty. God is called beautiful, God is called justice, God is called mind, God is called cloud, stone, rock, rain, dew. He goes through all these images and then he ends up — it's stunning, you'll fall off your chair — by saying that God can be any creature at all and none of them. God is in every being, so every being is, in some way, a book about God. Every being is, in some way, a story, an image of God. Whether you're talking tiger or elephant or galaxy or star or you or me, we're all an image of God. Yet also, God is none of these things."

When we see the divine in all things, we are experiencing the *via positiva*. The *via negativa*, Matthew explains, is our experience of God as nothing, "the black hole, the mystery that has no name and will never be given a name."

In just the last hundred years, our images of God have been torn apart by forces as disparate as the women's movement, the environment movement, the civil rights movement, two world wars and countless local scuffles brought, in violent, bloody color, into our living rooms. Scientists have split the atom, learned that space is curved and that the universe has grown from pinprick size to encompass a trillion galaxies. Eastern religion has infiltrated the West and the West the East. Colonial powers have fallen and indigenous cultures have risen up, each offering a unique cosmology. All we've held sacred is up for grabs. Nothing is certain.

"Our generation is passing through an immense cultural shift," Matthew adds, "and always, when this happens, the previously contained images and names for God start tumbling and losing their power. You had Nietzche anticipating this in the nineteenth century, talking about the death of God. Then, in the late 1960s, we had theologians speaking of the death of God again."

Yet out of this miasma, he believes, "divinity will emerge and utter its new names."

"Even today," he says, "we are hearing new names for divinity. We now know of one trillion galaxies, so God's home is much bigger than we ever imagined and populated by all kinds of beings we're just getting to know. Every being is a revelation of divinity, if we listen with an open heart.

"Our job is to keep our hearts open and learn the new names for divinity. One shift in our time has been the shift from God as Father, to God as Mother as well and, of course, God as the mystic child. Now, we can also see divinity in terms of black holes, in terms of interconnectivity and as the mind of the universe.

"It's not about losing God or slaying God. It's about finding our own beings. Eckhart says that all the names you give to God come from an understanding of yourself. So, as we change our understanding, which you do during a big cultural shift like this, whole new images are going to flood out. If Eckhart is right and the names we give to God do come from understanding ourselves, then if we can broaden, deepen and make more beautiful our names for God, we'll be making ourselves deeper, broader and more beautiful as well."

Matthew's favorite images of God are sometimes abstract, sometimes tied to nature.

"I experience divinity as a presence," he says. "Everything is in God and God is in everything. The fish is in the water and the water is in the fish. That's divinity. We're in God's grace and grace is in us. These are the images that I think are effective today. Also beauty. The medievals all talked about God as beauty. Aquinas says God is the most beautiful thing in the universe. It is a shared beauty with every being. Aquinas also says that beauty yearns to be conspicuous, which explains why the world is so conspicuously beautiful. Divinity is putting itself out there."

The way forward, Matthew says, is neither to run shrieking back to the security of the fundamentalist religions nor to build barricades of dogma. The mystical journey involves embracing the darkness and keeping our hearts and minds open for hints of a new dawn. These, he believes, abound in the world today.

"That's where I think our moment in history is so special," he says. "We can't just take the religious forms we have, East or West. We have to take the new creation story from science and the ecological story and the moral issues of racism and sexism. We have to call on the wisdom of our religious traditions and we have to call on the native traditions also. Then, we have to create new religious forms. We have to string it all together with our imagination and creativity.

"Our species has often done this. After all, Buddha was an historical figure. He reinvented the Hinduism of his day. Jesus reinvented the Judaism of his day. Luther and company tried to reinvent the Christianity of their day, as did Francis of Assisi and Hildegard of Bingen in the twelfth century. Obviously, we have to reinvent our religion and today it's a global thing. It's not just about Christianity getting its house in order or Buddhism getting its house in order. We're all in this together."

This is why Matthew Fox battled so long and hard to remain in the Catholic church.

"I think it is going out of business in its present form," he admits, "but it does have a lot to offer. There are the gospels, Jesus, the prophets and the mystics, some of the symbols and metaphors and ritual. All that is very rich and much needed at this time. I fought the Vatican for ten years, not because I agreed with them but because I didn't want to turn Western religious tradition over to their ideology. The model I used was Rosa Parks, who would neither leave the bus nor go to the back."

Finally, of course, he was evicted from the bus. After much soul searching, he has concluded it was heading irrevocably in the wrong direction. He is proud, he says, to have been thrown over by a pope who is "making such a fool of himself over issues like birth control." Matthew's initial anger at the church's betrayal has been supplanted by excitement at the new possibilities which are opening up in his life.

"I felt that they had made me a post-denominational priest in a post-denominational time. I don't think denominations are the issue today and I don't think most young people know the difference between a Lutheran and a Presbyterian and an Anglican."

Matthew decided he had three options:

"One was to hide under a rock, which was what they wanted me to do and personally, that's fine. I don't have to be an acting priest. The second was to do what Leonardo Boff did in Brazil. He stood up and said, 'Make me a lay person again, I can't take these attacks.' Then, I thought, a third option would be a lateral move, to become an Episcopalian, and I chose that. I thought it was the most creative move and I figured that, since they'd ordained me twenty-seven years ago, I might as well put it to some use."

Fortuitously, while he was still deliberating, a radical group of Anglicans, from Sheffield in England, turned up in San Francisco and knocked on Matthew's door. All in their twenties, they had taken on the task of recreating the mass using contemporary rave and techno music and multi-media technology. As a result, they had crowds of six hundred turning up to their "planetary masses" every Sunday. They fired this fifty-four year old post-denominational priest's enthusiasm.

"It's a phenomenon," he insists. "I asked them, 'How could I help you?' and they said, 'We're the generation that will understand your work. Become an Episcopal priest.' So I said, 'Well, this is synchronous,' because I'd just finished my new book and the last chapter was on how we need new ritual today. By putting on these masses, we're going to reinvent the church from the inside. That's powerful because that's how you change cultures. That's how we'll bring religion along, kicking and screaming, into the post-modern age."

Within days of that meeting, Matthew Fox had made an appointment to see the Episcopal bishop in San Francisco. He has now boarded another bus, through his ordination as an Episcopal priest. Meanwhile, thirty-six members of the Sheffield community were winging their way to San Francisco. They staged an immensely successful planetary mass in the cathedral and plans are underway to establish a community and ritual center in the Bay area.

"The Episcopal church has given me room to continue my work and that's what it's all about," Matthew smiles and pauses, as the day's first rays of sun struggle through lifting fog to light on a gaggle of teenagers outside. "I refuse to give up the work," he adds finally. "I believe it's important, especially for the next generation."